GunDigest GUIDE TO
Customizing Your
AR-15

Kevin Muramatsu

Published by

Gun Digest® Books, an imprint of F+W Media, Inc.
Krause Publications • 700 East State Street • Iola, WI 54990-0001
715-445-2214 • 888-457-2873
www.krausebooks.com

To order books or other products call toll-free 1-800-258-0929
or visit us online at www.gundigeststore.com

ISBN-13:978-1-4402-4279-3
ISBN-10: 1-4402-4279-8

Edited by Corrina Peterson
Designed by Dave Hauser
Cover Design by Kevin Ulrich

Printed in U.S.A.

10 9 8 7 6 5 4 3 2

Table of
contents

DEDICATION

BROWNELLS. MOST OF THE STUFF SHOWN IN THIS BOOK WAS PURCHASED OR OTHERWISE RECEIVED FROM BROWNELLS AND, AS WITH MY LAST BOOK, HAS PROVEN TO BE MOST USEFUL FOR THE CREATION OF THIS WORK. THANK YOU VERY MUCH, AND PLEASE, PLEASE, PLEASE STAY IN BUSINESS. FOR ALL OF US.

ACKNOWLEDGEMENTS

The following persons or businesses have assisted greatly in my acquisition of stuff and photos of stuff for this book. Larry Weeks from Brownells (of course), John and Mel from JP Enterprises, Brian from Wolf's Den Gun Shop in Hugo, MN; Clay from Bills Gun Shop in Hudson, WI; Your Mom's Basement (internet cafe, not really your mom's basement, though theoretically it could have been }:-]), Clifton Wayne from Monsterman Grips, Alan Thordsen from Thordsen Customs, Bruce Blatchley, Rachel Muramatsu, and to all the small businesses that have produced products that have been included in this book. Sorry if I forgot to mention any other major contributors. Please let me know if I did.

INTRODUCTION

Few firearms draw forth the mix of admiration and derision than the AR series of rifles (and pistols now). Certainly, with a firearm that begins its major use in the military, opinions will be sharp and often in sharp contrast, particularly if said firearm was used in extensive combat, as the M-16/M4 series has seen.

While we will explore a bit of the history and utility and other stuff related to this rifle later in this volume, it should be noted, with some amount of pride, that the M-16, in its various guises and upgrades, in some form or other, has served the U.S. military for almost sixty years. Since the early commercial years of the Colt SP1 up until modern days, the popularity of the AR-15 in the hands of the civilian community has grown in leaps and bounds. Since the expiration of the Clinton "Assault Weapons" ban the growth has been nearly exponential. Since the election of President Obama, the growth has been insane.

The wonderful free market has taken advantage of this meteoric increase in popularity. How many manufacturers build copies or variants of the Remington 700 receiver? You could probably name a handful of them and you would be naming a significant percentage. Compare this to the AR series. Well over 100 firms manufacture at least a lower receiver, firms small and large. This is not including accessories such as handguards, stocks, and barrels. There are far fewer of those entities, but still a significant number. Since the receiver is the serial numbered part, and therefore the regulated part, any law abiding Joe can purchase a lower receiver and build an AR that matches his heart's desire. Indeed, this is one of the reasons that the AR series has gained such a following: because it is eminently suited to personalization. I mean, why would I be writing this book if this was just some run-of-the-mill rifle? We've found that a lot of people will pay $100 – even $400 for a single piece of machined aluminum upon which to build their first dream gun. With only a few exceptions, these lower receivers are of good quality, cut right, and are an excellent item with which to begin.

This is not to say that a complete rifle is not an option. Certainly, the new AR owner is going to go first for a complete firearm, almost always a rifle or carbine. Even there, the choices are many. "Which AR should I buy?" is a very common question.

Ultimately, the reason for the huge aftermarket support, and to some degree the overall popularity, is that the gun is semi-modular. Swapping out upper receiver assemblies or if you like, barrel assemblies, can alter the entire scope of the AR's use. A self-defense carbine in 5.56mm can, with the manipulation of two captured pins, be changed into a Varminter/prairie dog shooter in .204 Ruger, or a long range target rifle in 6.5 Grendel. A little more work makes the stock M4-style carbine into a virtual precision carbine, with the replacement of the standard handguard with a free floated handguard and/or the installation of a match trigger kit.

We'll explore the entire range of things you can do, the installation of a selection of the popular choices, and the means to maintain the AR system of firearms so that it remains your happy little friend.

To save time and annoyance, though this will probably gin some up in a segment of the readership, there are a number of posed photos in this book used to illustrate a product or concept. I have chosen to do take these photos without eye or ear protection PRECISELY BECAUSE THEY ARE POSED!

Finally, it's pretty much impossible to cover all the stuff that could have been included in this book. I did my best with my time and resources to cover a broad spectrum of parts, accessories, and brands. For the record, I concentrated on several companies whose products I most like and have had the greatest experience. This should not be seen as a purposeful rejection of other manufacturers' products or services. We all develop preferences and opinions based on experience and part of the point of this book was to introduce the new AR owners to a sampling of the vast amount of quality resources available to them. So if it seems like I'm in the bag for a few manufacturers, you would be correct. I try to be objective, but like most other media sources, sometimes biases just seem to shine through. There are no low quality parts in this book. Everything has been used firsthand or if not by me, by a close colleague. All but a very few of these products are also made by American small businesses in America, and I'm very proud of that. While I have no objection to foreign-sourced stuff, I'd rather have stuff made in a free country, if I can help it.

Kevin Muramatsu
The Garage Shop
MN

P.S. I wore T shirts from www.takinglibertees. com intentionally for the posed photos. Check them out.

The AR and Why

Since you have picked up this book, whether for study or perusal, I think it's safe to assume that you either own or are considering owning an AR-15 or related rifle. You will generally be in good company. The AR-15 and its big brother the AR-10 and all the patterns derived from them just happen to be the most popular thing in the gun universe at this time. Part of this is because the guns are so adaptable. Partly it is because of a growing self-defense mindset among Americans and the desire to have the best equipment possible for that purpose. Also, in part, a lot of people previously did not have them and, because of recent events, want one before they are banned.

We'll address each of these points in this first chapter, but before we do so, a bit of history is necessary to bring you up to speed. After all, the AR platform is over sixty years old now, from its inception and original construct. Because of the controversy surrounding it (if you are unaware of this controversy, you will understand shortly), this little mini history lesson should help to straighten things out a bit and give you a better appreciation for the endurance of the AR, and even some of the people responsible for it. This will not be exhaustive, more of a summary really. More emphasis will be placed on recent developments than the specifics of the early years.

The ultimate AR accessory!

THE EARLY YEARS

A very smart man named Eugene Stoner designed the basic AR platform. His rifle was the first, at least the first successfully, to incorporate several features that we consider commonplace today. Until that point, these were not found together or at all on rifles, including military rifles. This story really starts with the AR-10. The AR-10 was designed by Stoner while he worked for the Fairchild Aircraft Corporation. Students of the history of the military/industrial complex will note that Fairchild was also responsible for another superb American weapons system, the A-10 Thunderbolt II (Warthog) close support aircraft, yet another object that has proven its worth over the last fifty years, and continues to do so.

Eugene Stoner, the inventor of the AR-15/AR-10/M-16.

The first feature of his rifle was the incorporation of synthetic materials in the composition of the furniture. Plastics had been quite common prior to this time, but had mostly been restricted to the fabrication of pistol grip panels, such as seen on the Colt 1911 pistol and the Walther P38 pistol, replacing the wood panels. Plastic grip panels were cheaper than wood and so began to be adopted by various militaries during the inter-bellum period of the twenties and thirties. However, wood still was the material used for the stocking of rifles and shotguns till well after WWII. Stoner incorporated plastics into the AR-10's buttstock, pistol grip, and handguard, replacing the formerly common wood

(above) A rifle sales wall in Bill's Gun Shop and Range in Hudson, Wisconsin. The entire wall is actually three times bigger than this and is completely dedicated to modern sporting arms. Every single firearm in this image is an AR-15 of some sort or another. This is not atypical with larger gun shops. Twenty years ago this would have been fantasy. Now it is reality and retailers like Bill's have helped make it possible.

(below) This is the opposite partial wall from the previous picture of Bill's Gun Shop and Range in Wisconsin. There are two other stores like it in the Twin Cities area of Minnesota and the both have a similar display of AR-15 lower receiver assemblies, stripped lowers, upper assemblies, and accessories.

(left) Even small reloading-centric shops like the Wolf's Den Gun Shop in Hugo, MN, have a selection of ARs and other Modern Sporting Arms. They also sell better than traditional rifles.

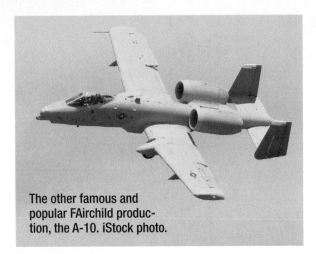

The other famous and popular FAirchild production, the A-10. iStock photo.

furniture. This was a pretty new idea and, later, the joke went that the AR was made by Mattel, or Kenner, or [name your toy manufacturer and place it here]. A nice wood stock is something of beauty and comforting solidity, and soldiers and civilians alike were used to seeing walnut or birch on their rifles, not plastic that made a hollow echo when you tapped on it. But the advantage of using plastics was hard to ignore. Plastic is much lighter than walnut or other hardwoods used in gun stocks and significantly cheaper to produce.

The second feature was the use of what has come to be known as a "direct impingement" gas system. Apparently Stoner did not consider this a true direct impingement system (like seen on earlier post WWII rifles such as the French MAS 40 series), since the bolt and carrier assembly is literally a gas piston. He was right, but the term has stuck as applied to the AR series of rifles and is unlikely to go away. Anyway, the point is that conventional gas-operated rifles have a forward reciprocating piston housed in an gas block, that then acts upon an operating rod which initiates movement of the bolt ("short stroke piston"), or they have an operating rod that incorporates a piston into its tip where the operating rod is attached to the bolt mechanism ("long stroke"). Stoner's design simply tapped gas from the barrel, channeled it through a simple hollow tube, back into the guts of the bolt carrier in a cavity behind the bolt. The gas expanding in this chamber caused the bolt to press firmly against the chamber, while the carrier itself moved to the rear to then unlock and then withdraw the bolt to cycle the gun. This system translates to less mass in the gun which facilitates a lighter overall weight, and particularly in the front of the gun which facilitates better handling. Furthermore, since there is no reciprocating mass (like a big piston or op rod) banging around attached to the barrel, this rifle is inherently very accurate, as there are fewer stresses placed on the barrel as the bullet passes through it.

The third feature was the low bore axis. This

Here you see two totally different design philosophies: a tilting style locking bolt from an FN-FAL and a rotating bolt head from a large frame AR.

As you see here, you can look straight down the top of the stock (okay, slightly to the side) and draw a straight line all the way to the muzzle. This aids in muzzle and recoil control.

allows a recoil impulse straight into the shoulder. Traditional style rifles use a stock that has drop to it, leaving the barrel itself above the shoulder, contributing to the majority of the muzzle-rise experienced when shooting. The low bore axis placed the recoil impulse lower and essentially removed the pivot point, or fulcrum, at the shoulder that traditional designs experience upon firing, and thus reducing muzzle rise. This also necessitated the vertical pistol grip so the rifle could be held comfortably.

The fourth feature was the combination multi-lugged rotating bolt head and barrel extension. The vast majority of rifles to this point used a system where the bolt would have two or possibly three lugs and would lock into the recesses in the receiver, with the barrel then screwed into the front of the receiver. A multi-lugged bolt, in this case seven (eight if you include the non-bearing lug on the extractor), allows several things. The first is a short rotation distance for locking and unlocking. Any centerfire rifle must have a locked breach for safety reasons. Without getting into a huge amount of science here, this works well in a self-loading rifle and we'll get into that and other reasons in a later chapter. The barrel extension meant that the bolt locked into the barrel rather than the receiver, making the fabrication of the receiver much easier and cheaper (a linear tube), and therefore…

…the receiver could now be made of something other than steel. Since all the pressure is contained completely within the steel bolt/extension system, something with much lower tensile strength could be used in the receivers, like aluminum alloys. This further served to lighten the rifle. Indeed the original AR-10, chambered in 7.62x51 NATO, weighed less than seven pounds, about the average for the current batch of .223 carbines. It is not uncommon to find AR-15-style rifles today that have receivers,

There is a popular but somewhat crude retort to the notion of banning guns: If guns cause crime, then spoons make people fat. It is used to illustrate the important and valid point that tools do not commit crimes or perform actions without the input of human direction. Even robots that perform tasks without direct supervision do so according to the human programming that has been built into them. Banning a tool, in this case the firearm, may indeed reduce the number of suicides or crimes committed by firearms, but that crime will simply be committed using another tool, such as a baseball bat or knife, or automobile, or pills. Indeed, more deaths, both intentional or not, are attributed by the U.S. Government's own data to these causes than to firearms already.

The original AR-10 looked like this. You may note the charging handle in the carry handle and the very slim handguards.
Photo internet sourced, www.dogswar.ru.

upper or lower or both, made from polymers and carbon fiber.

The origin story goes from the AR-10 prototype on to the AR-15 prototype. Late in the '50s, Armalite submitted the AR-10 to the Army trials that were seeking to find a replacement for the M1 Garand. They did not succeed. Fairchild and later Armalite divested itself of the rights to the gun and sold them to Colt. Colt continued to push the downsized AR-15, chambered in .223 Remington, and finally had success as the Vietnam War began to really heat up.

In its brilliance, rather than issuing the rifle and ammunition as it was designed, the Army decided to alter both the rifle and its ammunition, most notably changing the powder specification. The powder change resulted in critical malfunctions because it caused the cyclic rate of the rifle under full auto to increase significantly. This, and the failure to issue sufficient cleaning supplies and instruction on the rifle's use and maintenance, resulted in the rifle gaining a sour reputation among the early users in the military. However, as the kinks were ironed out, cleaning equipment issued, and instruction commenced, the rifle became a very effective tool for the infantryman. Exhaustive histories of the AR-15/10/M-16 can be found from a multitude of authors. Controversy continues to this day on its reliability, its ammo, and other specifics that we aren't going to go into a great deal of detail here. What we will do, however, is explore the suitability to the civilian market, and the cornucopia of support for the gun, including maintenance equipment, accessories, ammunition, and other great stuff that will help you to make a wise buying decision either on the firearm itself, or on the supporting cast of equipment and knowledge.

POLITICAL ISSUES

Before we go into the fun stuff, we really should examine the politics that seem to surround the AR series of rifles and other "black" rifles that are

gaining in popularity. Particularly, it is important to analyze the use (or more accurately, the lack of use) of these "black" rifles, or MSRs (Modern Sporting Rifles, the common term for the entire spectrum), in violent crimes. This is the primary argument used to promote the restriction of such firearms in the civilian marketplace.

Certainly, internationally the AK series of rifles has been used to commit more acts of violence, more mayhem, and more mass murders, than any rifle in modern history. Also certainly, that has no bearing on this discussion, as this is the United States of America, not Africa or Asia. Unlike in most third world regions, we are a nation that is ruled by laws, and more importantly, a nation with a majority population that is willing to be bound by those laws, even if adherence to those laws can be very personally inconvenient. Especially when those inconvenient laws are criminally stupid, like most gun control laws happen to be.

Analysis of the federal government's own data shows that ARs, AKs, or anything else in the so-called "assault weapon" category are used in crimes with such infrequency as to completely debunk the above argument entirely. More violent deaths are perpetrated by the deadly use of bare hands, such as striking or strangling by far than are perpetrated by the use of an MSR. However, if you repeat a lie often enough, people will believe it, hence the reason that the "used in crimes" argument persists. This is not to say that MSRs are not used at all in crimes. In fact, several high profile shootings and mass shootings were initiated with such rifles, which served to keep the object in the spotlight, so to say, and to give such firearms an undeserved stigma that the political left continues to exploit every chance they get.

Without getting too partisan here, it should be noted that, even if they were used in significant, even most, cases of violent crime, it would still not justify the removal of the type from personal ownership. What a criminal does with his gun should have no impact on what a law-abiding citizen does with hers. The sad fact is that existing gun control laws do nothing to address the use of the criminal's gun, except to perhaps increase his punishment. Rather they serve to deny the law abiding from a product which can be and often is of use to them, and is of no threat to anyone else. These are uses that, because of the nature of the law-abiding citizen, do not violate the law. Therefore, the imposition of a gun control law affects only the law abiding, which are precisely NOT the people that are causing the problem to begin with. The kind of logic that suggests we ban an object (in this case firearms, but there are other examples) because of the misbehavior of a minority of a population is beyond asinine, demonstrating either the pure, gleaming incapability of thinking rationally (an indicator that you should not be making decisions for anyone), or demonstrating a desire to control the law abiding population for nefarious or selfish personal ends (an indicator that one is not to be trusted).

So, why the rant? If you purchase an AR-15 you should be well informed as to the state of the laws that apply to the ownership thereof. In most states there are none. In others, like my home state of Minnesota, a permit (simply acquired) is necessary for an AR or handgun. In others, they are virtually forbidden. It is then ironic that in those places where restriction is the greatest, the highest concentrations of violent crime are present. If you live in a freer state, you can enjoy AR ownership and all the attending benefits thereof. If you live in a restrictive state or city, where the masters do not trust you with ARs or firearms of any kind, or where your neighbors are unable to think rationally, well, you find yourself screwed over. My sympathies are upon you. You are missing a treat and you are living in a system that limits your rights because of insecure peoples' insecurities, and because of the desire of powerful people to remain in power over you, disregarding your input.

While the existence of stupid laws is infuriating, that does not mean that they should be violated. We live by law, not by decree, and laws can be changed peacefully over time. Until then, make sure that the guns you own, or are about to own, conform to the statutes of the area in which you dwell. Unfortunately, many jurisdictions limit the type of AR you can own. They do so based upon either cosmetic issues or functional issues that have no relation to their suitability for anything.

A common example would be banning the use of high capacity (really, standard capacity) magazines, or even limiting the number of cartridges that you may have in them. This is like banning high horsepower (really, standard horsepower) engines in a Porsche to only 300 horsepower. You may not have a car that can exceed 70 mph; no one needs such a thing. Guess what? It's none of your friggin' business what I need, nor are you in any

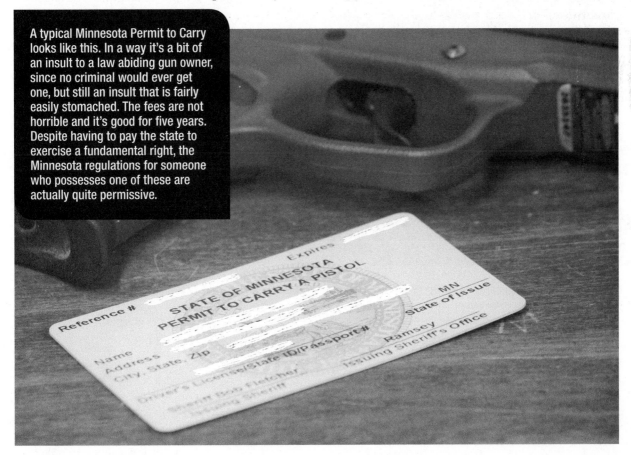

A typical Minnesota Permit to Carry looks like this. In a way it's a bit of an insult to a law abiding gun owner, since no criminal would ever get one, but still an insult that is fairly easily stomached. The fees are not horrible and it's good for five years. Despite having to pay the state to exercise a fundamental right, the Minnesota regulations for someone who possesses one of these are actually quite permissive.

The anti-gun activists like to use a very broad definition of children. If any of you are parents and have taken your children to a pediatrician sometime in the last few years, you may have been asked or been given a small survey asking if you have any firearms in the home. The ostensible justification for such a random, seemingly unrelated question is this: according to the American Academy of Pediatrics, a left-wing activist group masquerading as a physicians association, firearms are the second leading cause of deaths of children. What they don't say (and unfortunately most pediatricians don't bother to research to find this out), is that when they say "children" they mean children up to the age of 23 or 25 (depending on the study). The connotation of the word children is always that of adolescents, not teenagers, not anyone over 18 years of age. They have to include up to the ages of 23 or 25 to get the stats and numbers they need to make this statement. The vast majority, upwards of 90% of these numbers, include the deaths of gang members between the ages of 16 and 23 or 25. Um, a 21 year old gang member fighting over drug distribution turf is not a child. So the moral of the story is to verify crazy talk, because even a two-second perusal of this stat should indicate to anyone with an ounce of common sense that it is off somehow. If your pediatrician asks this, take the time to explain that, first, it's none of her business, and second, how the political element in this country has skewed her numbers to get her to become a sleeper activist for their cause. I guarantee that she does not consider anyone over 18 or even 8 or 10 years of age to be a "child."

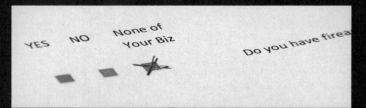

This is how I respond when a doctor asks if there are guns in my home.

position to determine such a thing. Yet politicians and gun banners never cease attempting to limit how many rounds you can have in your gun at one time based upon "need." It's just like with a high speed car. I have the ability to easily exceed 150 mph, but I do not because I am willing to obey the speed limit of 70 mph for a number of reasons, not the least of which is safety and concern for other drivers. If I ripped through an intersection next to a grade school, I would never be able to stop soon

No one needs this car or the muscle under the hood.

istock photo

enough to avoid hitting child in the crosswalk, a child that would certainly die if that event occurred. In the same way, I might have or desire a 60-round magazine for my AR-15. I am capable of killing at least 60 people with that if I so wished, but I won't, because I am a law-abiding citizen with a healthy respect for the rule of law, the societal and cultural bases for those laws, for human life, and for a personal life lived outside the cold, gray, concrete walls of a penitentiary. A heck of a lot more people are killed by irresponsible driving than by the use of MSRs like AR-15s.

Another example is the protruding pistol grip. The sole purpose of a protruding pistol grip is for the user to safely and comfortably control the firearm. The reason they are there is necessitated by the low bore axis we talked about earlier, which aids in controlling recoil and muzzle rise. Apparently this is an icky feature and only terrorists need to use one. Again, this is asinine. Banning a feature that makes the rifle MORE controllable is based on bizarro logic.

Collapsible or folding stocks. Collapsible stocks allow multiple people to use the same rifle comfortably, or allow the same person to use the gun comfortably when he has more or less clothing on. Pretty simple. Folding stocks are just cool. They allow the rifle to be stored in a smaller space or allow it to be carried as a smaller package. There are several legitimate uses in combat but that is not the point.

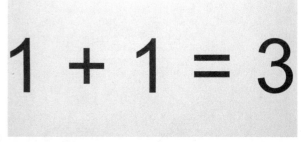

1 + 1 = 3

Bizzarro logic.

Collapsible stocks make the same gun shootable for the large frame of an adult and the small frame of a child.

Bayonet lugs. If you can find me any story where a criminal used a mounted, fixed bayonet to commit a violent crime I will be astonished. Likewise, if the restrictors would have us believe that a bayonet lug was inherently dangerous, I would truly love to see the data on all the drive by bayonettings that are apparently rampant across the inner cities.

Threaded barrel muzzle. A threaded muzzle allows you to attach things like flash hiders, muzzle brakes, or – the spawn of the devil – sound suppressors (silencers). Since only criminals or terrorists need things like that (I guess muzzle brakes are the exception pretty much anywhere), you shouldn't have the ability to mount one of them. Particularly the silencers. As we have all seen from movies (everything in movies is true) silencers are only good for assassinations. Yeah, not really. What they are really good at is preventing early onset of hearing aid use. In most countries with strict firearms regulations (pretty much all other countries) the guns are heavily regulated but the silencers are completely unregulated, and indeed their use is considered good manners, since your neighbors won't be hearing all the gunshots. It kind of makes sense that a criminal that is going to shoot someone is going to do so whether he has a silencer or not, and the law abiding citizen who is not going to shoot someone will not do so whether or not a silencer is attached to his gun.

Now the really crazy thing about all these is that the bans that are enacted address these items as the "bad" things that make guns bad. Functionality has no weight to these decisions, other

If you ask a gun banner, this feature can only be used by assassins.

than misunderstanding the utility of the items and making up completely farcical facts about the features to demonize them. They can't really ban the basic gun very easily, but they have been much more successful banning the useful items from being incorporated into the firearms. This results in the parts being treated as purely cosmetic, and you will find that the firearms will still be available, just minus the "bad" parts. Functionally the gun is otherwise identical. A semi-auto is a semi-auto no matter how many parts you force me switch around to make it less scary looking.

This was the angle taken during the federal "assault weapons" ban that ran from 1994 to 2004. AR-15s didn't stop selling, they were just sold with fixed stocks, no flash hiders, and 10-round magazines. The guns and the aftermarket support were available before and during the ban. However, that market didn't really explode until after the ban expired (it had a sunset provision, which is good, because it had no effect on violent crime at all). Then and up to the present, the market has gone truly nuts. There are so many options for modding and upgrading the AR platform that it really is mindboggling. As we go through the chapters in this book, we'll explore a number of them, but it's simply impossible to get to everything in the space available. Generally I can say that the vast majority of the available items are of good quality and, of those, almost all of them are manufactured domestically. As with anything, there are a few items that are kind of stupid and make you scratch your head, wondering why, or in what universe is it worth that much money. Well, I'm simply going to ignore those, and you will just have to trust that my subjectivity is acutely correlative with objectivity in these cases.

So, onward we go into the AR universe.

A Remington 742 and a .308 AR. These are the same thing with different clothing, functioning essentially the same way.

CHAPTER 2

Safety Stuff and Tools for the AR Series of Firearms

I t's kind of important to go over some safety items that some of us may take for granted. The target audience for this book is not really the guys that have a bunch of these guns already. It will likely still be of use to them, but mostly I'm talking to the new buyer, or the buyer that may have purchased his first receiver or rifle or upper at some point since the last couple election cycles. A lot of people have begun and are well into the transition from the traditional hunting rifle or pistol/revolver to the Modern Sporting Rifle or MSR. I really hate that acronym and type designation because it's kind of a propaganda term, but it is a true description of the type, particularly with the AR platform. It really can do just about anything for any type of lawful use of a firearm, over a vast array of disciplines, so I'm going to swallow my distaste and go ahead and henceforth use the term "MSR" as needed.

Let's start with the basics of gun safety and move on to more specific things after that.

THE THREE RULES

The National Rifle Association has three basic rules of gun safety. You will often see other organizations or manufacturers use ten or more, but those are hard to remember. Stupid. Safety rules should be simple and few, and the three NRA rules cover all the others that other people mention

specifically anyway. Three is easy to remember and therefore are much more likely to be remembered. Except maybe by trap shooters. They always forget the first one.

Rule 1: Always keep the gun pointed in a safe direction.

A safe direction is defined as a direction where there is not something or someone that needs an extra hole. If that means up, then point the gun

(opposite) While this is a pic of a range setting, "downrange" is a term used to describe a safe direction to keep the muzzle of your firearm pointed toward. At a range, it is easy to figure out what that direction is; it can be more tricky when not at a designated range.

(top left) This shooter's trigger finger is properly off the trigger, since she's not ready to fire yet.

(left) This shooter's trigger finger must be ready to fire, since her finger is on the trigger. Otherwise, it shouldn't be there.

up. If it means down, then point the muzzle down. If that means there isn't one, then put the gun down with the muzzle pointed in the air and walk away. Don't wave the gun around carelessly; it makes other people rightfully nervous. Don't point it at anyone unless you want them to point one back at you, because that is likely to happen. Don't point it at the dog, cat, or at guy in the back seat or you will have a Boondock Saints or Pulp Fiction moment to remember that isn't funny at all. An adjunct to this rule is that you need to make sure you are aware of your environment. Don't walk in front of a guy aiming a gun downrange. He may not see you and pump a round past your wandering butt. I know it's hard to believe, but that is exactly how the friend of a former vice president got shot in the face with a 28 gauge. Neither guy was taking this rule quite as much to heart as he should have.

Rule 2: Always keep your finger off the trigger until you are ready to shoot.

This is admittedly difficult to learn, because your index finger is naturally going to drift in to the trigger guard, but you have to train yourself to not do that. Make yourself consciously place your finger outside the trigger guard, away from the trigger. The primary safety is your brain and its interface with your finger. Get control of it and keep that finger to the side until you are on target and ready to make a hole. It should literally make you nervous anytime you see someone resting their finger on the trigger, ever. It should make you mad every time you see some moron in a movie doing it, and that is where most people have received their gun training: sitting in front of a screen. You have to counteract that training and do it right. Don't even thing about touching the trigger until you are ready to shoot.

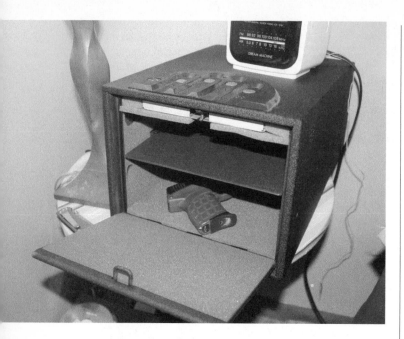

Rule 3: Always keep the gun unloaded until ready to use.

With a concealed carry gun you should be carrying it loaded. If you don't trust it to not fire with a round in the chamber when you carry it, then you should get a gun that you are comfortable with and ship me the gun in which you are not. I will happily pay for shipping. However, since most ARs are kept for hunting, target shooting, or actual in-home defense, you should keep them unloaded

except at the range or if you think the gang is invading your home. If you must have a loaded gun next to your head to sleep soundly, make it a pistol. If you don't have time to get to your rifle in the event of a home invasion, then the perps are likely already standing over our bed and you won't have the chance to get to your rifle anyway. A pistol is much more useful on this occasion. If it's an AR pistol, well then so be it. Otherwise, when storing the AR, keep it unloaded, and you are much less likely to have an "oopsie" later on. This is particularly vital if you live in an apartment building or have children in another room. You want to develop the mindset that "guns are always loaded" so that whenever you pick one up, you check the chamber to see, and that whenever you hand one to someone else, you hand it to them with the bolt locked back to demonstrate that you have just done so. Included in this rule is to keep unauthorized persons away from the guns. This includes your kids, other people's kids, and the neighbor you can't stand but invited to the block party anyway. Lock up the guns and they will not get at them, nor will the burglar who decides to check out your house when you are on vacation in St. Thomas.

OTHER SAFETY ISSUES

So you're a tough guy. You don't need no stinking earplugs or safety glasses. If you are that tough then you probably don't need a gun to defend yourself, so just ship your guns to me. I'll pay for the shipping. If you are not that tough, then you will want a set of ear plugs and some shooting glasses. Plugs are great and cheap and work. Some folks don't like to have things that aren't tongues

(above) This pistol, while loaded, is ready to fire. It is a home defense gun and is loaded accordingly. It's also accordingly stored in a combination locked pistol safe.

(right) These big ear muffs are the most effective means of protecting your hearing, short of using a sound suppressor. Purely passive types have been around for a long, long time. The electronic muffs are now almost omnipresent (and finally affordable) and can dampen the loud while amplifying the soft. This is great when you are at a range and would like to hear the range commands easily.

(below) Plugs tend to be somewhat less effective (and comfortable) than muffs. But they are sufficient for most guns that don't use muzzle brakes. You might want to combine plugs and muffs for the big-bored compensated firearms like .50 caliber rifles.

stuck in their ears so they will generally go with the ear muffs. Both plugs and muffs are available as purely passive designs (traditional), or as modern electronic devices that selectively filter out loud harmful noises. The really nice thing about electronic devices is that they allow you to hear normally otherwise, making it easier to hear the important range commands or engage in friendly conversation while someone else is shoot-

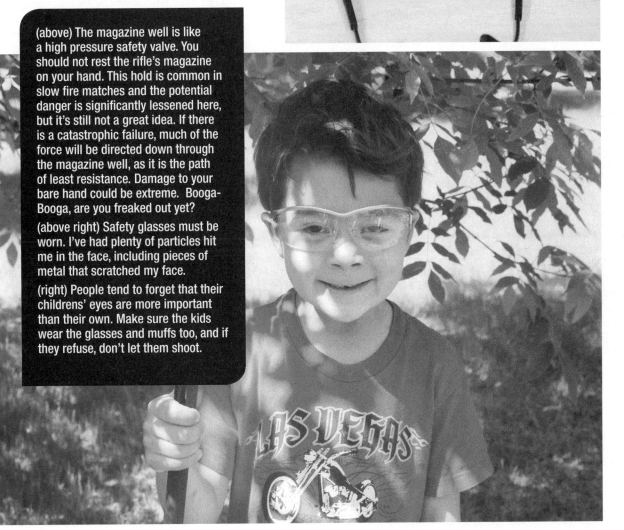

(above) The magazine well is like a high pressure safety valve. You should not rest the rifle's magazine on your hand. This hold is common in slow fire matches and the potential danger is significantly lessened here, but it's still not a great idea. If there is a catastrophic failure, much of the force will be directed down through the magazine well, as it is the path of least resistance. Damage to your bare hand could be extreme. Booga-Booga, are you freaked out yet?

(above right) Safety glasses must be worn. I've had plenty of particles hit me in the face, including pieces of metal that scratched my face.

(right) People tend to forget that their childrens' eyes are more important than their own. Make sure the kids wear the glasses and muffs too, and if they refuse, don't let them shoot.

ing in proximity. The upside to the plugs is that they rarely protrude and will not get in your way. The muffs can on occasion get bumped around and, since they add a couple of inches to your head width, can interfere with some types of shooting or shooting positions.

Firearms can have problems, hence the existence of gunsmiths. Depending on how much you shoot and what you shoot you may even have a catastrophic failure in your gun at some point. This usually happens to people who put huge amounts of rounds downrange, like the competitive shooters. They almost always get a "Kaboom" at some point. The AR is well designed and if you have such an event, the majority of the force is going to go to the sides and down through the magazine well. So don't support your gun by resting the magazine on your hand.

Whatever happens, there will be lots of hot gas that can be kept out of your eyes by shooting glasses. Even normal shooting will result in some gases or small particulates, so the glasses are always useful. As with hearing protection, glasses should be treated as essential items that you will not go without. I'll warn you in advance, it might take you awhile to find properly-fitting glasses and ear protection. The glasses should fit closely to your face with only minor clearance or none at all (honestly, goggles are best). Muffs should seal fully to your head; if the cup doesn't seal you will lose a great deal of the sound attenuation that you would have if the muff was sealed properly. Everyone's face and head shape is different from everyone else's.

If I just started you worrying about catastrophic failures, please stop. They are avoidable and we will address these as we proceed through the book, and the point of good preventative maintenance is to keep bad things from happening.

READ THE MANUAL

I shouldn't have to say this but reality is often different from what we would like it to be, and let's face it, there are a lot of lazy people. If your gun has a user's manual, then you need to read it. Read it thoroughly and if you don't understand it, find someone to help you. The manual tells you just about all you need to know about your firearm. How to operate it, how to clean it, how to take it apart, are all included, and if you read and obey the manual you will save yourself time, money, and frustration later when your gun stops working and you wind up having to bring it to a gunsmith to fix because you didn't read that part about not using steel cased ammo (or whatever, pick something).

READ YOUR USER'S MANUAL! If you got a used gun with no manual with it, get on the inter

This is the book of all knowledge that hardly anyone bothers to read. Read your fudging manual!

net and print the manual off the manufacturer's web site.

Here are a few other useful items of safety equipment. You don't necessarily need these, but you do necessarily need the safety glasses and ear protection.

1 Respirator. This will, if worn, keep out dust and paint or whatever. If you are going to paint your gun, wear a respirator. Also used when sand blasting.

2 Latex or nitrile gloves. This is to keep the crud and solvents away from your skin. Solvents that clean guns real well, like acetone and lacquer thinner, not super good for your hands and fingernails, and really aren't good for you in the long term anyway. Gunk and residue that is coming off the gun also for some reason doesn't come off your fingers nearly as easily as a glove coming off your hand. Get some rags made of tee-shirt material. Cheap and effective.

3 An apron is a good thing to have. I don't particularly like them because they give me headaches (pulls on my neck) but it's still something just about anyone can use. So, no picture. If you don't know what an apron looks like, send me all your guns. I'll pay shipping.

4 Lead wipes. You are going to get lead residue on your hands. Use the lead wipes to get it off before your baby starts chewing on your fingers. Every time you shoot you should wash your hands before doing anything else. If not the wipes, then at least with soap and water.

5 First aid kit. If you have a garage shop or something like that, a basic first aid kit in proximity will come in handy when you slam your thumb in your M1 or when you let the slide on your pistol spring forward before you got the meat of your palm out of the way.

Now for some tools of the AR trade.

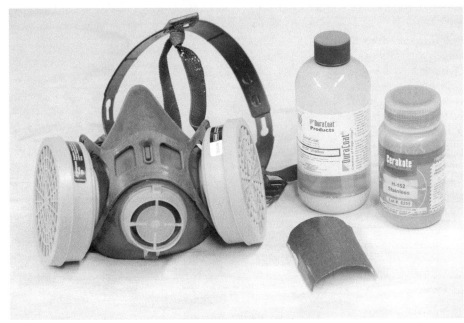

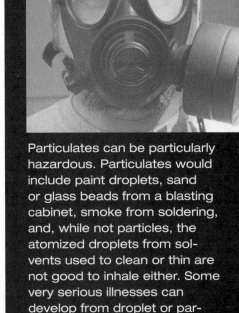

Particulates can be particularly hazardous. Particulates would include paint droplets, sand or glass beads from a blasting cabinet, smoke from soldering, and, while not particles, the atomized droplets from solvents used to clean or thin are not good to inhale either. Some very serious illnesses can develop from droplet or particulate ingestion so the use of respirators, or at the minimum of a mask, is mandatory if you want to live to old age.

(top) If you decide to refinish your rifle, which is a commonplace thing, you will need to wear lung protection as well as eye protection. Inexpensive paint respirators like these are available at any hardware store.

(middle left) Keeping the crud off our hands will be appreciated by your wife. Gloves and rags will help with that.

(middle right) De-leading wipes are handy to have.

(right) This first aid kit put together by the author is more complete than necessary for a vehicle/range kit, but hey, the author is a bit paranoid. The bag itself is a Maxpedition Sabercat Versipack. It's pretty much a buttpack but can be attached to larger containers if necessary. It's spacious enough for paranoid people and extremely well made.

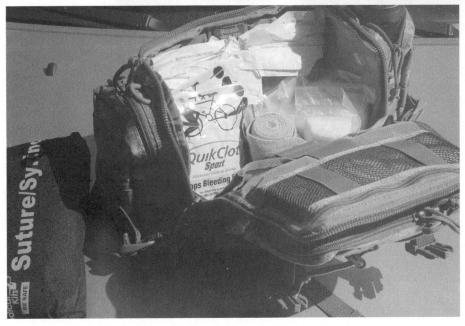

TOOLS

1 **Digital Camera.** Digital pictures are free. Take pictures. Take lots of them. While ARs are very easy to assemble, it doesn't hurt to have a visual reference if you need one. Pins will insert backwards and the wrong spring has been known to be inserted here rather than there. If you do this type of thing a couple times, it will become second nature, but until then take pics of everything.

2 **Vise.** Some sort of vise with padded jaws is a must. Most of us do not have three hands, and a minimum of three hands is needed to work on a gun. The padded semi-soft jaws will cover the hard steel jaws and prevent the vise from damaging the gun. There are a lot of vises made for use in the gun industry, but for starters just a regular bench vise from the hardware store will suffice. As long as you get the jaw pads.

3 **Lower receiver vise block.** This can be purchased from Brownells or you can make your own by trimming down a piece of wood, 2x4, or using an old magazine and filling it with something rigid like cement. There is no place on the lower receiver of an AR that allows clamping with a vise without harming the receiver

4 **Upper receiver vise block.** There are several versions of this. Some retain the upper by means of the takedown pin holes. Other's wrap around the receiver like a clamshell. Another pinches the upper receiver between the jaws with the receiver on its side, and another goes into the receiver and locks in to the barrel extension. All will work, but the latter two are the best.

5 **Gunsmithing screwdriver set.** This you must have. Gunsmithing screwdrivers have a hollow ground tip, not the taper tip that conventional screwdrivers sport. Taper tips chew up the fancy delicate screw heads on the gun screws, and hollow ground tips do not. Nobody wants buggered up screws showing on their gun, nor do they want the value loss inherent in having what is now a defective part. The Craftsmans in your garage are not going to cut it. Gunsmith screwdriver sets also come with a much wider range of widths and thicknesses to fit the large variety of screws that exist in guntown. There are two sets that I can recommend without any reservation. They handle maybe 99% of the screws that you will find on firearms, the Brownells MagnaTip sets and the Wheeler Engineering Professional set. Fortunately there are few screws on ARs and many of them are actually hex or torx heads.

(top left) Use it when you take something apart.

(left) To work on your AR you must have one of these.

(below left) To work on your lower receiver, you must have one of these. Note one is simply the steel tube from a crummy old mangled magazine.

(above) Upper receiver work requires upper vise blocks. Seen here are the JP Vise Clamps and the Brownells/Peace River upper block.

(below) Brownells and Wheeler Engineering make great screwdriver sets. The small Wheeler Engineering set is a fantabulous addition to the range bag.

6 **Hex wrench sets.** You are much more likely to find hex screws, and some torx screws too. Hex (Allen) wrenches, and Torx tips are a must, both standard and metric.

7 **Punches.** Good high-quality steel punches are necessary for removing pins. Standard punches are the basic and you will use them. Furthermore you will need roll pin punches and pin holding punches. Roll pin punches have a little nubbie on the tip that sits inside the roll pin. These punches reduce (but not eliminate) the damage taken when driving roll and spring pins in and out. The pin holders have shallow hollow tips that hold the pins so you can get them started in the holes. For the non-gunsmith, they are not completely necessary. It should be noted that the more modern the gun, the higher the ratio of spring or roll pins to solid dowel pins.

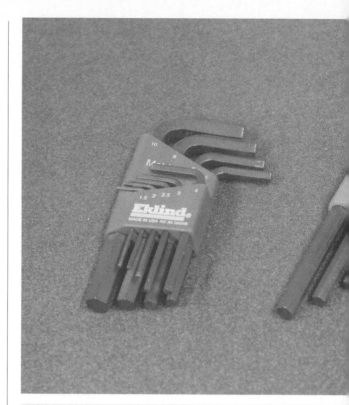

8 **Hammer or mallet.** Go to Brownells or Mid-wayUSA and buy a soft face hammer, like one of the dual brass/nylon heads. Most of these models are heavy enough to dislodge any part you will find on a gun. The heads are replaceable so when you chew up the nylon end, you can order a replacement head. On ARs, you will do very little pounding. The worst is removing the taper pins on the front sight/gas block assembly. The most common is to lightly tap out the fire control pins. You may need a heavier hammer for the taper pins, but the light dual faced hammers are more than sufficient for the FC pins. A very small steel ball-pien hammer is also sometimes handy.

9 **Work mat and solid bench.** The kitchen table won't cut it. A good heavy garage or workshop bench is needed, for stability and sturdiness. A work mat to help catch parts as they fall out is also a requirement. These nicely inhibit bouncing parts from skipping off the bench onto the floor. Throw in some magnetic trays and you are golden.

10 **Hand drill.** You will use this for cleaning the chamber and lug recess in the barrel extension. There is no better way to do this without the drill. If you don't have one get one. Thirty bucks at the hardware store.

11 **Fire.** A plain old propane torch from Ace will be all you need. You are not going to be welding, but you might need heat to uncure the thread locking adhesive that is often applied to certain parts of ARs. The propane flame can also slowly heat up the parts to expand them to make them easy to take apart, particularly if there is a lot of dirtiness involved, or if the parts are aluminum.

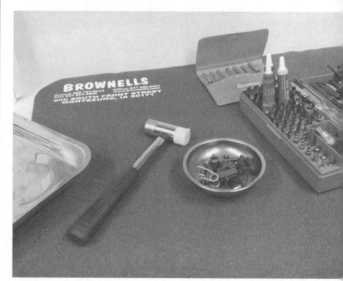

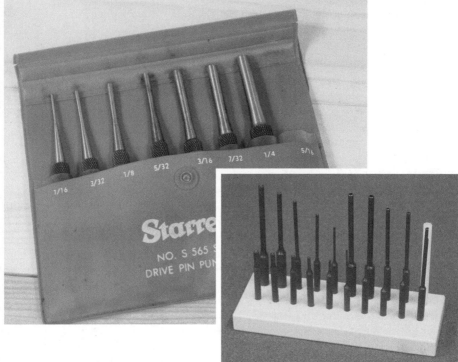

(above left) Hex wrenches (Allen) are more and more necessary to gun work. Get some.

(above right) Try pounding out pins with your fingertips. It don't work too good. (inset) Roll pin punches.jpg: Spring and roll pins require these punches. Just get them, alright?

(left) Small gunsmith hammers, one steel, one with interchangeable, not-steel, heads.

(bottom left) Work spaces benefit from non-bouncy surfaces. A fabric mat like this one from Brownells fits the bill.

(below) Easy chamber cleaning tool this drill is.

(below right) Loc-Tite removal device.

12 **Bench Block.** A plastic bench block for pin removal is a handy item, particularly for installing the front sight tower and the trigger guard. The holes allow the pins to pass completely out of the gun while still maintaining full support for the parts. Brownells makes a specialty block shaped to receive the front sight on an AR.

13 **Airbrush.** If you get into refinishing with DuraCoat or Cerakote or Alumahyde or something like that, you will need an airbrush at a minimum, and an HVLP gun at most.

14 **Bore sighting equipment.** Lasers and optical collimators are great tools and are all but necessary for scope mounting. But if you aren't mounting your own scopes then there is no point. Since most rifle owners have attempted to do so, thinking the $35 bucks a gunsmith might charge is a rip off (it so isn't) there are a lot of boresighters in private hands. The mandrel types of boresighters are not appropriate for ARs. They are not tall enough. Use a magnetic or laser boresighter for ARs.

15 **Headspace gauges.** If you are in a position to change out barrels you will need headspace gauges. Alternatively, they can be rented, as can reamers, from several companies on the net.

16 **Multi-tool.** This can unjam or fix in a jiffy. Keep it in your range bag or rifle case so it's handy when you need it.

17 **Pretty much anything else.** The possibilities are endless and it's your money. There are other specialty tools for ARs that you may decide you like or need.

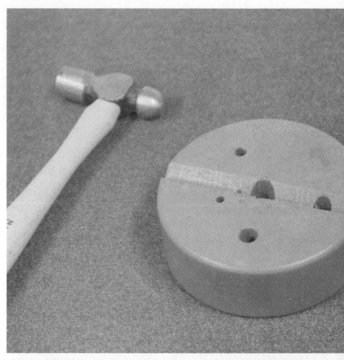

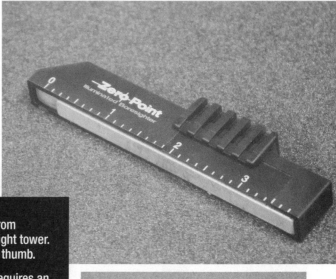

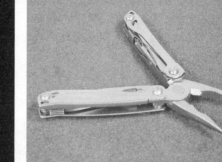

(top left) The block on the right is from Brownells, for removing the front sight tower. The other one is for smashing your thumb.

(top right) Small scale refinishing requires an airbrush. Easy and relatively cheap.

(middle left) If you mount your own optics, then a boresighting tool will save you ammo.

(middle right) Rebarreling your own rifle will require a set of GO, NOGO, and FIELD gauges.

(bottom left) If this is on your belt, you will not regret it. This is a Multitasker AR specific multi-tool that you can get at Brownells.

(bottom right) Other AR specific tools include, but are not necessarily limited to, an action wrench, a handguard removal tool (very convenient), free float tube wrench, stock wrench.

How it Works

There are a vast number of AR-type rifles in existence but, with the exception of a couple, they all operate in the same manner. So let's look at the cycle of operation of the AR-15 and how the shooter interacts with it, so that we can understand how the whole system works.

LOADING/UNLOADING

The trigger is located in the normal place, at the top front of the pistol grip. Above and behind the trigger on the left side is the safety/selector lever. On semi-auto guns it is a safety. On full auto it is both a selector and a safety lever. On a semi-auto it rotates 90 degrees, with the lever pointing straight to the rear on SAFE, and pointing down when on FIRE. The lever is on the left side of the lower receiver, making the AR series easier used by right-handers. The shooting hand thumb is simply raised in order to interact with the lever, pushing it down to bring the gun to FIRE and pulling it to the rear to SAFE it. It will rotate accordingly. Please note, and this is very important, that the safety lever should not be able to go on SAFE if the gun has been fired and the hammer is resting forward, i.e. the gun is not cocked.

Only a few of the many variations, but they all work the same (mostly).

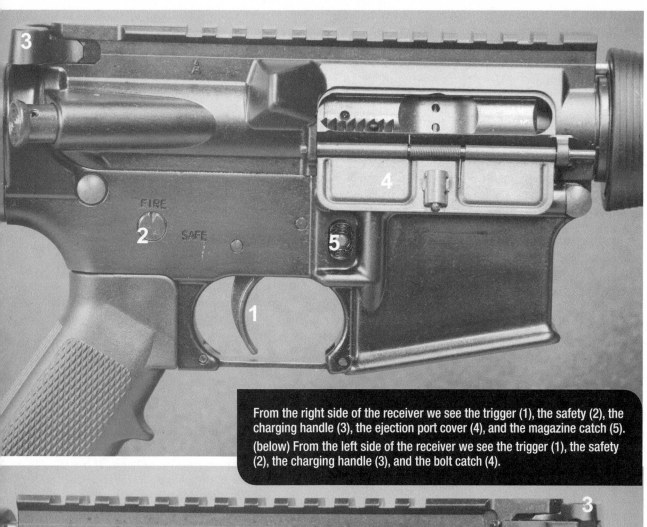

From the right side of the receiver we see the trigger (1), the safety (2), the charging handle (3), the ejection port cover (4), and the magazine catch (5).

(below) From the left side of the receiver we see the trigger (1), the safety (2), the charging handle (3), and the bolt catch (4).

The gun is loaded by inserting a magazine that has cartridges in it into the magazine well and raising it until it locks in place. The charging handle is then pulled to the rear all the way until it stops, and released to slam forward by the force of the buffer spring in the stock, loading a round into the chamber.

To unload the AR, eject the magazine by depressing the magazine catch button on the right hand side of the lower receiver, then pull the charging handle to the rear to extract and eject the round in the chamber. If you desire, the bolt can then be held open by seating an empty magazine in the magazine well, or you can do the same thing by pushing in the bottom of the bolt catch on the left side, then pushing the charging handle back home manually to latch it back in place.

CYCLE OF OPERATION

You really should get to know this. Understanding how the system works will help you understand what might go wrong and how to fix it if it does. Every repeating firearm will have some variation of what amounts to a common cycle of operation. Meaning that when you fire an AR a number of things happen in a very specific order to make the whole thing work the way it should, safely and effectively. Okay, here we go.

1 **Firing.** This is where you have a loaded magazine and chamber, safety off, and you pull the trigger. The hammer is released and it rapidly rotates up and forward and strikes the rear of the firing pin. The firing pin then strikes the primer on the back of the cartridge case and causes it to ignite the powder in the case. The powder is rapidly converted to gas and this expanding gas pushes the bullet down the barrel. The bullet at some point

in the barrel will pass a gas port where some of the propellant gasses are tapped off from the barrel to be used to continue the cycle to the next step.

2 **Unlocking.** The gas that has been tapped from the barrel is shunted through the gas tube that lies above the barrel and travels back into a cavity in the bolt carrier just behind the bolt itself. The gas expands in this area, pushing the carrier to the rear and simultaneously pushing the bolt tightly into the barrel extension. As the bolt carrier begins to move to the rear it begins to rotate the bolt in the barrel extension by means of a cam slot and pin. When the carrier has moved about one half inch to the rear, the bolt is fully unlocked from the extension and the entire bolt and carrier assembly can continue to the rear and begins the next step of extraction. Also at this point, the carrier is no longer in contact with the gas tube and no further gas is introduced into the system. The carrier continues moving under its own momentum until it is stopped by impacting the rear of the stock extension tube in which it is contained.

3 **Extraction.** When the bolt is fully unlocked (from step 2) and begins to move to the rear, the extractor hook on the right side of the bolt pulls the fired cartridge case from the chamber, "extracting" it completely from the barrel and presenting the case to the ejection port. If insufficient gas enters the system, extraction will not be completed and the bolt carrier will not experience it's full range of rearward motion, and will close again under the force of the buffer spring, sometimes pushing the spent case back into the chamber, sometimes jamming the mouth of the spent case against the barrel extension.

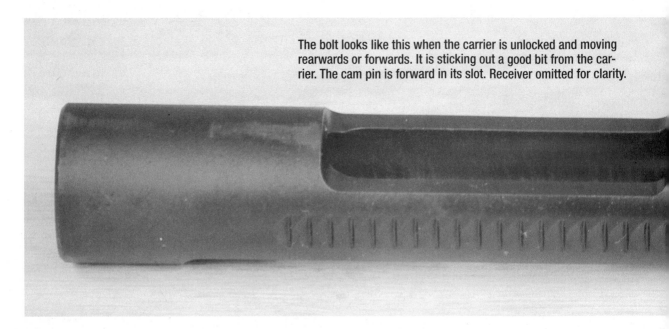

The bolt looks like this when the carrier is unlocked and moving rearwards or forwards. It is sticking out a good bit from the carrier. The cam pin is forward in its slot. Receiver omitted for clarity.

The bolt has pulled, or extracted, the spent case from the chamber and in this picture is about halfway through its rearward movement.

The bolt has moved far enough to the rear for the case to clear the front of the ejection port. Now the ejector, which has been under spring tension, can push the case out to the right and out of the receiver.

The bolt carrier assembly, as it is extracting and ejecting the spent case, is also recocking the hammer with the underside of the carrier. When the carrier is pressing down on the hammer, the trigger is completely out of contact with anything, until the carrier moves forward far enough to remove contact with the hammer and the hammer comes to rest on the disconnector.

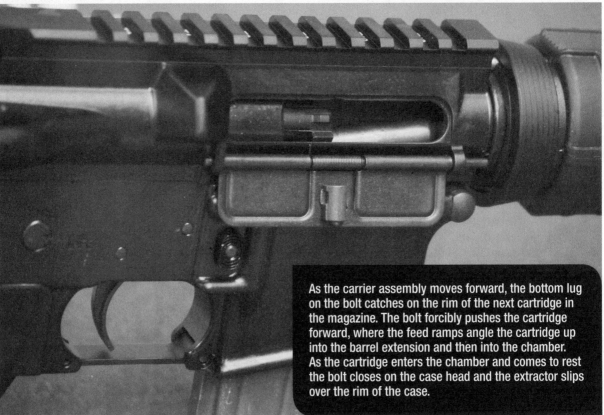

As the carrier assembly moves forward, the bottom lug on the bolt catches on the rim of the next cartridge in the magazine. The bolt forcibly pushes the cartridge forward, where the feed ramps angle the cartridge up into the barrel extension and then into the chamber. As the cartridge enters the chamber and comes to rest the bolt closes on the case head and the extractor slips over the rim of the case.

4 **Ejection.** When the front of the case clears the front edge of the ejection port, the case is thrown (ejected) from the gun out in to the surrounding environment, clearing the system for another round to be fed into the chamber. The ejector mechanism is inside the left of the face of the bolt itself, composed of a plunger and spring. When a cartridge is chambered and held in place in the bolt face, the ejector spring is compressed, then released as the extracted round clears the ejection port. Ejection can be affected by the bolt carrier moving too swiftly or too slowly.

5 **Cocking.** As the bolt carrier moves to the rear it also rotates the hammer to the rear again, the hammer being caught by the disconnector hook. The hammer does not reconnect to the sear again until the bolt carrier is most of the way closed again and the trigger has been released.

6 **Feeding/Chambering.** The bolt carrier's rear travel is stopped by impact with the rear of the buffer tube. The buffer spring is now compressed as a result. The spring expands and pushes the bolt carrier assembly forward to strip off another cartridge from the magazine. This cartridge is pushed into the chamber, at which point the bolt stops against the barrel extension, and the carrier continues forward. The cartridge will always have to move forward and up, a fairly complex movement. Bullet shape, poor resizing during reloading, damaged mag feed lips, bolt velocity, and mag spring condition will all affect how well a firearm feeds and chambers, and all must maintain the ideal balance for a firearm to be considered reliable.

7 **Locking.** The carrier continues forward, and in a reversal of the unlocking step, the cam pin and slot cause the bolt to rotate in the barrel extension so that the lugs of the bolt are placed in front of the lugs in the barrel extension, fully locking the bolt into the extension. It is this lug interaction that locks the bolt closed on the chamber to seal from the resulting pressure from firing. This is what keeps the system contained and the expanding gas away from you.

The reason the cycle of operation is included in this chapter is to provide a better understanding of how a semi-automatic rifle functions. Even basic knowledge of the steps and what happens during each step will prove to benefit the owner immensely. Identification of malfunctions will be simpler and more accurate, and the resultant safe handling practices will improve measurably as well. I've seen many gun owners, experienced and amateur, do some insanely dangerous things with their guns when a gremlin gets in the works. We want to avoid these activities, and intimate understanding of the cycle of operation will go a long way to accomplishing this goal.

The bolt stops either from contact with the cartridge or (ideally) from contact with the rear face of the barrel inside the barrel extension. The extractor is engaged on the rim of the case. The carrier continues forward until it comes into contact with the barrel extension. This causes the cam pin to rotate the bolt into a locked position, as seen here. The bolt is pushed into the carrier, and the cam pin is fully to the rear of its slot.

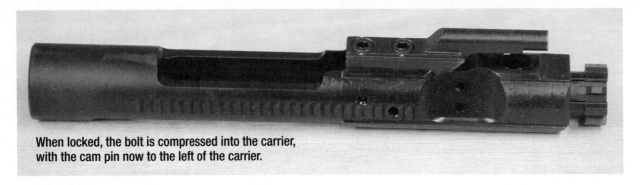

When locked, the bolt is compressed into the carrier, with the cam pin now to the left of the carrier.

GAS SYSTEM LENGTH

At the risk of getting a little too technical, I want to talk a bit about the differences between gas system lengths. The new or prospective AR owner may have heard of or even engaged in the debate between carbine, mid-length, and rifle length (I suppose pistol length too) gas systems and their benefits or deficiencies.

The original M-16/AR-15 rifle used a 20" barrel with what came to be known as the rifle length gas system. The gas port in the barrel that is used to tap gas from the bore, is about 13 inches from the bolt and seven inches from the muzzle. This allowed the rifle's pressure curve to be ideal for the 55 grain bullet that those guns used, and the 20" barreled guns are extremely reliable. This pressure curve, based on the pressure at the gas port and the pressure at the chamber, is an indication of what is exactly going on in the bore when a shot is fired. For example when the powder is ignited and starts to push the bullet down the bore, there is a great deal of chamber pressure but no port pressure. There is no port pressure until the bullet moves past the gas port. When this happens, a certain amount of high pressure gas is passed through the port and that gas then travels back down the gas tube to unlock the bolt. There is still significant chamber pressure, but not as much as when the bullet was still in the throat of the barrel. Once the bullet exits the barrel, the chamber and port pressure rapidly decrease to zero, negating any further introduction of energy (gas) into the system.

Remember that the whole point of a firearm is to contain and direct pressure in a very confined manner in or-der to send downrange a projectile at high enough velocity to make a hole in something. It must also be used to operate the action. In either case, that pressure can't be too high or too low or things don't work right. Too little pressure and your gun will not cycle; too much and you can have bad results up to and including catastrophic failures and malfunctions.

This brings us to the carbine length gas system that the vast majority of 16" and less barrels use. Most of the ARs sold on the market today are 16" barrels, so this paragraph should concern you. The reason for concern is that the 16" barreled carbines are more problem-prone than the 20" barreled rifles. Here's why. The gas port is only 7 1/4 inches from the bolt, but is fully 8 1/2 inches from the muzzle. This means the gas port has to be smaller for two reasons. It's closer to the chamber and the higher attendant pressures that will be

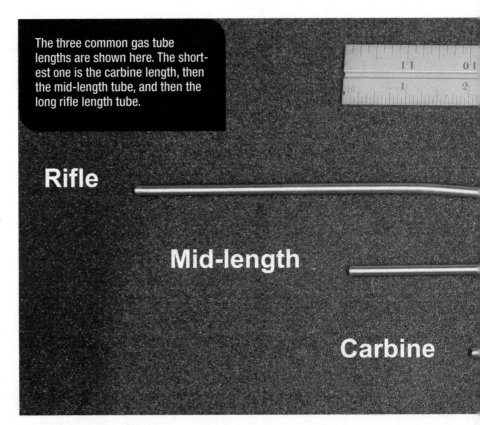

The three common gas tube lengths are shown here. The shortest one is the carbine length, then the mid-length tube, and then the long rifle length tube.

Rifle

Mid-length

Carbine

transferred through the gas port, and it's farther from the muzzle which means there is more pressure building up behind the bullet before it leaves the muzzle. This means a shorter gas tube as well. The shorter distance and higher temperatures and pressures mean that the bolt is trying to extract the case from the chamber sooner than would be the case in a 20" barreled rifle. This places much more stress on the extractor and the case rim itself. One of the most common malfunctions in the carbine gas system guns is the failure to extract, usually caused by the case head (the very back part containing the rim) separating from the case body, leaving the body in the chamber, or the extractor

This is what the front end of the gas system looks like in a standard AR rifle. The gas is diverted from the gas port through the gas block, and then to the receiver via the gas tube that is pinned into the block.

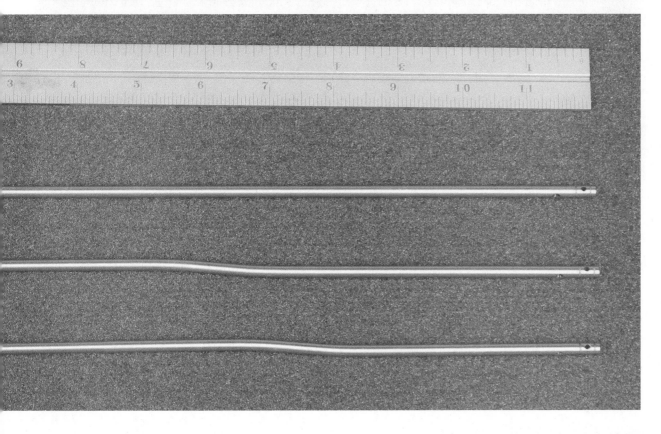

Gas tube

Adjustment screw hole

Retaining pin

Gas port

Clamp screw holes

ripping the rim from the case head itself. Furthermore, the hook of the extractor has a reduced life as well and can break off.

There are several treatments for this symptom. The first is to increase the reciprocating mass of the bolt carrier. You can't really make the carrier more massive, but you can make the buffer heavier. Indeed there are H1, H2, H3 and 9mm buffers. In that order, they are increasingly heavier than the standard carbine buffer. This increased mass slows down the speed of the system (cyclic rate), generally allowing the extractor to impart much less stress onto the case rim because more time has allowed the case to contract again, away from the chamber walls. Heavier power buffer springs can assist in this process as well, but if taken too far can make the rifle more difficult to manually charge.

The second option, like the first, is to treat the symptom rather than the problem. This approach is the most common and takes the form of using higher compression rate springs in the extractor, and/or the inclusion of a squishy insert inside the spring to enhance its tension. The extractor spring is then more difficult to compress, which makes it grab the case rim more firmly, or rather, makes it more difficult to skip off the rim. This makes

it more likely to result in a torn rim, where the extractor simply rips the section of rim off, instead of popping around the rim. This does nothing to reduce stress placed on the extractor hook; if anything, it increases it. So while we have increased extraction reliability with the increased spring tension, the breaking of the rims and the extractor hooks remains.

The third and best solution addresses the cause of the problems rather than the symptoms. This is to move the gas port farther down the 16" barrel several inches. This slows down the system by the very fact that it is farther away from the chamber. It also addresses the high port pressure seen in the M4 style barrels because of the large stretch of barrel past the gas port. Having the gas port further from the barrel and closer to the muzzle, in a nutshell, balances the system out in a way much closer to Stoner's original 20" barreled design. Rifles with this "mid-length" system work much more reliably than the carbine system, and incidentally also have a greater sight radius, which promotes better accuracy. Armalite has a series of Technical notes on their web site, number 48 being the most pertinent to this subject. I highly recommend spending some time on that resource page.

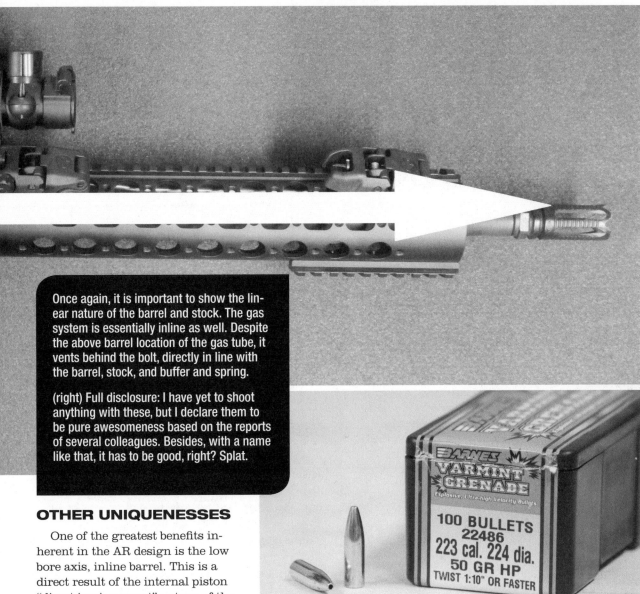

Once again, it is important to show the linear nature of the barrel and stock. The gas system is essentially inline as well. Despite the above barrel location of the gas tube, it vents behind the bolt, directly in line with the barrel, stock, and buffer and spring.

(right) Full disclosure: I have yet to shoot anything with these, but I declare them to be pure awesomeness based on the reports of several colleagues. Besides, with a name like that, it has to be good, right? Splat.

OTHER UNIQUENESSES

One of the greatest benefits inherent in the AR design is the low bore axis, inline barrel. This is a direct result of the internal piston "direct impingement" nature of the rifle. Other than the fire control components, all the moving parts move directly in line of the bore axis. This means that you can have a rifle that is very inherently accurate because there are no other parts rattling, stressing, or flopping around in connection to the barrel. The gas is simply channeled to the bolt carrier, expanding inside the carrier which then moves directly in line with the bore. Stoner further placed the bore so that it was aligned with the heel of the buttstock, thereby directing the entirety of the recoil impulse directly into the shoulder, rather than over it. We've already sort of mentioned this, but it bears repeating because of its relevance. Recoil, felt recoil that is, from a .223-class rifle is already close to negligent. However, the addition of further recoil mitigation, such as muzzle brakes, additional weight to the gun, and reduced mass carriers and buffers,

among other things, reduce it to the point of ridiculous. It truly is a thing of beauty to take a shot, feel only the tap of the buffer against the stock, and see the red blooming result in the scope as the Varmint Grenade atomizes a gopher at 50 yards.

Unfortunately, this low bore axis creates a high sight axis for lack of a better term. The sights and therefore any mounted optics are consequently quite high over the bore axis. This is generally not considered optimal, as greater separation of the two can complicate the ballistic calculations when target shooting, and force the shooter to expose more of himself to return fire in those cases of combat. Flat top mounts have helped to lower the optics from those days when everything had to be mounted on top of the carry handle. We will address these things in greater detail in later chapters.

Pistol Grips

he original AR-15 pistol grip was what is now considered the "A1" grip. Very similar to the current standard "A2" grip, it was distinguished by slight dimensional changes and the significant difference of being smooth with no finger nub. The A2 grip has a large and, in my opinion, poorly placed finger groove projection. If you have fingers twice the thickness of mine, the A2 grip might be comfortable for you.

WHY CHANGE?

Well, somebody back when finally decided that the AR-15 A2 style pistol grip really wasn't all that comfortable. Since I have yet to meet someone who admits to liking it, I can imagine why people started filing the finger bump thingy off. Problem solved and more people were happy. Pretty soon, other variations of grips started appearing, with completely different designs becoming very popular. While I hear there are a few people happy with

The classic A2 pistol grip that most factory rifles and just about all lower parts kits are shipped with.

(below) An evil protruding pistol grip, compared to a more traditional pistol grip on a traditional hunting rifle.

the stock A2 grip (usually folks with fatter fingers, or generals who don't have to use them), many are not, and we now have a generous selection of quite inexpensive pistol grips, such as the models from MagPul, Hogue, Ergo Grips, CAA, and the list goes on. Mostly, these grips are under $20 and can be obtained easily, and come in a variety of colors. All because the A2 grip came with a finger nub. If you want, you can still get an A1 grip.

Perhaps we should first explain why the pistol grip is there and, quickly, what it is. It is a hand-filling section that protrudes from the bottom of the gun, like would be seen on a pistol, and is generally close to vertical. This is what you will see on most other Modern Sporting Rifles and increasing numbers of more traditional rifles and shotguns. There are two main reasons to use a protruding pistol grip.

The first relates to the desire to lower the barrel in relation to the shoulder to better control recoil

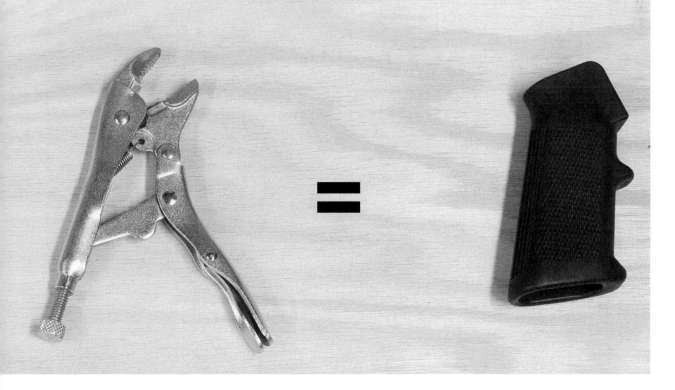

impulse. Most traditional rifles' stocks contact the shoulder below the barrel line. This is the primary cause of muzzle rise when firing a gun. You are essentially using a lever that has an off-center pivot point. Lowering the barrel so that the recoil force is directed straight into the shoulder minimizes muzzle rise. However, a traditional pistol grip incorporated into the stock is less than comfortable when it is combined with a low bore. So low bore axis guns like ARs, AKs, HKs, basically anything derived from modern military rifles, are equipped with protruding pistol grips so that holding the gun is more comfortable and practical. We mentioned this trait in an earlier chapter.

The second function is related to the first. Your hand is pretty much perpendicular to the length of your forearm. Keeping your hand nearly vertical also allows your arm to control recoil better. For example, try punching something with your hand closed in a fist, impacting on your knuckles. That's how it's supposed to work. Now try it this way. Punch something really, really hard, but instead of impacting on your knuckles, angle your wrist forward so that the

impact hits the top of your fist on the thumb and index finger. Your hand isn't designed to do it that way, is it? It functions the same way with a gun and pistol grip, albeit in a less dramatic fashion.

So you see, there is a reason for putting protruding pistol grips on guns, including guns that don't traditionally have them. Contrary to what the lovely Mrs. Senator Feinstein says as she waves AKs

This beavertail hogue grip forces your hand into a slightly more vertical angle and lengthens the trigger reach a little bit. Good for thick-fingered dudes with carpal tunnel, though oddly, it is for my small hands more comfortable than the standard Hogue grip. It also has a little projection to fill the void behind the standard trigger guard.

This Monsterman grip is not considered a protruding pistol grip and is California legal, for those who cannot escape and still wish to own a compliant AR. Photo courtesy Monsterman Grips.

(left) The basic MagPul MIAD grip mounted to a rifle, this time in OD green, one of several colors available other than black.

(left middle) This image of a MIAD black basic kit shows the extra pieces.

(left bottom) The CAA grip as compared to an A2. Big, big difference. It is loosely styled on the HK pattern of pistol grips from the old G3 and 90 series of rifles.

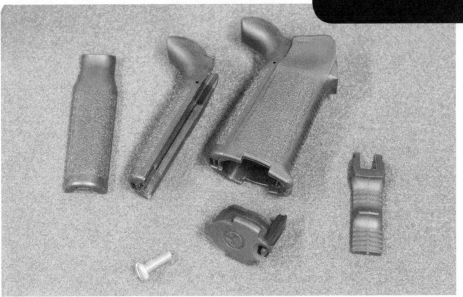

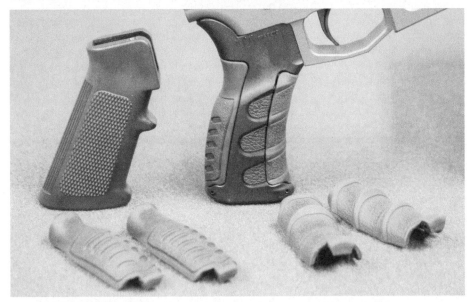

market has, of course, flipped the bird to such silly notions and created ever more interesting solutions. I won't get into too much detail here, but the intent is to remove the idea of a protruding pistol grip and replace it with something that is either incorporated into the stock, or looks nothing like a protruding pistol grip but still sort of fills the same function. The MonsterMan grip and the Hammerhead grip are two of the most obvious examples that were designed for use in California. These grips allow the shooter to legally use detachable magazines, rather than have fixed mags. The FRS-15 stock is a new example where the grip and the stock are one piece and avoids the problem of a protruding pistol grip altogether.

Let's dig a little deeper into the standard options. The original

around the U.S. Senate, it's not to make it easier to shoot from the hip without aiming. Comfort and recoil reduction are always desirable and the pistol grip in any of its forms contributes to the improvement of those qualities in the action of shooting.

Ironically, legislation has continued to evolve ways to bar citizens from nice things and the

Hogue pistol grip is one of the most popular, being overmolded with a rubberized coating that gives it a high grip friction factor. But it still has finger grooves in it that don't really fit people with small fingers very well. Hogue has since begun producing a grip that doesn't have finger grooves, and also a more vertical and bottom-trimmed model as

The Stark grip is probably the most divergent of the standard type of AR grips. The hand is very vertical and the trigger reach is extreme. It's a good grip for bench shooting with really light triggers, or for dudes with really big hands.

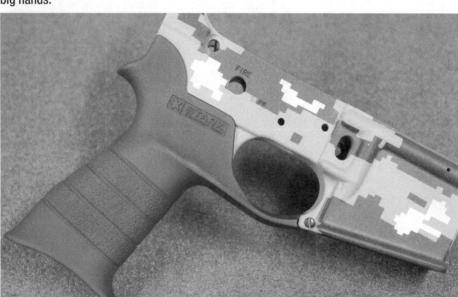

grip to very slightly adjust to your hand.

Another fun possibility for the rifles is the modular grip, of which there are only currently two prominent in the marketplace. The MagPul MIAD grip is the original and has replaceable back straps and front straps that slide into the main body. The trigger guard insert on the original Deluxe models is unfortunately no longer available. The unfortunate part we will discuss later in the chapter on building your AR. The MOE trigger guard has superseded the trigger guard insert. The CAA Universal Pistol Grip is similar, but where the MIAD is a straight grip, the CAA Universal has a slight curve to it and looks more like the pistol grip from an HK rifle. There are folks who like the curved nature of these grips. In fact, this grip and the Ergo grip from Falcon Industries are quite comfortable in the hand. Well, some people's hands, anyway. It's all personal preference. I know guys who use only one and no other brand, and others who are not too horribly picky.

A unique model is the Stark Industries grip. Very not-AR looking, it is big, increases the trigger length-of-pull, and has a more vertical angle to it. It is rather well suited for big guys with big

well. The Extreme series uses laminated G-10 and related synthetic materials to create some strikingly attractive grips. Hogue grips are often used as OEM products by rifle manufacturers because of the popularity and the low price point.

A similar item to the Hogue grip is from MagPul, the MOE+ grip. This grip is also overmolded, but is otherwise just like the standard MOE grip. As mentioned previously, the rubbery surface increases the traction on the grip. Even when wet, the pistol grip is still very solid in the hand, and the overmolding also gives a little, allowing the

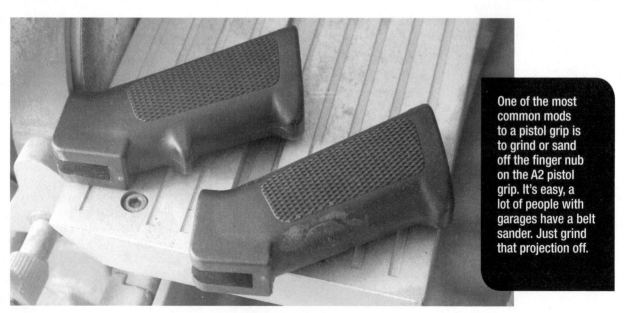

One of the most common mods to a pistol grip is to grind or sand off the finger nub on the A2 pistol grip. It's easy, a lot of people with garages have a belt sander. Just grind that projection off.

hands and long fingers.

The really nice thing is that most of these models, regardless of the model of gun that they are designed to fit, are almost always attached by one or maybe two simple screws, or maybe a screw and nut combination. But either way, it is a very simple matter to take off the old grip and install the new one. Best of all, you rarely need more than a rather large sized flat-bladed screwdriver. The reason a flat-bladed screwdriver-headed screw is used is for ease of tool availability. Despite the superiority of hex and Torx head screws and bolts (which some manufacturers use anyway, thank God), it is much easier to find flat head screwdrivers in anyone's tool box, less so with the better hex and Torx heads. It should be noted, if not already realized, that there are a lot of things on these guns that are leftovers from the military and the M16, most of them being positive. This is not one of them.

You will find the largest assortment of grips is available for AR-15s and AR-10s, with those for the AK-type rifle close behind. You will even find otherwise identical models for the AK to use AR grips. But that is a story for the AK chapter.

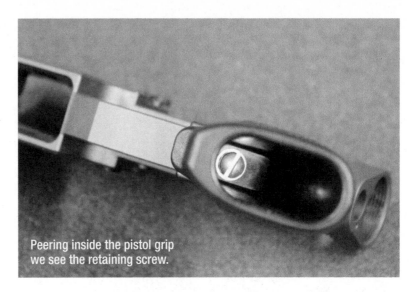
Peering inside the pistol grip we see the retaining screw.

INSTALLING A PISTOL GRIP ON AN AR

As mentioned a few paragraphs ago, AR grips are generally retained to the lower receiver of the AR via a slotted dome-headed screw that is an inch long. It will usually have a star lock washer underneath it that digs into the plastic of the grip to hold the screw tight. Unscrewing this screw completely will allow the grip to be removed. At the top of the grip on the right side is a small hole that contains the spring for the safety detent. This is the spring and detent that keeps the safety or se-

As the grip screw is loosened, the safety detent spring will become untensioned. Don't lose the spring or the detent in the hole above it.

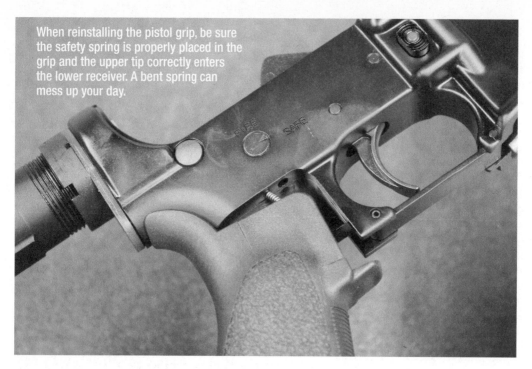
When reinstalling the pistol grip, be sure the safety spring is properly placed in the grip and the upper tip correctly enters the lower receiver. A bent spring can mess up your day.

lector in the receiver and gives it the click tension that keeps it on SAFE or FIRE. Loosening the grip screw partly (about halfway really) will completely remove spring tension on the safety, even though the spring's top end may still be sticking into the lower receiver. This process is often necessary to remove the trigger from the lower receiver.

Sometimes the trigger's safety tail will not clear the safety body and the safety will have to be partially removed to get the trigger out. To move the safety body partially or completely out, the detent must be dropped down in its hole, which requires the safety detent spring tension be released, which requires the pistol grip be partially removed. Following all this?

So let's replace the POS A2 grip with a not-POS Hogue grip. Completely remove the grip screw from the lower receiver and pull the grip off the receiver. Remember that the safety detent and spring will be free to fall into a crack in the floor,

The front pin is a spring-loaded detent and just needs to be depressed and the guard pulled down. The rear pin must be punched out and extreme care must be used to fully support the trigger guard wing or it will break off. At that point you will have to use a grip with an integral trigger guard.

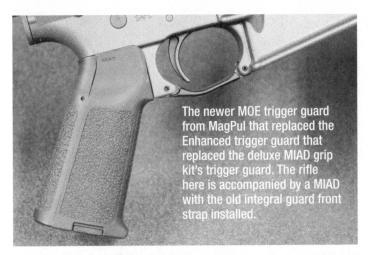

The newer MOE trigger guard from MagPul that replaced the Enhanced trigger guard that replaced the deluxe MIAD grip kit's trigger guard. The rifle here is accompanied by a MIAD with the old integral guard front strap installed.

so catch them as they come out. Or even better, hold the receiver left side down and bottom slightly raised and the detent itself will stay in the receiver. Pull the spring from the original grip and insert it into the hole in the new Hogue grip. Roll the receiver onto its left side and slide the new grip onto the spine on the bottom of the receiver. Doing this will keep the spring in the grip and the detent in the receiver.

As the grip goes on, ensure that the spring goes into the hole in the receiver or this whole process will be messed up. You can kink the spring if you don't get it into the hole and then Hulk the grip down. It

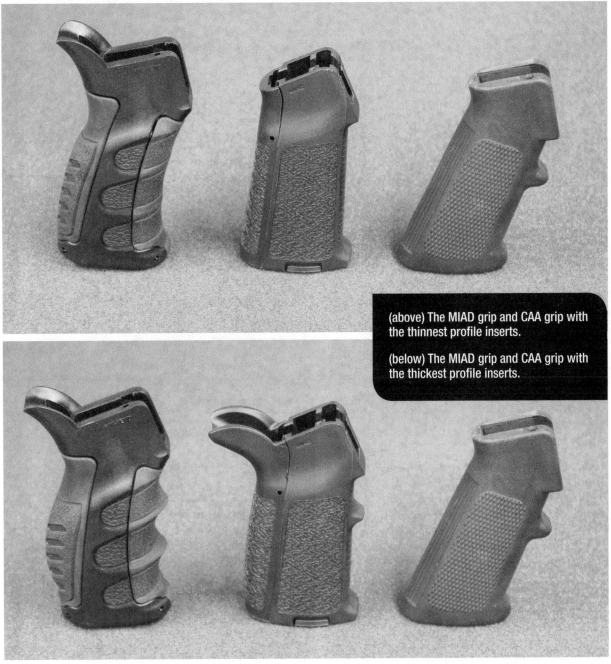

(above) The MIAD grip and CAA grip with the thinnest profile inserts.

(below) The MIAD grip and CAA grip with the thickest profile inserts.

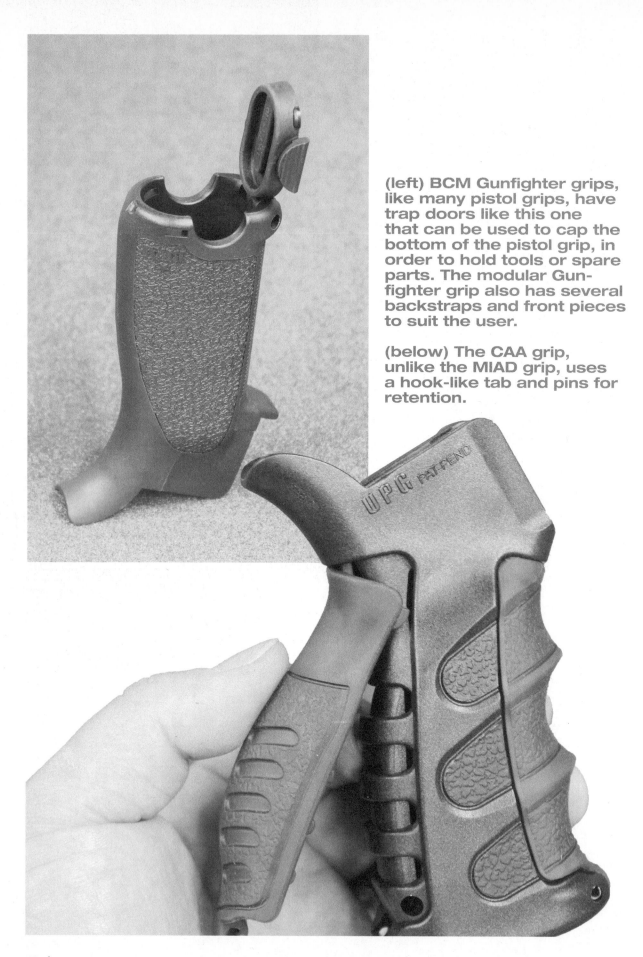

(left) BCM Gunfighter grips, like many pistol grips, have trap doors like this one that can be used to cap the bottom of the pistol grip, in order to hold tools or spare parts. The modular Gunfighter grip also has several backstraps and front pieces to suit the user.

(below) The CAA grip, unlike the MIAD grip, uses a hook-like tab and pins for retention.

won't work right then. With the spring in the hole, push the grip fully into place and use the same screw and washer to tighten the grip down to the receiver. That's pretty much it for the standard replacement.

The discontinued MagPul MIAD Deluxe pistol grip had the option of a trigger guard front strap. The grip came with several front straps that could be slid in and out of the front of the grip, just like the basic MIAD kit has. Well, the reason I mention this is that to use that trigger guard you had to remove the aluminum trigger guard that the lower receiver normally has installed. You depress the detent pin holding the front of the guard in place, and drive out the spring pin holding it in at the rear to remove the trigger guard. Or even better, don't even put the normal trigger guard in at all; then you won't have to remove it. By the way, this same process is used almost to a tee to install the MagPul Enhanced trigger guard and the Stark Equipment Group pistol grip. The grip with the trigger guard is installed after the original guard is removed. The new grip is tightened fully by the grip screw, and as you do this the new grip's trigger guard should slide right into place. These grips come with a small set screw that you install through the hole at the front of the trigger guard area of the lower receiver (right where the detent pin was). It self-threads. Installing this screw then secures the front end of the trigger guard and you now have much larger volume to insert your fat trigger finger, or to insert a finger with a glove on it.

It would be horribly remiss of me to not detail specifically these modular pistol grips. The first was the basic MIAD, with three back straps and two front straps. One of the back straps is thin and has a flush contour at the top. The other two back straps have what has come to be known as a beaver tail, even though it looks nothing like a beaver-tail. It is essentially a thumb webbing raiser that changes the grip a bit. It forces your hand at the thumb webbing area back and down slightly. This makes the grip feel slightly more vertical and also makes the guys with long fingers happy because it pulls the hand back. The grip circumference is also made larger. The medium and large straps both have this feature with differing thicknesses. The front straps simply allow you to have a finger nub like on the A2 grip or to have a smooth contour. Anyway, these options can be changed around willy-nilly if desired by removing the grip entirely for the front straps, or simply by manipulating a latch at the bottom rear of the grip for the back straps, which will slide down off the grip.

The other well-known modular grip is the Universal grip made by Command Arms Accessories. This model is generally shaped with the palm-swell style of the HK pattern grips, with the exception that you can make the swell larger or smaller, or

The word "grip" as used in anti-gun legislation has two definitions: the "pistol grip" that the firing hand holds (which is evil); and anything that would protect the support hand from being burned from contact with the barrel.

By these definitions they could ban almost any firearm, since every firearm has some provision to protect the hand from being burned from barrel heat. On most pistols it can be interpreted as the slide itself, and on any long gun it can be interpreted to mean whatever you hold onto with your support hand that isn't the barrel. Virtually all long guns have a forend or hand-guard where the support hand gains purchase, and it is always around or under the barrel.

Words mean things. Don't let some morons in suits use them against you.

add or remove finger grooves on the front. The front and back straps are rubbery but the grip body is hard plastic, giving the whole thing a variable feel. The beavertail projection is fixed on the body and the overall feel is much more vertical than the A2 grip. Both front and back straps are held in place by spring pins at the bottom of the grip, the tops of the straps having a hook.

All of these grips are hollow-cored of course. They must be in order to run the attachment screw through them. There are aftermarket options to cap or plug these hollow cores, and a few such as the MagPul lines come with plugs anyway. Some of these plugs have fittings to stick spare parts or batteries allowing them to be used efficiently as storage areas.

Stocks

W e shall now turn our attention to buttstocks. We are talking all kinds of flavors here. There are fixed stocks, folding stocks, collapsible stocks, and combinations thereof, but for the most part, what the AR world sees are fixed and collapsible stocks.

Most ARs come from the factory with basic A2-style fixed rifle stocks or simple collapsible M4 stocks. The trend recently is to make buttstocks that incorporate special features, with compartments, often watertight, that allow the owner to stash useful items like oil bottles, beef sticks, smokes, prophylactics, spare batteries for their red dot sight, or a couple last ditch rounds, or to cut down the rattle by putting in a tensioning or locking mechanism in the adjustment system.

Fixed stocks seem to be less common than collapsible stocks. A common alternative to the standard A2 stock is the skeleton stock made by ACE called the ARFX. It is very lightweight and incorporates a foam rubber cheek pad that makes it much more comfortable under the face. Most of the Ace stock lineup makes use of the foam pad and it is unique to that brand. If you have a hunting AR and you want a stock eminently suitable to that purpose, regardless of the prey, this is the ticket. I hunted for several years with a 6.5 Grendel chambered rifle. The stock was one of these ARFXs. When the temp is sub-freezing and you are lining up your shot, that foam pad is heavenly. I know people are going to say "you won't notice when you are about to shoot, with the stress and all" and I say BS. I noticed it every time, or rather I noticed the lack of a cold plastic shell on my cheek. It removed the potential distraction of 18 degree F toy plastic.

The LaRue RAT stock has a large easily-pulled ring used for the adjustments. Rotating the little knob at the front of the stock 90 degrees allows the ring to be pulled all the way back to fully remove the stock from the tube. This sucker is a tough, tough stock with a nice cheekweld section and rubber butt pad.

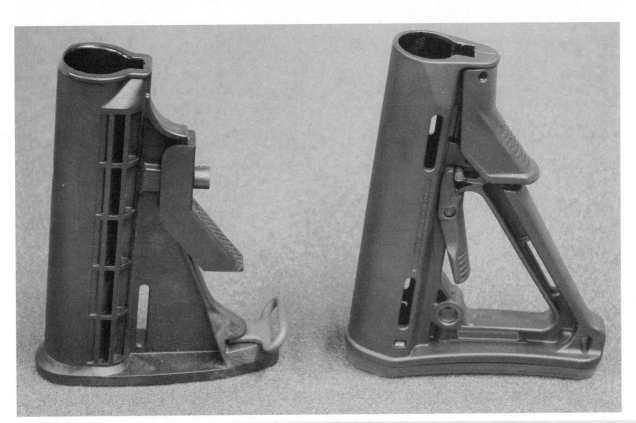

(top) The CTR stock next to the M4 stock it replaces. General profile is very similar, but still significant enhancements are present on the CTR.

(right) While the A2 stock is very serviceable, it is often replaced. One of the more common replacements is the ARFX skeleton stock from Ace. It's relatively low priced and looks pretty cool too. The foam pad/buffer tube cover is for the ARFX is not shown.

One of the most common things to do is to replace a rifle-length fixed AR stock for a carbine collapsible stock. Up until the end of the ban, and continuing on in the states with their own bans, everything had a fixed stock. Even normally collapsible stocks were pinned in place to fix them because, apparently, only terrorists need a collapsible stock. The advantage to a collapsible stock is not to hide it under a trench coat, as several politicians have intimated. Rather, it is to adjust the stock's length to the wearer's body, whether because he or she has a thicker coat on while out hunting, or it is somebody else's body altogether. Going to an adjustable stock loses you little, including expense, and gains you a great deal of flexibility. The same rifle can be comfortably and safely fired by the 6'3" father, the 5'8" wife, and the 4'5" twin sisters, one after the other with just two seconds of easy adjustment in between shooters. Furthermore, collapsible stocks do not require alteration to fit to anyone, unlike a traditional wood stock. The AR collapsible stock is so proven, useful, and prevalent that adaptors have been made to attach it to just about every other common rifle and shotgun in existence. Shotguns have it, AKs have it. Heck, even German guns have it. And you know what they say about Germans.

LET'S LOOK AT A FEW: FIXED

I want to point out that the following items that I am going to cover are not the only ones on the market. They are simply the ones that I like the most. Since everyone has different preferences there may be disagreements on the particulars. But since this book is directed more toward new owners, instead of the experienced AR owners that are already set in their ways, it is my desire to relate what I believe to be high quality and high usefulness in the products covered, based on my preferences and my experience. By all means look around; there is plenty to find and I can only begin to cover all the stuff that is available. As we look each example you will find that, with rare exception, they will all mount in the same way as others in their class of stock, just like the pistol grips did in the last chapter. This will not hold true in the next chapter when we discuss the handguard/forend situation. So as you see the awesomeness unfold before your eyes in pictures and words, keep in mind that if it's a fixed stock, it probably goes on the same way as all the other fixed stocks, but I will make note of major differences as we go.

The standard A2

The fixed rifle stock that you will find most commonly in this day and age is the basic A2 buttstock. This is a derivation of the original known, of course, as the A1. The biggest difference functionally is the longer length of the A2, roughly an inch longer. This is perfectly in line with the current

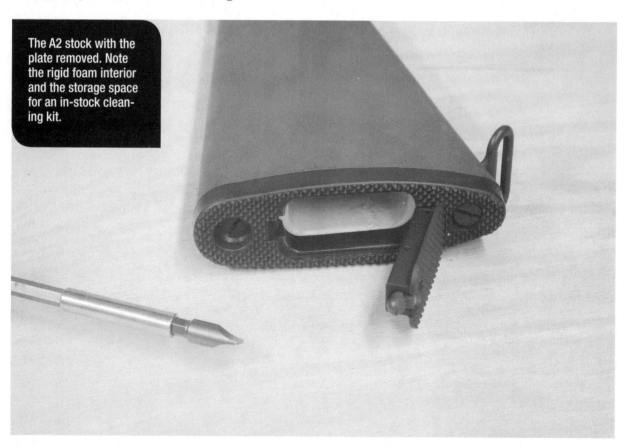

The A2 stock with the plate removed. Note the rigid foam interior and the storage space for an in-stock cleaning kit.

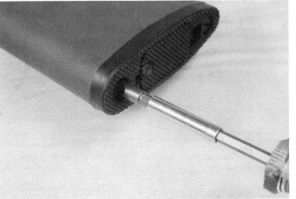

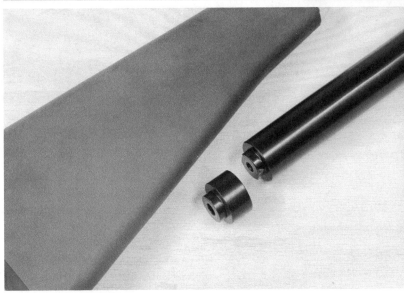

(top left) To change the stock, remove this screw at the top of the stock. Take care not to bung it up. It happens pretty easily. Use a screwdriver that is somewhat less wide than the length of the slot and one that closely matches the thickness of the slot.

(top right) This spring is retained by the stock. Don't lose it.

(left) The A2 stock uses a one-inch aluminum spacer behind the buffer tube. You will not need it for the A1 stock or any of the aftermarket replacements.

trend of making stocks that have gigantic lengths of pull, because apparently the average American is 6'8" tall. It's really bad with the Benelli stocks. The fixed pistol grip stocks they put on the tactical guns are over 15 inches LOP. IN. FRIGGIN. SANE.

The A2 has a rigid but lightweight foam core surrounded by a plastic shell. The core has a cavity in it that is just begging to contain a cleaning kit, as did the earlier M1 and M14. And so it is, a multiple section kit is issued for the M16 that fits perfectly in that cavity. The stock is enclosed by a heavily checkered plastic butt plate that has a trap door in it, as did the earlier M1 and M14. It slips on over the buffer tube and is secured to the tube by a flat head screw at the top rear of the butt plate. The screw at the bottom of the plate simply holds the sling loop onto the stock toe.

To remove the stock to replace it with something with a higher coolness factor, simply unscrew the top stock screw. Please note that the stock holds a spring and detent in the receiver. At the bottom right of the rear face of the receiver, just below and to the right of where the buffer tube enters the lower receiver, is a hole for a detent plunger and spring that retains the rear takedown pin. If you aren't careful, you will lose this spring. The

detent usually stays inside, but the spring can easily fly forth with gusto. It doesn't hurt to have a couple sets of these springs and detents on hand as spares. The new stock must then be pushed straight on to the receiver so that this spring does not get kinked. Oh yeah, there should also be an aluminum spacer insert that is inside the stock. This insert represents the difference in length between an A1 and A2 stock and must be in the stock tube hole behind the buffer tube when the A2 stock is mounted. If you are using an A1 length stock (most fixed aftermarkets are A1 length) you will not need the spacer.

The Ace ARFX

This is my favorite fixed stock. It is skeletonized, meaning you lose a hair of rigidity, but it is lighter weight and has that wonderful foam rubber cheek pad/sleeve around the buffer tube. It attaches to the receiver in the same way as the A2 but getting it on requires a special step. This is one of those times that compressed air is not only convenient, but really crazy convenient. Here's how you mount this stock in less than a minute. Place the stock ring on the tube, and slide it halfway up the tube to the receiver. Shove the foam tube on

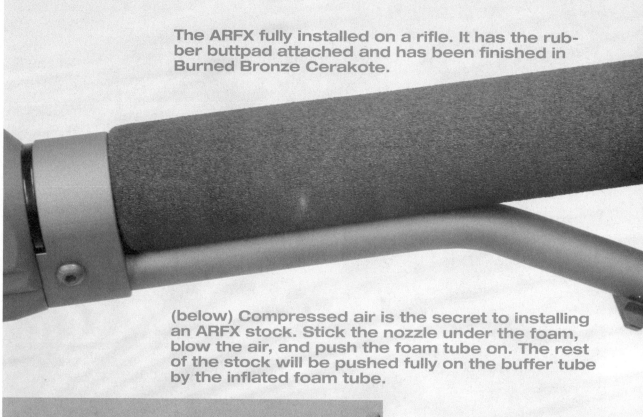

The ARFX fully installed on a rifle. It has the rubber buttpad attached and has been finished in Burned Bronze Cerakote.

(below) Compressed air is the secret to installing an ARFX stock. Stick the nozzle under the foam, blow the air, and push the foam tube on. The rest of the stock will be pushed fully on the buffer tube by the inflated foam tube.

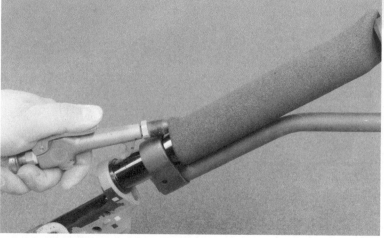

as far as you can easily get it with your hands. Then place the nozzle of your compressed air gun under the front lip of the foam tube. Blow the air in there while simultaneously pushing the tube forward from the rear. It will just slide on as if it had a large airflow expanding the foam (which it does). The foam will push the stock ring forward as well. Stop when the butt plate hits the tube, then fit the plate over the tube and push the whole thing forward so it is seated against the receiver. Then use the air to budge the foam tube as needed to cover any remaining exposed buffer tube, and then screw the stock retaining screw in. Did. Done. Under one minute, no oil, grease, or spit needed.

You also have the option of making the stock

longer by adding a squishy rubber pad to the butt plate. But for most guys that will make the stock too long and that pad really grips on your jacket and can actually get in the way. For some reason it also tends to pick up dog hair. Must be the static electricity buildup. This stock will work great for all kinds of hunting or pseudo-hunting situations like deer, coyotes, prairie dogs, and you name it. Very comfortable stock.

MagPul PRS

This is the other highly popular stock mod for the AR. The small frame AR-15 style and large frame AR-10/SR-25 style use different models. The cheek piece on the large frame models is a little shorter to accommodate the longer charging handle of the large frame guns. This cheek piece can be raised or lowered by means of a thumbwheel mounted in the middle of the stock. For most folks, the lowest or almost lowest setting seems to work, but you can really raise it up if you need to accommodate high scope rings and huge optics objective lenses.

The butt plate is also adjustable to lengthen the stock as needed or desired. For example if you are

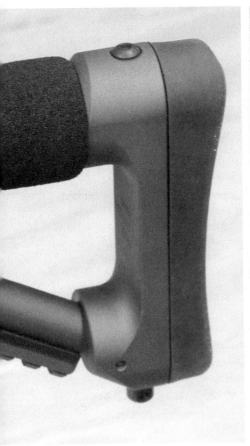

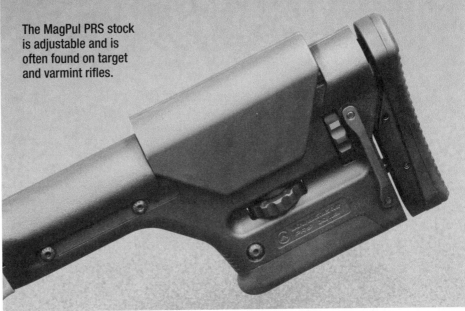

The MagPul PRS stock is adjustable and is often found on target and varmint rifles.

shooting standing or off hand in some way, you might keep the stock short. When you then shoot off the bench or prone, you can lengthen that adjustable stock to keep your eye in the right spot for the optic. Sure, you can adjust it to different users at will, but it is really shining through when you can use it to compensate for different shooting positions. Like the other stocks, it attaches by means of a ¼-28" screw at the top of the rear of the stock, but you first have to take off the thin rubber pad that covers the hole. Once that screw is tightened, you can also snug up the two screws that hold on the forward sling loop. This will snug the stock to the buffer tube as well.

The PRS also has a dandy pull-off section with a hidden Picatinny rail under it. This is for mounting a monopod on the stock. While this is a fairly expensive stock,

priced at right around $250 retail, it is worth every penny. It is also a bit heavier than the average stock, which helps to balance out the longer thicker barrel commonly used in conjunction with it.

MagPul MOE

MagPul also makes a line called the MOE. There are many products in this line, but the one of concern here is the full-sized fixed MOE rifle stock. This is a direct replacement for the A2 stock, has the same length, and is priced under $100. It has a large compartment in it as well and has a snappy look to it. The butt plate opens to the side like a door, rather than the trap door style of the A2, and it does not use the aluminum spacer behind the

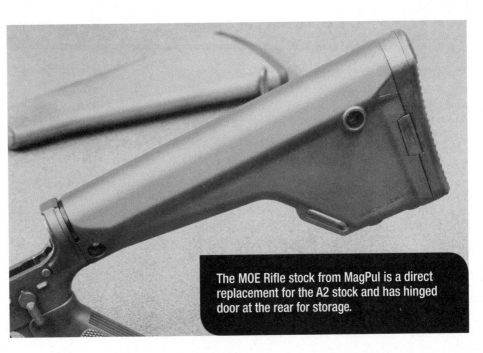

The MOE Rifle stock from MagPul is a direct replacement for the A2 stock and has hinged door at the rear for storage.

buffer tube. Like other MagPul stocks, it comes with push button QD sling swivel mounting points on either side. The inclusion of these mounting points makes it much easier to attach or detach a sling. We'll cover slings in a later chapter.

LET'S LOOK AT A FEW MORE: COLLAPSIBLE

Standard M4

Most factory-produced rifles and carbines are shipped with the standard M4-style stock. I say

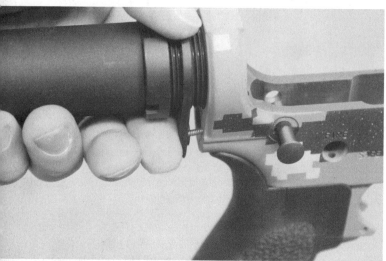

"style" because they can vary a little bit, and to some extent, most of the aftermarket stocks that replace the M4 stock are at least loosely based on the M4 stock, which is itself based on the CAR stock from back in the later years of the Vietnam conflict. The M4 is essentially a CAR stock but made of plastic rather than aluminum, and has a larger butt footprint to it.

The standard rifle stocks fit onto a buffer tube that is perfectly cylindrical and runs pretty much the full length of the stock. Carbine stock tubes are different. The tube that the CAR and M4 stocks fit onto has a rail along the bottom that contains depressions for a plunger to drop (actually, raise under spring tension) into. Also this style of tube is shorter and is only long enough to reach the rear of the stock piece when the stock is fully collapsed and as a result uses a shorter buffer. And while the rifle tube is simply screwed in, the carbine tube is retained via a lock plate and castle nut. We'll get into that tube and buffer stuff in a later chapter, too.

Anyway, the carbine and CAR tubes usually allow four to six positions for the shooter. If you want a short stock then collapse it all the way. If you want a long stock (as long as an A2 stock), then open it all the way. A simple lever on the bottom of the stock piece can be pinched and the

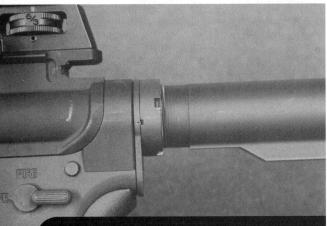

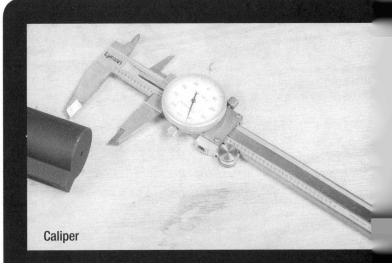

Caliper

There are two sizes of collapsible stock tubes for ARs. The "Mil-spec" version is the most acceptable for the mil-spec-is-all crowd. There is also the "commercial" version that many companies use for their rifles. They are not compatible, so if you are taking off an M4 stock from your mil-spec tube to replace it with, say, a LaRue R.A.T. stock, your tube must be a mil-spec tube. Some companies, like MagPul, offer products in both sizes. The mil-spec tube will measure 1.14 inches in diameter (not including the locking rail underneath) and the commercial tubes will measure 1.17 inches in diameter.

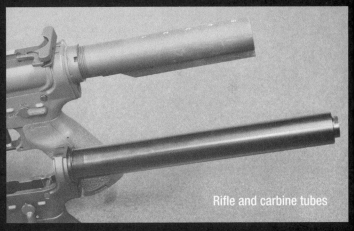

Rifle and carbine tubes

(opposite bottom) The carbine stock tube is screwed into the receiver just like a rifle tube, and the buffer retainer must be depressed to allow the mouth of the tube to settle over it.

(opposite top) When the tube has been screwed in and is holding the buffer retainer, the tube rail should be oriented down and the retainer plate needs to be pressed flush to the receiver. It is very important that the takedown pin detent spring is not damaged, but pressed directly into its hole. Align the tube then push the whole plate forward. If you like, the hole can be threaded to 4-40 threads and a 4-40 x 1/8" set screw can be used to retain the spring. The spring will need to be shortened by ¼ inch, and be sure you don't break the tap in the hole.

(top) The nut should then be tightened down by hand to the retainer plate. At every step, be sure the stock is vertically aligned with the receiver. Use an M4 stock wrench to torque down the nut. Medium strength threadlocker (small amount) can be used if desired.

(above) The nut should be staked in place using one of the staking grooves, if the nut has them. Displace material from the retention plate into the groove on the nut.

Side by side, the rifle and carbine extension tubes are quite dissimilar, but serve the same functions, to contain the buffer and spring, and as a mounting point for the buttstock.

Side by side the two sizes of carbine extension tubes look alike, but short of measuring them with a caliper, you can usually determine by subtle differences in the shapes. Commercial tube has definite step up just behind the threads and has an angled back plate. The mil-spec tube generally has no step (or a minor one) and a flat back plate.

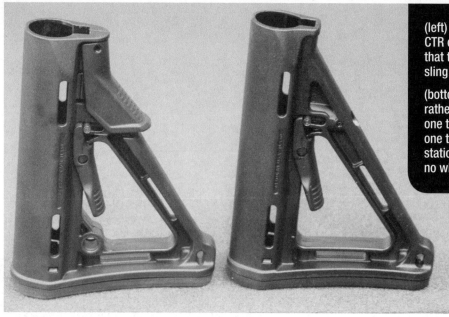

(left) The MOE is on the right, the CTR on the left. Identical, except that the MOE has no lock or QR sling attachment point.

(bottom) The MagPul UBR is a rather heavy carbine stock, but one that is very solid, rugged, and one that keeps the cheek piece stationary, meaning you will lose no whiskers to it.

MagPul MOE and CTR

These two direct replacements for the M4 stock are virtually identical, but the CTR adds a lock that removes any tangible rattle in the assembly. A lever similar to that on the M4 is used to adjust the stock and the lock is just forward of it, looking for all the world like a second adjustment lever. The MOE has no lock or QR sling socket and is a bit less expensive as a result, but both are well under a Franklin and are good deals.

stock slid forward or backward. Some people find these stocks noisy as they rattle a bit, and thus, the aftermarket pool of stock sweetness grows at a healthy rate every year.

This is a good point to mention that you should be aware (very aware, as in never ever forget aware) that there are two diameters of carbine extension tubes. The mil-spec model is approximately 1.14 inches in diameter and the commercial versions are 1.17 inches in diameter, and ne'er shall the two be compatible. If you replace your stock for another carbine stock (whatever the brand or style) make sure you acquire the correct one. Most manufacturers produce both sizes.

Falcon Industries F93 and MagPul UBR

These two stocks are closely related. The F93 was the original collaboration between Falcon and MagPul and was sold for a time as the MagPul M93. Falcon Industries continues to sell the product. The brilliance of these stocks is that the cheek piece of the stock assembly is stationary, with the foot of the stock attached to the section that slides underneath the cheek piece. Here's why it's brilliant. You don't lose whiskers in any of the joints or interfaces. Every time I put my face on an M4 stock I lift it from the stock minus at least three face quills. A consistent cheek weld can be maintained.

Another neato feature is the ability to bypass or lock down certain positions. You can set the maximum length to something other than the

In a brilliant effort to conform the AR-15 to developing legislations in several states, the Thordsen Customs FRS-15 stock was born. This is only one example of the modifications made to the AR to conform to nonsensical, ineffective laws passed in a hurry without proper consideration or debate. In fact, this stock, which attaches where the standard pistol grip is supposed to be, is quite practical and comfortable. Kudos to the companies like this that spend the time and resources to develop these alternatives.

default, or something greater than the fully collapsed position. They are both a bit on the heavy side, and attach somewhat differently. The F93 uses a more traditional carbine tube style of attachment that is integral with the cheek piece, using a plate and castle nut. The UBR attaches to what is essentially a shortened rifle receiver extension/buffer tube that is carbine length rather than rifle length. It attaches in the same way as the standard rifle tube, with the tube screwed into the lower receiver and the sleeve screwed onto the tube like an A2 stock would be attached. Like the PRS, these two items can be used to counterbalance a heavier profile barrel and still allow length of pull adjustments.

Vltor makes the Modstock that is very similar in length to the original A2, but with the addition of modular compartments at each side of the cheek rest. You can store a lot of batteries in there. The stock can be used with the compartments, which are watertight, without anything, or with the optional large cheek pieces that do not contain compartments.

Vltor ModStock

Vltor (pronounced like OOL-tore) came on the scene some time ago and offers both fixed and collapsible stocks. What generally sets them apart is the cargo capacity set into them. The stocks have a tubular watertight compartment that runs along each side of the stock below the cheek rest area that can hold several batteries, for instance, securely. Models could also be purchased with hinged compartments at the toe of the stock as well. You can hold a lot of stuff in these stocks. They attached to the lower receivers in the usual ways.

As mentioned before, this list has been less than exhaustive, but does give a good idea of the variety that is available. There are more yet, but it will be left to the reader to investigate those items. There are some that are rather funny looking, but are fully and completely sensible when it comes to function. I seriously think that some manufacturers deliberately make things weird looking just to make the gun appear more unorthodox. Others will be straight vanilla styling and functioning. There are very few "bad" or low quality aftermarket parts for the AR. There are so many good ones to choose from that the occasional poor quality part usually disappears because no one wants to purchase unproven crap.

Barrels: The Heart of the Gun

The barrel is the heart of any firearm, particularly the rifle. There would be no firearm without the barrel since it is the barrel that makes it possible to project a projectile with specifically directed force, safely, with enough power to make a hole in things that might not want holes put in them.

Because of their function, barrels need to have great strength. There is a tremendous amount of pressure generated in a modern rifle barrel, and only steel has shown to be a suitable material in the modern world. Sure there are other alloys that could theoretically be used, but they would be a lot more expensive to use. The earliest forms of rifle or gun barrels were made from other materials than steel, such as various forms of iron, brass, and bronze. Indeed brass and bronze were being used up through the 19th century in artillery barrels. There are recent forays into using titanium alloys for barrel material in pistols.

Different kinds of steel might be used. The most common steel used to make modern barrels is called AISI 4140. A similar material, 4150

is also commonly used. These two steels are the most widely used non-stainless steel materials and compose the majority of barrels manufactured today, regardless of the type of gun they are on. Stainless steel is used as well in the form of several versions of the 400 series of stainless steel. What's the difference beyond the obvious? Well, the stainless steel is of course less vulnerable to rusting and corrosion than the non stainless steel, also known as Chrome-Moly steel. You will find both options in the AR world, and if you are building your own rifle, or are possibly replacing a heavily shot barrel, you will want to know the differences and the advantages of each.

This new pistol from Taurus, the View, has a fully Titanium barrel, likely the first production firearm to do so. Not yet available for ARs.

CHROME-MOLYBDENUM

The "41" in 4140 means the steel (iron + carbon makes steel) is alloyed primarily with Chromium and Molybdenum (CM), hence it's common moniker of "chrome-moly." This has proven to be an excellent barrel steel, somewhat resistant to corrosion and heat. It has a high tensile strength and is easy to manufacture. However it still must be surface finished by Parkerizing, Blueing, or other oxidation process, or painting to give it a protective skin, or it will rust fairly quickly.

In the AR realm, you will find these barrels in all sizes, thicknesses, calibers, and contours. The majority of AR barrels are manufactured from 4140 or 4150 (more carbon in it), and the vast majority of carbine barrels are made from 4140. Often, as in the case of the barrels supplied to the military, the bores and chambers are also chrome plated to further battle the insidious threat of corrosion. This usually adds a bit to the cost of the barrel, and in the temperate climate that covers the majority of North America, you don't really need it. If you find that you can afford a lot of ammo and you like to do mag dumps in really humid weather, say in the Everglades or something, then you might want to insist on chrome plating. The same goes for guns repeatedly taken through large temperature transitions, like deer hunting in the cold, in and out of the cabin and such, where a large amount of condensation may appear in the barrel.

STAINLESS STEEL

Stainless steel, so it is said, was specifically invented for use in barrel steel, to make barrels that would be less vulnerable to climatic effects. A stainless steel barrel, with all other things being equal, is going to be more expensive than a CM barrel, on the order of 10-30% usually. There are a several reasons for this. It is simply more expensive to make stainless than CM, for one. Another is that stainless is often more difficult to machine to contour, so that will bring a raise as well. A third is that it is a good enough reason as any to charge more for a "premium" product. There are benefits. Stainless is generally considered to be slightly more inherently accurate than a similar CM barrel, and you have far greater corrosion resistance than CM ever will. Be warned, however, that stainless steel will still rust, particularly if it is exposed to an etching agent, like some solvents, acids or, oddly enough the liquid contents of a test fire snail trap.

A typical chrome-moly barrel. It is machined and then mag phosphated (parkerized), though nowadays might have some sort of salt nitride treatment instead.

The typical stainless steel barrel below is kept in the white, sometimes with a high polish, but usually left in its machined state.

SO WHAT MAKES A RIFLE A RIFLE ANYWAY?

A rifle has a rifled barrel, duh. Okay. The word "rifle" refers to grooves in the bore of the barrel that make the bullet spin as it goes down the barrel. It wasn't until the mid to late 18th century that appreciable numbers of rifled barrels were in use. Firearms have been around since about the middle of the 14th century in the most primitive forms and crude artillery pieces predated even that. In those three centuries the barrel bore was smooth and the barrel was made by wrapping a sheet of iron around a mandrel and forging the edges together to form a hollow tube. When the European armies began to arm their soldiers with large numbers of what became known as muskets (muzzle loading, smooth bored long guns), someone quickly noticed that you couldn't hit jack past twenty or thirty yards. The musket balls just kind of developed a mind of their own as soon as they left the muzzle. The solution was to pack a bunch of guys into a block or double or triple line and tell all the guys in the front to let go at the same time. Then you might hit a few guys on the other side. After that you fixed bayonets, and went back to the oldest combat model in the books, fighting like a real man, with a spear.

See, the gunsmiths of

This was one of the least accurate unrifled firearms, a blunderbuss. You could just shove whatever you wanted down the barrel. It was effectively an early high-spread shotgun.

the day could turn out smoothbores pretty quickly but rifles were another story. Rifle barrels had to be drilled and then the rifling cut into them. This made rifles much more expensive. A colonial power could purchase a number of muskets for each rifle purchased and it made much more sense to buy five or ten or twenty guns for the price of one rifle. Furthermore, there were large supplies of peasants that could be conscripted to carry those guns. It was more financially acceptable to arm and lose three illiterate cannon fodder conscripts than to arm one guy with a rifle. Especially because a rifleman could only shoot maybe once a minute compared to the three shots per minute of a good trained musketeer. The tight fitting bullets often had to be hammered down the barrel and this takes a while. It wasn't until the American Civil War (War Between the States, Northern Aggression, whatever you want, man) that rifles were standard issue and the real slaughter began. This came about because of a leap forward in bullet technology, which we'll briefly cover in the Ammo chapter later.

Cut rifling

The style of rifling in those early rifles is still used today in modified form. It's called "cut" rifling. It works this way. A barrel blank of appropriate bore diameter has a cutting tool pulled through it which cuts (gouges, really) the rifling grooves in the barrel, usually one at a time. This method has become incredibly precise and many shooters consider this process to still produce the best accuracy of the several rifling methods available today. As before, it tends to be more expensive than the other methods and is not use by most barrel makers, but is used by what are considered to be some of the best barrel makers in the country.

Grooves

Lands

Rifling looks like this, seen at the muzzle.

Broach cut rifling

Similar to the cut rifling is broach rifling. Really it's very close to the same thing, just that instead of cutting grooves one at a time, the broach that is pulled through the barrel cuts them all at the same time. This is extremely common on pistol barrels and much less so with rifle barrels.

Button rifling

This is the most common type of rifle rifling today, and the type most often encountered in AR barrels. The rifling in this type of barrel is not cut, but is formed by a "button" that is pulled through the barrel. The button forms all of the grooves simultaneously by forcing its way down the barrel, displacing the metal to form the grooves. This is also the cheapest way of making modern barrels, hence its omnipresence.

Hammer forging

This is the newest common method of barrel manufacture. The barrel blank has an oversized bore. A hardened mandrel that looks like the reverse image of the rifling pattern (because it is) is placed inside the bore and the blank is passed through a hammer forging machine. The series of hammer blows literally bangs the bore down so that it mirrors the mandrel. The mandrel is then removed and you have a nice new rifled barrel, and the forging process makes the barrels very strong. This is a relatively inexpensive means of rifling a barrel, as long as you do a heck of a lot of them. The hammer forging machines are ungodly expensive to purchase so usually only the big dog manufacturers have them, like FNH, Glock, and Steyr. AR barrels made by FNH and Daniel Defense and a few others are hammer forged.

BARREL EXTENSION

The AR series of rifles have barrels that are screwed into barrel extensions. This barrel extension is where the bolt rotates and locks into in order to close the breech of the rifle. This extension has eight lugs with gaps separating them and two feed ramps. The gaps are for the lugs of the bolt to pass through and the feed ramps are for guiding cartridges into the chamber from the magazine.

The feed ramps have been improved since the original rifle was produced. It was found, presumably since the M4 cycled faster because of its inferior gas system that rounds were not always reliably feeding from the magazine. Essentially, the magazine spring could not keep up with the speed of the bolt, barely. So the M4 feed ramp was optioned in that made the feed ramps in the extension slightly steeper or deeper and then continued into the upper receiver, so that the feed ramp crossed both the receiver and the extension. If a bullet tip wasn't quite raised up far enough, it would still hit the extended feed ramp and angle up as it should to feed into the chamber.

As we mentioned in an earlier chapter, the use of a barrel extension was brilliant, as it allowed the receivers to be manufactured of a lower strength material such as aluminum, rather than steel, making the rifle much lighter in weight. It further

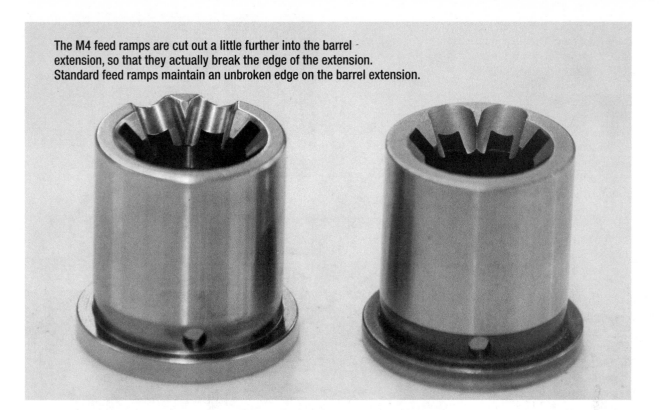

The M4 feed ramps are cut out a little further into the barrel extension, so that they actually break the edge of the extension. Standard feed ramps maintain an unbroken edge on the barrel extension.

kept the system completely linear, using a rotating bolt head, which contributed to several positive factors. It is also a fairly hard place to clean unless you use the chamber brush. We'll get further into that little story in the cleaning chapter.

BARREL LENGTH AND CONTOUR

By far the most common barrel is the M4-style 16" barrel. I say M4-style because it's kind of funny looking with multiple diameters along the barrel between the gas block and the muzzle, the most obvious one being a couple inches in front of the gas block, and it is the deepest as well. This barrel duplicates the M4 barrel used by the military with one very important difference. The military barrel is 14.5" in length, but the standard civilian M4 barrel is 16" in length to comply with the National Firearms Act. Otherwise the contour is identical. The deep cut in the barrel is meant to be a mounting point for the M203 grenade launcher. In order to make the rifle look as much like the real M4 the contours are maintained on the 16" barrel. Also usually left intact is the bayonet lug on the bottom of the gas block/sight tower. It is completely useless on the 16" barrels, and its presence is why the military went with the carbine gas system in the first place. It is on the 14.5" barrels in just the right place to mount a bayonet, with the same amount of barrel sticking out as a 20" standard rifle. On the 16" barrels it is too far back on the barrel to actually mount the bayonet. This is what is so funny to me about the people who want to ban

bayonet lugs from these guns. You can't even effing use them anyway. It is a purely cosmetic issue on an M4 barrel.

Mid-length barrels are growing in popularity, which is good, because they work better. Usually you will find these barrels with a heavy contour under the handguards. I can't figure that one out, because there is no point. That kind of contour is useful on a long barreled target rifle but under a carbine handguard it just adds weight with little advantage beyond slightly better heat dissipation. Accuracy is not substantially improved by this contour. It is my recommendation that if the mid-length barrel you get is this big, then have a gunsmith turn it down to .650-.750". There are excellent examples of barrels in this category, particularly those from JP Enterprises and Ballistic Advantage. These high end barrels will regularly shoot groups under ¾" when used in conjunction with a free float handguard. Armalite long ago converted carbine barrel production to mid-length from carbine length gas systems.

The M4 is not the only carbine length barrel in common use but is the most common. There are others such as lightweight barrels that have an outer diameter of .625" as opposed to .750" on the M4 and M16 barrels. These barrels sacrifice some precision for a significant improvement in handling and overall weight reduction. Some barrels are simply straight contoured without the M4 silliness in front of the gas block. Most manufacturers offer one or more or all of these options and this might wind up making the decision to purchase a hair more indecisive feeling. Don't feel bad. This is the side effect of having so much choice. It's a good problem to have. In the end, even though the M4 style is, in my opinion and others, a second choice to a mid-length barreled rifle, the sheer commonality of the M4 style is a potent selling point and you may not immediately find a non-M4 barrel when you want to build your gun or replace the old barrel. Or you may just want to keep it simple and replace with a like example.

"Rifle length" barrels tend to be 20-24" in length, though some places are a little different. For example JP Enterprises uses 18" barrels with rifle length gas systems and they also have offered 22" barrels, something that was unique to JP. On the other hand, most companies that offer 18" barrels choose to give them mid-length gas systems and only offer 20" or 24" barrels. The original AR-15 barrel was a 20" long .625" in diameter pencil barrel. The contour was thickened when reports came in that barrels were getting bent from impacts. Some places, like most of the big name companies, only use carbine gas system barrels and 20" rifle length gas system barrels. As mentioned, there is a complete glut of companies that make AR stuff, including barrels, so the options are plenty.

The most common way of barrel changing is simply to

Yes, even the big .50 BMG can be placed on your AR-15. This upper uses a side feeding magazine and is bolt action. You remove the buffer and spring from the lower, and the upper of course, and drop the .50 upper in their place. Recoil with the large muzzle brake is less than many 12 gauge shotguns. The concussion is something else entirely.

The ever present M4 profile looks like this, with the big grenade launcher mounting groove forward of the gas block. The barrel under the handguards is typically ¾" in diameter.

push two pins, take the entire upper assembly off and replace it with another. It's quite common for a guy to have two or three uppers for every lower that he has. Or for an owner to only own one AR but have an M4 upper, a long varminting upper, and maybe something else to suit his fancy. It is the quickest and easiest way to change calibers and purposes and this is part of the reason that many upper assemblies are sold without the lower. Everything up to .50 BMG can be found in upper assemblies. There's really not much more to say about switching upper assemblies, since it's so easy to do. There should be compatibility among all manufacturers and except for the cases where companies make the fit intentionally tight, there should be no problem slapping one upper from company A onto the lower of company B. Remember that there are large and small frame guns; essentially the .223 is small and the .308 is large.

These three barrel extensions illustrate differences in different rifles. The .308 barrel has a much larger diameter extension than do the .223 and 9mm barrels. The 9mm barrel doesn't have an extension, really, since it is a blowback operated gun and has no bolt lock-up. The "extension" is machined into the barrel.

BARREL EXTENSIONS

Before we get too far into the mechanics of this I should make note of a teensy little factoid that many people, particularly new owners or almost new owners may not quite grok yet. Generally speaking (there are now a couple of rather expensive examples), if you want a .223 and a .308 you need two different guns. The .223 (small frame) and .308 (large frame) have different magazine well sizes.

You can't stick a .308 magazine with .308 cartridges into an AR-15 small sized frame. Obviously, it's the same in reverse. The upper receiver thus is also longer on the .308. You cannot (again, with one or two expensive exceptions) criss-cross the upper assemblies. You need two guns.

The barrel extension of the AR-15 small frame barrels measure a nominal one inch in diameter. The AR-10 large frame barrels measure 1 1/8" in diameter. This doesn't mean you can't have a .30 caliber barrel in the small frame receivers. The .300 Whisper and AAC Blackout cartridges are

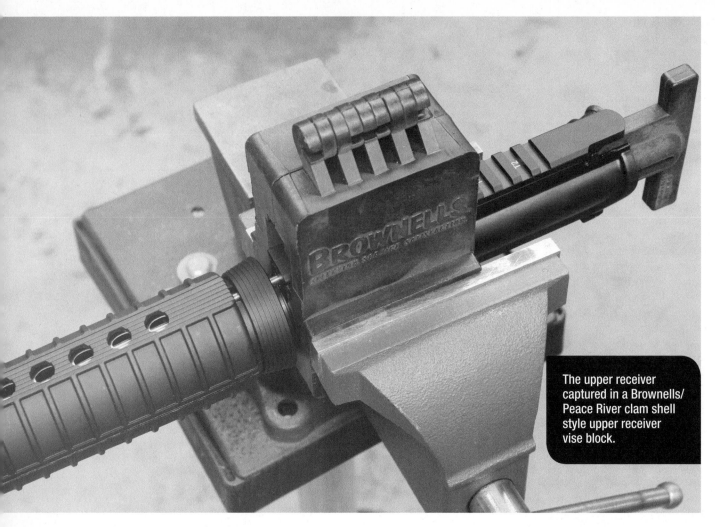

The upper receiver captured in a Brownells/Peace River clam shell style upper receiver vise block.

meant for the small frame, as is Remington's .30 Rem. AR cartridge that probably no one besides gun writers have ever heard off. Anyway, just so you know, the barrel extensions are different, so if you want a .308 rifle you have to get a large frame model like the Armalite AR-10 style or DPMS LR-308 / Knight SR-25 style rifles.

This doesn't really limit you in any way. There are several other options of chamberings of which advantage can be taken. For example, one of the first options that someone (Colt) came up with was to make an AR in 9mm Parabellum. But I'm getting ahead of myself. Ammo and caliber choices come in a later chapter. For now let's assume that we are changing out a .223 Rem M4 barrel and replacing it with a similar model.

CHANGING OUT A BARREL

We will approach this from the aspect of barrel replacement. If you are building your own upper receiver, then you simply disregard the disassembly portion of this section. If you aren't building an AR then you are behind the game. The usual pattern is that a dude will purchase a factory as-

sembled rifle. Then he/she will change it to better fit their useful or cosmetic need so that it very shortly becomes completely unique. Then he/she will build one from scratch totally in their mental image; because why the heck not?

The first thing you need for barrel removal is a sturdy bench vise. The second thing is a good set of receiver blocks or clamps that will allow you to grasp the upper receiver without damaging it. You will be instilling a fair to heavy amount of torque onto the receiver and you will want it to not be bent when you are done. There are several options. The most common one is the Peace River style of clamshell and insert vise block. The plastic shell folds around the upper receiver to encompass the upper receiver and an insert that fills the bolt carrier and charging handle channel area to prevent crushing. It works well and can be used with any standard dimensioned forged upper receiver like would be found on 90% of small frame rifles, both flat topped and with traditional carry handle.

Another style is the approach taken by JP Enterprises with their Universal Vise Clamps. This set is actually a set of magnetized vise jaws. The flat topped upper receiver is placed so that the rail is contained in one jaw and the front receiver lug (the one that the front pivot pin goes through) is held in the other. The receiver is thus held sideways. This orientation will not crush and as such the vise can be clamped quite tightly onto the receiver with no worries. This set can be used with any flat top receiver, whether it is a forged model or a billet model. As long as it has the top rail it will work. Oh, yeah, it will also work with the large frame receivers as well. Both the JP and Peace River sets hold the receiver directly in between the vise jaws. Keeping all the force exerted on the receiver between the jaws makes the entire set up much more stable, and stable means less likelihood of damage.

The third style is the Reaction Rod style first made by Geissele Automatics. This resembles strongly the barrel extension wrench used to torque on the barrel extensions to the barrels. The back half of the rod is clamped into the vise jaws with the rod inserted into the receiver. The rod holds the barrel extension, so that the torque placed on to the barrel nut is transmitted to the extension only, removing any stress placed onto the receiver. While you have to try very hard to do it, you can snap the receiver threads off the receiver. This cannot happen with the Reaction Rod. Furthermore, it will work with any receiver as long as the correct rod is used for the appropriate frame size.

The fourth style is one that I don't recommend. It involves a Delrin block that is inserted up into the upper receiver and retained by means of cross pins going through the takedown and pivot pin holes in the upper. The block bottom is held between the vise jaws. This arrangement is far less rigid than the previous three methods and if you use it for barrel changing you will be imparting a good deal of force to those receiver lugs. Not the ideal way to do things.

You will need one of the several different versions of the AR action wrench. DPMS, Olympic, and Smith Enterprises make some really good models that have multiple functions built into them, but in this instance you just need the end with the big round semicircle in it. It has teeth that interact with the standard teeth on the standard barrel retainer nut. This nut, if the gun looks like an M-16 or M4 has the delta ring assembly around it. You have to remove the plastic handguards from the barrel to access the barrel nut. Certain hand-

The upper receiver captured in a JP Enterprises two piece vise clamp. This unit can be used for both small frame and large frame upper receivers.

guards that ship with proprietary barrel nuts will often have their own wrenches included with the handguard. But we will assume this time that you are replacing the existing M4 barrel with another, and that the standard handguard is also equipped on the rifle.

Place the upper in the vise. Remove the bolt car-rier assembly. Remove the handguards by pulling the delta ring to the rear and removing the bottom handguard half, and then the top handguard half. This can be done easily with a tool designed for the purpose, but it is not necessary. The gas tube will have to be removed from the gas block, or the gas block/front sight assembly will have to be removed from the barrel. On the basic, standard M4 and AR-15 rifles, it is a heck of a lot easier to remove the gas tube from the gas block than the other way around. Drive out the small spring pin in the gas block and throw it away. You will need a new one to replace it when the gas tube is reinserted. Pull the gas tube to the rear in order to pull it from the gas block, then rotate it 90 degrees so that the bend in the tube causes the front end to hang to the right of the gas block. Pull the tube forward from the receiver and out. If the gun has been shot a lot, the powder residues may have effectively glued the tube in place. There are tools designed for this occasion but a pair of pliers can be modi-fied to grab the tube without crushing it so that you can get a good grip on it. The barrel nut can-not be removed with the gas tube in place.

Apply the action wrench so that the teeth in the

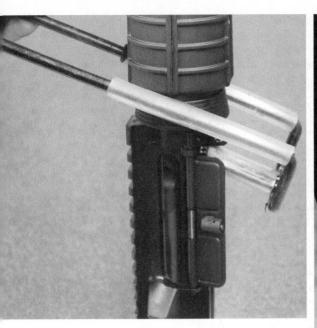

(left) The handguard removal tool is one of those unnecessary tools to have, but it sure makes it easy to pry back that delta nut.

(below) The wrench will fit on two ways, correctly with all wrench teeth engaged, or incorrectly with only two teeth engaged. Don't do it incorrectly.

(bottom) If the nut is super stuck, like if some jerk used thread locking compound on the threads, you may need more leverage. This pipe gives leverage. Just push down (or up, depending...) very, very slowly.

wrench fit precisely with the teeth on the barrel nut. You will have to push against the spring tension of the delta ring. It may take some force to unscrew the barrel nut. The recommended torque for this nut is 30-100+ foot pounds and they will run the full length of that range. If you cannot budge the wrench, DO NOT SMACK IT WITH A HAMMER! Get a length of pipe, three feet is plenty sufficient, place the pipe over the

wrench handle and gently attempt to loosen the nut again. The pipe will give you the leverage and control necessary to do it right without excessive force. The teeth on the nut can break and then you are going to be stuck.

When the nut is loose, unscrew it all the way from the receiver threads and the barrel should be able to be pulled from the receiver. The clam-shell type receiver blocks may need to have some vise tension loosened as well as that type slightly pinches the receiver. It may also be that the builder of the upper used thread locking compound around the barrel extension. If this is the case, you will need to apply heat with a propane torch to the receiver threads to burn away (uncure; is that a word?) the thread locker. When you see a fair amount of wispy white smoke, then you have probably applied enough heat. Don't inhale the wispy white smoke. If it still is stuck like a tick, then you will need to tap the barrel from the receiver, and the best thing to use for this is one of the cleaning rod guides available on the market. The guide can be inserted in place and then tapped on the back end with a hammer, gently (kind of) dislodging the barrel. Make sure you clean out the crapped out thread locker (and the entire receiver, really; it's a good time to do so) before you insert the new barrel.

As I just commented, now is a good time to detail clean

If you did not want to remove your front sight to get the barrel off, and want to use the existing delta ring/barrel nut, you can't. The nut is stuck but you can still use the delta ring. You will have to disassemble this assembly, and you can easily do so with split ring pliers. Remove the split ring and the rest can be removed toward the rear of the nut. I mean, the nut will totally fall right off.

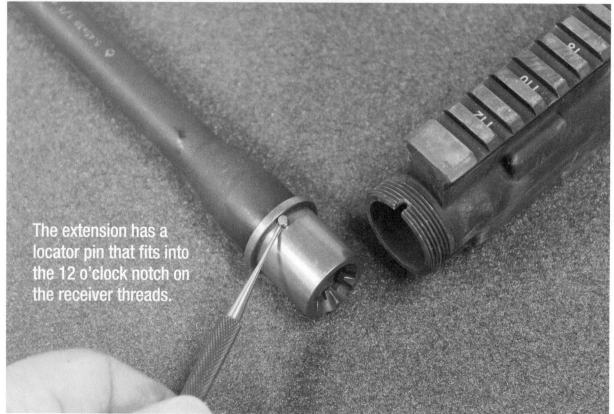

The extension has a locator pin that fits into the 12 o'clock notch on the receiver threads.

Disassembling the delta ring is easy. The split ring pliers should be set to expand rather than compress, meaning when you squeeze the handle the tips will separate. Simply insert the tips in the holes of the ring, pinch slightly to displace the ring and slide it off the back. The spring will slide off and then the ring. Simply reverse these actions to install the ring, spring, and split ring back onto the new barrel nut.

(top) Looking through the receiver, back to front, you can see through the gas tube hole. If it looks round then the barrel retaining nut is properly aligned. If it doesn't look round, you are either too far, or not far enough.

(above) This is what the gas tube hole should look like when the barrel retaining nut is properly aligned.

the upper receiver. The hole through which the gas tube passes in to the receiver has a tendency to get quite cruddy and now is the only time that it can be cleaned decently. If you don't care about that then, well, you should grow up. Clean is better and the build up here can easily get on you or your stuff in short order because it is relatively exposed. It's entirely possible you had no need to remove the front sight tower from the barrel. Many new barrels already have the barrel nut (minus the delta ring) on the barrel, but for those barrels that don't, you may need the existing barrel nut for the new barrel or handguard. Let's assume for now that you are replacing an M4 barrel with another, newer M4 barrel. The nuts are generally already on the barrel.

You will have to disassemble the delta ring assembly and reassemble it on the new barrel retainer nut. See sidebar for this procedure. Once the delta ring assembly has been reassembled, you can insert the new barrel extension into the receiver. Be sure to do so slowly and in a controlled fashion, as the extension has an alignment pin that fits into the notch at the 12 o'clock position of the threads. Then hand thread the nut onto the receiver threads and snug it tight. Follow this up

Headspace gauges are essential for determining headspace (easily). They look the same, but these three gauges, GO, NOGO, and FIELD are all different lengths.

by using the action wrench to tighten rather than loosen the nut. The torque spec varies by manufacturer, but you can go with 30 – 100 foot pounds. It may behoove thee to acquire a commercial torque wrench (you can get these at local hardware stores; Brownells even has them) until you get a feel for it. Truthfully, most people in the real world get it tight, "uumph" tight, and then go to the next tooth notch for perfect alignment. This typically results in a torque spec in the 60 – 70 foot pounds range. Of course everyone's "uumph" is different, hence the wisdom of the torque wrench if you have not done this before. Heck, I bet you could borrow one pretty easily too.

Now you have to line up the holes in the compression spring, retainer ring, and delta ring itself with the tooth notch aligned to the receiver hole.

At this point you can reinsert the gas tube, and then the handguard pieces.

To a great extent, bolts and barrels, even from different manufacturers are quite compatible and will headspace safely with each other. There are exceptions, and many companies offer matched barrel/bolt combinations. While because of this very tight standardization on this issue, I'd like to tell you

Headspacing can be done when the upper is already assembled. Remove the extractor and then reinstall the bolt in to the carrier and the carrier into the upper. Drop the gauge into the chamber. The carrier should completely close and the bolt fully lock up on the GO gauge. Look at the underside of the upper assembly for the clearest picture.

The carrier should not close on the FIELD gauge, though generally if it closes on the NOGO you will be fine for a while. However, if you have the option of using a different bolt that will not close on the NOGO gauge you should pursue that option. There should be a significant space between the front of the carrier and the barrel extension.

that you don't really have to worry too much about headspace, but it is still a very wise thing to check the headspace when you have installed a new barrel. You just never know if you caught the edges of the tolerance runout. Frankly, when you install a new AR barrel, you might as well install a new bolt too.

Waaaallll, I should probably define what "headspace" actually is. It is one of the most important measurements on any firearm. Because of the high pressures involved in centerfire cartridge chambers, there is a range of measurement in the barrel chamber that is safe, and the rest is considered not safe. It is necessarily a narrow range, measured in the thousandths of an inch, often less than ten thousandths; in other words, less than the average person can resolve with MK 1 eyeballs. For the purposes of the new gun owner, or new barrel changer, it can be devolved to the usage of three gauges. GO, NOGO, and FIELD gauges are standard for any chambering and will tell you whether that barrel is in the spec as determined by the Sporting Arms and Ammunition Manufacturers' Institute (SAAMI) or its European counterpart, the CIP. The difference between the GO and NOGO with a .223 Rem/5.56mm gauge set is only .003". You simply insert the gauges and determine whether the bolt closes or not. It is best to do this prior to assembly as it is just a tad easier when the barrel is not stuck into a receiver. Remove the extractor by pushing out the extractor pin, and ideally the ejector as well, but you can get by leaving the ejector in. Make sure the chamber of the new barrel is clean. Drop the GO gauge into the chamber and place the bolt behind it, attempting to "lock" the bolt into the barrel extension. Basically, stick it in and see if it will rotate. Rotation by finger pressure only. If you can't turn it by just using your fingers, it doesn't pass. Don't use a tool in the cam pin hole to crank it around. If the bolt will rotate to lock (bolt lugs behind the extension lugs) then the bolt passes the GO gauge. Do the same thing with the NOGO gauge. If the bolt does not rotate with the NOGO gauge inserted, then you are shiny and you can go ahead and assemble or pass check your build; you are ready to shoot. If the bolt rotates with the NOGO inserted, then you should then perform the check with the FIELD gauge. If the bolt rotates with the FIELD gauge, then you need to find a new barrel or bolt or both. FIELD indicates that headspace is longer than is considered safe, and you will see symptoms of such in the form of broken case heads, gas leaks, and other malfunctions. Not safe or close to ideal.

If the FIELD gauge does not pass but the NOGO gauge did, then you are still okay to shoot the barrel, but you should pay attention to the cases when they are ejected and picked up for signs of excessive headspace. Obvious bright lines around the case head about a quarter inch from the rim (case stretching), popped primers, consistent light primer strikes, case head separation (rim and back quarter inch of case rips off case body) and damage to the rim from extractors not seating on the rim properly. You are unlikely to notice anything like this until the headspace is into the FIELD category, but it's still safe to check. Your headspace will not likely change significantly for a great many rounds. The gauges are good to have even if you aren't a gunsmith and you can purchase the set for less than $100 from Brownells and you can even get a full incremental match set if you want for around $200.

This can still be done after assembly, but you will have to use the entire bolt carrier assembly, and it's harder to feel the whole thing, but it will work if you forget to headspace before assembly, or are not able to do so. Feel free to take it to a gunsmith to have headspaced. The fee will likely be minimal, under $30, saving you the expense of the gauges if you don't want them. Plus any gunsmith should be more than happy to take your money for an easy job such as this.

FREE-FLOATING A BARREL

Free-floating a barrel does not refer to riding the Niagara Falls inside one while naked. It means installing a rifle barrel so that no contact is made between the barrel and anything else, except where it enters the upper receiver. Free-floating a barrel is arguably the single most effective thing you can do to a rifle to make it more accurate, often substantially. It is very common in the AR series of rifles. In fact, there are very few aftermarket handguards that aren't some sort of free-float tube replacement for the standard two piece plastic handguard. While we will wade into the handguards pretty deeply in a later chapter, I want to go over the very pointed point of free-floated barrels right now in the barrel chapter. About the only time you will find the traditional plastic handguards is on the big named manufactured M4 and AR-15/M-16 style of carbines and rifles. The basic stuff. The smaller boutique builders and to a small extent, the optioned out models from the big guys are pretty much exclusively equipped with free-floated barrels and the appropriate handguards. This generally also means that the guns are without front sight towers and are more optimized for optics and back up iron sights. If there is no obvious contact between the front of the handguard and the barrel, it's likely free floated.

I've already made the minor point that free-floated barrels are more accurate than barrels that are not so mounted. So...how come? Basically, it's this. When things touch the barrel, a pressure point of sorts is placed on the barrel so that the barrel har-

(top) With the top handguard piece removed, you can see the steel free-float tube beneath it. The overall appearance remains the same as the non-free-floated standard rifle.

(bottom) This sling swivel attachment is moved from the front sight to the FF handguard, seen here. This one was modified slightly to accommodate the JP adjustable gas block/front sight tower.

monics are changed. When a bullet goes down the barrel, the barrel vibrates to its own tune. Barrels of the same design will have similar harmonics but no two barrels will ever be the same, just like no two people are exactly the same, even identical twins. While the schematics (like the twins' DNA) may be identical, other things happen very quickly. One twin brother was punched smack in the face and got a broken nose because his twin brother was an insufferable jackass, and the offended party figured punching the first brother was just as good as punching the twin brother that was a jerk. Now they are different because the first brother has a crooked nose. Of two barrels, one might have a big dent right in front of the gas block because of being dropped. They are technically the same barrel, but…they're not.

Barrels will, as long as you are shooting the same bullet, vibrate consistently, unless something touches, presses, hangs from, or pulls the barrel to alter the barrel harmonics. A great example is a sling. People can sling up so tightly (particularly CMP guys) that they will significantly change their bullet's point of impact, compared to not slinging up. This is why free-floated barrels with free-float handguard tubes are handy because the sling can be attached to the handguard, placing no stress whatsoever on the barrel.

Since I mentioned CMP shooters, I might as well cover the typical (or not so typical, in my case) CMP/DCM National Match rifle barrel setup. There are two inviolable rules for a rifle in this kind of (popular) competition. The trigger must have at least a 4.5lbs pull, and the shape or silhouette of the rifle must match an issued rifle, in this case an M4, M-16A2 or A4, or if you are an old timer, an M-14 or M1. That means two-piece plastic handguards, A-frame front sight tower and gas block, A1 or A2 stock and pistol grips, and integral or detachable carry handle. There is a free-floating handguard tube that uses the standard handguard pieces that we will see in the next chapter. The barrel usually chosen is a heavy profile (commonly an inch or more in diameter) behind the gas block with the standard contour after the gas block. Often the barrels have no compensator or threads at all and they are practically universally fabricated from stainless steel. The theory is that the heavy barrel is inherently more stable in offhand shooting than a lighter barrel, plus because of the thicker contour be more accurate. This is generally true. In combination with the heavy barrel, shooters also tend to add a few pounds of lead to the buttstock cavity to add more mass to the rear of the rifle for balance and additional stability. Ranges fired will vary from 50 yards to out to 1000 yards.

This barrel doesn't really have much practical competition use outside this field of competition. Most other AR competition disciplines incorporate

ARs can make good self-defense tools in the home. The shorter the better here, since you have to go through doors and stuff. One of the things that anti-gun activists like to say to somehow denigrate ARs is that they are scary looking and might frighten people, and it's true that many people with no experience with them experience an irrational but understandable fear. But if someone is in my house uninvited, then I want them to be afraid of me and my gun because I really don't want to have to shoot them. If the gun is scarier looking, so much the better.

movement and a rifle this heavy, while extremely accurate, is not an ideal choice for engaging multiple targets at multiple ranges while interspersed with movement. Plus, disciplines like 3-gun competition are almost always seen with optic equipped rifles. However, the usual accuracy found in these barrels makes them excellent choices for varmint shooting.

WHAT KIND OF BARREL SHOULD I GET?

Well we have already covered the CMP type of barrel choice. But let's go over some others just in case you are, like most new owners, somewhat conflicted over which type of AR to get, or more specifically, the length of barrel to get. The actual type of chambering will be covered in the ammo chapter.

Home defense

Generally speaking, the shorter the barrel the better the choice for this category for one simple

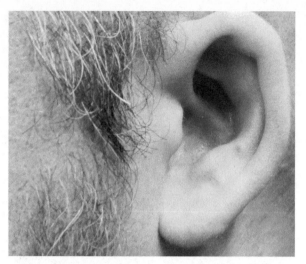

(above) Have you ever seen one of these bleed? If you shoot off a braked gun indoors (or under a shooting bay) with no muffs, you will acutely experience such a thing.

reason. Long barrels are difficult to maneuver in small spaces, like doorways, hallways and such. The wide selection of 16" barrels are ideal for this purpose. Even better would be the lightweight or ultra-lightweight barrel choices. They are much lighter than the standard M4 barrel and can be swung faster, and effectively used by physically weaker people better (theoretically; haven't seen any data on that one, can't really back it up). These barrels are going to be less inherently accurate than the standard contour barrels but in the home that will not matter, nor will having a free-floated barrel.

Better still would be to have a 14.5" barrel that has the permanently affixed flash hider, and you want a flash hider (flash suppressor) not a compensator or muzzle brake. Indoors, you will permanently damage your hearing using a comp and while it is a lesser concern than dying, it should still be a concern. The inch and a half of shorter barrel will be even nicer than the standard 16". People say that when you have to shoot at a time such as that, you never notice the gunshot.

Between the two carbines is a factory stock DPMS varmint gun with a 24" barrel. Used for small furry things that dig holes. Just add scope and bipod and you are ready to slaughter fuzzy, scurrying, little vermin at 400 yards.

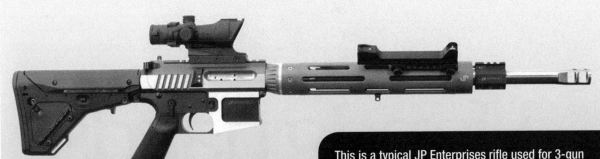

I believe them. But I also believe I'd like to be able to hear the cops coming too (or another assailant), and if I'm deaf from the gunshot that I didn't hear myself pop off, my ability to do that is severely compromised. Of course if you own a legally purchased sound suppressor (silencer) you have the best of the sound world, but it will add a few inches to the length of your barrel. Plus, the shorter the barrel, generally the louder the report.

These tend to be the choices seen used by law enforcement and security services as well. Most common are simply the M4 clones of which just about every manufacturer has a version.

Hunting

There is a spread here. Most dudes that shoot varmints such as gophers or prairie dogs (especially prairie dogs) will go for highest velocity and accuracy possible. This typically means a 24" heavy contour barrel, with handloaded cartridges designed to maximize the velocity. Sometimes the barrels move down to the 20" length for these purposes but the 24" (or longer!) is the standard for that sort of thing.

If you are shooting at the vermin of the canine world, the coyote, then most guys go shorter, topping off at 20" and often going as short as 16". Depends on how close you are shooting the things. The heavy barrel is still common here, and even heavy contoured 16" barrels are pretty common.

If you are going after big game, say white tailed deer or wild hogs, the short barrels, 16" to 18" .308 rifles are the most common with 20" coming in third. Lighter contours are the norm since no one really wants to carry any more weight than he has to when he's walking around in the woods.

Competition

Besides the CMP type of barrel are other sports in which the AR-15 has simply taken over and dominated. The 3-gun sports are with only a few exceptions owned completely by the AR. Barrels are usually of a lighter contour and more often than not of 18" or 20" in length. You gotta have the velocity to hit 500 and 600 yard targets, yet still be agile enough to engage multiple short range targets in the same stage. Hybrid barrels, thin under the handguard, thick past the gas block, much like the standard basic M4 contour without all the silly rings in it, like those made by JP Enterprises, are extremely common in this sport.

High Power is another paper shooter sport that has rifles often referred to as "space guns." Very long barrels with very precise sights are the norm here and there are no shape requirements in this one. Many barrels even have extensions called bloop tubes on the end so the sight radius can be longer than the barrel itself by up to a foot in length. Think of it as an eight inch long flash hider with a front sight mounted to it, but doesn't hide flash. These guns look really weird, but are accurate to insane ranges for a .22 caliber bullet.

I'm probably leaving something important out, but it's almost impossible to catch everything, and what has been mentioned encompasses the vast majority of uses that people buy ARs for.

CHAPTER 7

Handguards and Forends

Well, as anyone knows, a rifle is a firearm that is held with two hands. On the AR you have a great number of options for a weak-hand purchase. Traditionally, the two-piece plastic M-16 handguard style was the only thing around. The original M-16 handguard was triangular and had left and right side sections. When the M-16A2 model came around, the handguards went from triangular to round, with top and bottom sections. Even bigger a difference, the halves were interchangeable, which was a benefit to the supply officers in the military. There is debate on which was/is more comfortable to hold, but both styles are still used, though it is the round A2 style that is found on most factory guns, whether it be rifle, carbine, or mid-length.

The point of the handguard, of course, is to provide a convenient and ergonomic spot to place your support hand. The standard handguards will even have a heat shield inside the panels to protect

the support hand from the heat generated by the barrel, as well as vent holes at the top and bottom to help to circulate that radiated heat away from the barrel. Modern handguards made from aluminum alloys tend to lack heat shields but are very heavily ventilated to allow flow through the forend and around the barrel to enhance the radiating heat dispersion. They tend to have some sort of accessory mounting rail or rails as well. A rifle with no handguard is a rifle missing a key piece of its structure. Try holding that barrel with your bare hands after just ten shots. I triple dog dare you.

There's really not much more to say about the standard plastic-two piece handguards. They're plastic, they're two pieces, they have heat shields in them with vent holes on the top and bottom (I sort of feel like I said this already), and they are among the first things to be removed and replaced on any AR. They're also cheap to produce and purchase and are identical to the units attached to U.S. service weapons.

This is the heat shield that is found inside the typical plastic handguards.

FREE FLOAT OR NOT?

The reason the standard AR handguards are commonly removed is to replace them with free-floating tubes, in order to gain the floating barrel benefits as discussed in the last chapter. The accuracy of a rifle can be significantly enhanced by removing any outside stress from the barrel, and of course this means that you have to replace the handguard assembly with something else entirely.

With standard handguards, the rear of the pieces is held in by the delta ring of the barrel retaining nut, and the front of the pieces is retained by the cup just behind the front sight/gas block. With few exceptions, the front sight will have to be removed and this cup also removed in order to attach free-floating handguards (I'll cover one of the few exceptions later). The reason for this is that the barrel retaining nut has to come off in order to put on a new handguard assembly, since aftermarket handguard assemblies are almost universally in possession of their own proprietary nuts. This is

The piece that retains the front end of the handguard pieces will generally need to be removed, along with the front sight tower, when installing a free-float tube.

The quickest and easiest way to remove the front sight tower to add a free-float tube such as a long Daniel Defense Omega is simply to leave it and cut the top off above the gas tube. The free-float tubes will usually fit right over or over and around the shortened block.

This is a simple free-floating handguard. Unlike most, this DPMS tube's back end is in fact the barrel retaining nut, onto which the rest of the handguard is attached.

necessary because everybody has to do everything differently.

Incidentally, this is also a bodaciously opportune time to replace your gas block with something other than the standard A-frame gas block/front sight, assuming you want to use optics on the rifle. Since the number of choices for optics is huge and the prices are generally not too bad for some pretty good stuff, it's quite common for changes to be made here as well. Of particular note is that, by using a different, lower profile gas block, you can mount a much longer free-floating handguard tube to your rifle, with the gas block fully inside the airy confines of the tube. We'll get into gas blocks more in the "Operating Systems" chapter later on and the whole silly optics thing in the "Optics" chapter. It should also be obvious that, since we are removing the barrel retaining nut, this is also a fabulous time to put a new, better, or replacement barrel in the upper receiver.

TUBES, RAILS AND CROSSES

Usually we refer to free-floating handguards as "tubes" or "rails." Pretty much all of the earlier generations of free-floating handguards were simple tubes that attached to a similar-looking retainer nut, and this style is still quite common. These tubes were generally about two inches in diameter and often did not have vent holes in them. For ex-

ample, the Hogue overmolded rifle tube has mostly aluminum construction (like most) but also has the rubberized grip surface over a large portion of the tube. The standard DPMS free-float handguard is

a simple tube that is threaded onto a same-diameter nut that retains the barrel.

Many free-float handguards are tubes like the aforementioned, but with the addition of Picatinny rails at the 3, 6, 9, and 12 o'clock positions. When these hit the market they were the stuff, and became popular quite quickly. They had two potential detractions, depending on who you asked. The first was that the rails were in addition to the already two-inch tube, making the whole thing quite wide, sometimes almost three inches in diameter, particularly the railed tubes meant for mounting on .308 rifles. The second was accentu-

The usual way to fill uncomfortable Picatinny rails is to use these rail "ladder" covers. They are of flexible plastic, are usually pretty inexpensive, and are manufactured by many companies.

ated by the first, that is, the four rails tend to be fairly uncomfortable for ungloved hands to handle roughly. Sometimes those rails would cause abrasions, and were just not all that comfortable. The wider the tube, the more uncomfortable those naked rails were. The market adapted quickly with rail covers that snap into place on top of the rails, and what are known as "ladder" covers, that mount on, filling the rail gaps and thus taking away the rail edges.

Efforts have been made to reduce the diameter of some of these tubes. The first is simply to not make them tubes but something else. These typically are of a cruciform cross section and the perfect example is the Daniel Defense Omega Rail. When viewed from the front, it looks like a cross (the top rail is raised to the level of the receiver rail, the bottom of equal negative height). The width is quite thin, significantly thinner than the height. The vent holes and rail slots are machined into the "tube." A rear cup assembly is then welded to the tube, or is simply machined into the tube, that affixes to the standard barrel retaining nut. This is a free-floating handguard assembly that requires only the removal of the standard handguard pieces. The cup fits over the nut teeth on the top and bottom pieces of the handguard, which is also a two piece unit. Where it differs from the standard is that the pieces screw together after assembly on the upper and then tensioning set screws are tightened against the barrel retaining nut to fully make the entire assembly rigid. The Delta ring closes forward over the cup and gives the appearance of a replacement non-floating two-piece forend, but is in fact free floated. It is also suitable for use with a number of piston upgrades (pistons are covered in the next chapter). Naturally, because of the extensive machining necessary for this type of railed handguard, they tend to be quite expensive, $300 or more.

Another means of approaching this issue is the use of very lightweight "clamp on" types of handguards, and in the last couple years these have really gotten popular. Good examples of these are the Gen II SS tubes made by Midwest Industries. A proprietary barrel retaining nut, similar (a bit) in appearance to a standard nut, is screwed onto the receiver (and for the record, this nut has

(left) You can see here the cruciform cross-section (or is that redundant?) of the Daniel Defense Omega Rail. This model is a mid-length version.

(below) The top half of the Omega rail has been installed onto the barrel retaining nut. Note how the cup fits right on the toothed portion of the nut. The bottom half will attach the same way.

(bottom) The back end of the Omega railed handguard has a cup-like structure that fits around the barrel retaining nut, in a similar fashion to the standard handguard.

(top) Once both pieces of the Omega rail have been installed around the barrel retaining nut, the four large screws in the left and right rails can be installed. These screws join the top and bottom sections to form one rigid handguard.

(second) At this point, with the handguard halves secured together, the handguard should be perfectly aligned with the upper receiver. A fixture is priceless for aligning receiver and handguard rails. This is a fixture I obtained when installing an old piston gas block, and the manufacturer wanted to make sure I did it correctly. I still use this invaluable tool on a regular basis. PWS could probably sell these things if they still made them (hint, hint). It clamps the receiver and handguard rails tightly together, and perfectly too.

(third) The four set screws in the cup are the last things to tighten. With the pieces immobilized by the fixture, the four set screws can be tightened with little concern for alignment. Without such a fixture, the installer should snug each screw in an alternating, criss-cross fashion until they are tight, using a medium strength thread locking compound, with attention paid to perfect alignment of the handguard around the barrel. If the barrel exits the handguard precisely at the crucial (another cross word, FYI) crossing of the horizontal and vertical, the screws have been torqued correctly.

(bottom) The Omega rail fully installed on an upper.

to be perfectly aligned, in order to perfectly align the top rail of the handguard to that of the receiver) and the tube is pushed on over this nut. A pair of screws and a slot on the bottom of the handguard form a clamping assembly that is tightened down on the nut. The tube itself is ventilated and has an integral top rail even with the receiver, but is a bare fraction of an inch larger in diameter than the nut itself. These tubes measure well under 1¾" and are heaven for small-handed shooters, and as mentioned, are very lightweight with few exceptions. You definitely need to have a very low profile minimized gas block when using this type of handguard, and most do not accommodate piston systems. But you can easily get a sub-seven-pound rifle using a lightweight barrel and one of these handguards.

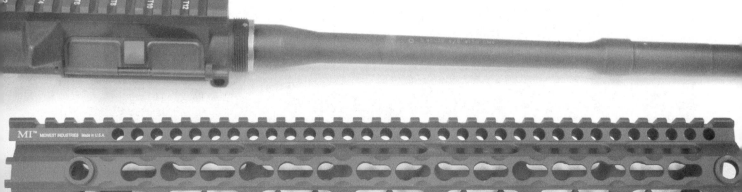

(above) The Midwest Industries Gen 2 SS rails are lightweight and thin. They are practically child's play to install, provided you are building rather than upgrading. If you are upgrading, you will have to remove the front sight/gas block, and the current barrel retaining nut.

This ruler should indicate adequately how skinny these railed tubes are. Even when you add a supplementary rail to the tube, it is still no wider than the normal standard four-railed handguard. Still the point was to not have extraneous unused rails, so you only need to add one exactly where you want one and still keep the very thin profile on the tube.

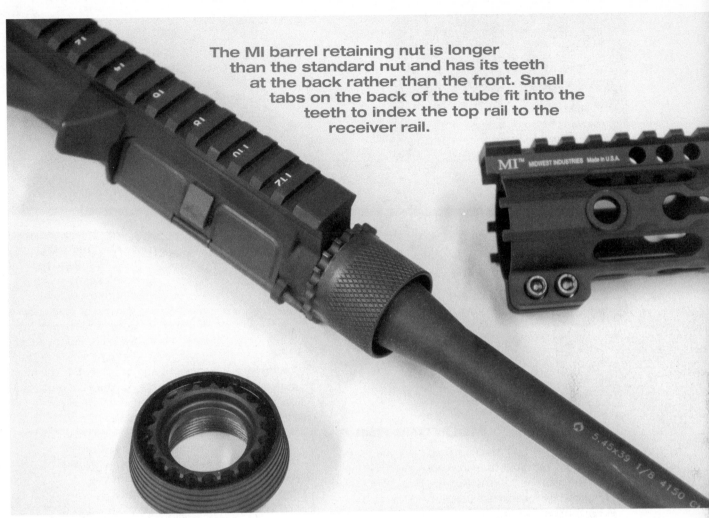

The MI barrel retaining nut is longer than the standard nut and has its teeth at the back rather than the front. Small tabs on the back of the tube fit into the teeth to index the top rail to the receiver rail.

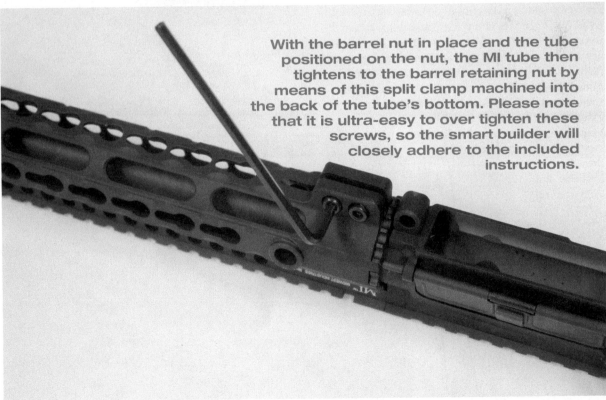

With the barrel nut in place and the tube positioned on the nut, the MI tube then tightens to the barrel retaining nut by means of this split clamp machined into the back of the tube's bottom. Please note that it is ultra-easy to over tighten these screws, so the smart builder will closely adhere to the included instructions.

This is the standard Picatinny rail design, allowing a great deal of location flexibility for things that used to be mounted rather inflexibly, or not at all. The MI rails are all equipped with rails.

(below) The MI handguards usually come with accessory rails, one of which has an interface for a QD sling swivel. They can be placed anywhere there are screw holes on the handguard.

MOUNTING RAILS

The standard for some years for mounting accessories to firearms such as the AR has been the Picatinny system developed by folks at the Picatinny Arsenal. It consists of rails integral or attached to tubes that are composed of a dovetail-style cross section with transverse grooves along the flat outer surface of the rail. This is the reason that certain handguards are simply referred to as "rails" even though the rails are only a component of the overall handguard. By far the most common integral rail is the top rail that is designed to literally be an extension of the optics mounting rail machined into the top of the upper receiver. These are closely followed by the four-railed systems. Less common are truly modular units that allow rails to be mounted at any point on the handguard tube by means of screw holes or slots. Short two- to four-inch sections of Picatinny rail can be attached where needed to mount a tac light or laser or whatever, leaving the rest of the handguard tube smooth and rail-free. For the most part, only a small percentage of the rails on a four rail handguard are ever used at one time.

The newest standardized means of mounting is called the Key-Mod system. It's not really new, since we've been using it for like, forever, on shelves and storage cabinets. A capped peg is inserted into a slot that on one end is peg-sized and on the other end is smaller than the cap but sized for the stem of the peg. The smaller end acts as a lock and is usually down in relation to the assembly and/or gravity. The Key-Mod when applied to a handguard shows a series of such slots with the small end facing forward. The rail or whatever accessory has the peg which is inserted in to the slot and the screw tightened down, locking it in place. The small end is forward since, under recoil, inertia would cause the accessory to remain in place, essentially moving forward in relation to the handguard tube, and thus should not pop out of the slot under recoil. If the slots were the other way, the accessory would eventually creep forward and then ultimately fall off. The Key-Mod system has not replaced the Picatinny system, and probably won't completely, as both are excellent systems, and they are pretty much apples and oranges anyway, but it is gaining in popularity since any accessory can always be added after the handguard tube has been installed. Standard modular tubes that use normal slots often require backer plates that can require removal of the tube for installation of the rail, and it is this style that may give way to the Key-Mod eventually. But I doubt it.

(below) Note the identical design to your shelf unit.

(inset) The original keymod concept, applied to non-shooty equipment.

(bottom) The backer plates used on the Key-Mod system can be left attached to the rail and inserted as a unit onto the tube, and then tightened. You should probably use a medium or low strength threadlocker on the screws.

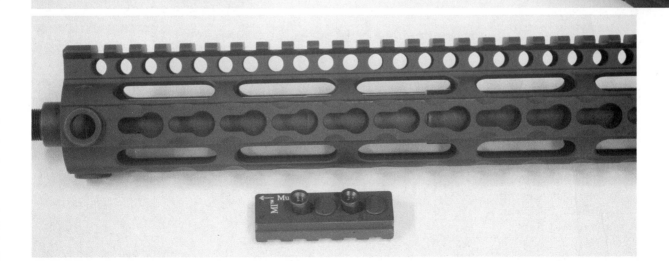

The upper assembly is secured in a set of vise blocks in the bench vise.

(below) These two tapered pins need to be driven out to remove the front sight/gas block.

CHANGING OUT: EXAMPLE 1

This is the typical process to change a standard handguard to a free-floated handguard. Start with no lower assembly. The upper assembly should be detached and in a bench vise. You will want to use your upper receiver blocks that we covered in the barrel chapter for this entire sequence. The first thing is to pull back on the delta ring to remove the lower piece. It seems just easier usually to do the bottom first. The piece should be lowered from the back and then pulled out of the cup at the front. Follow this up by then removing the top piece. You should now see an upper assembly with no handguard, with the barrel and gas tube naked and exposed to all creation. This is way easy with a forend/handguard tool. I will restate that I prefer to remove the gas tube at this time as well, so as not to risk banging it up when we start banging on the front sight block.

You will have to remove the front sight's tapered retaining pins from the bottom of the A-frame. They are TAPERED, which means they only go out one way, and some companies think it's just the coolest thing ever to really, really jam those things in there. Granted, you don't ever want them coming out without actually wanting them to come out, but they are often in there so tight that you might have to cut or drill them out. We're talking baby bunny under a porch step here. Sometimes you can get them out by putting the barrel or the

Brownells makes a mind-numbingly sweet bench block to use as a fixture for driving out these silly taper pins. It supports the A-frame handily and has through-holes for the pins to drop into. The reverse side is a mirror image intended to fixture the assembly up for driving the pins in.

sight tower in the vise and most times you can get them out using a specialty bench block. I wish I could tell you a universal way to get them out easily, but I can't. Some are relatively easy, and some aren't.

The specialty bench block to which I refer is the front sight bench

The nekkid barrel ready to have the retainer nut removed.

(below) The JP modular free-float tube has an inner and outer nut. The outer nut functions to tension the inner nut to the barrel extension, even though you will not really be doing anything to the outer nut other than lining it up. The tube then fits over the reduced diameter of the outer tube. The two nuts must be affixed prior to the installation of the gas block and tube.

block that Brownells sells. It is machined out so that the front sight tower will fit either way into it and you can hammer out the pins; even has directions on it.

You will want to support the rest of the upper on a similarly elevated surface for ease of use. By the way, they virtually always go out from left to

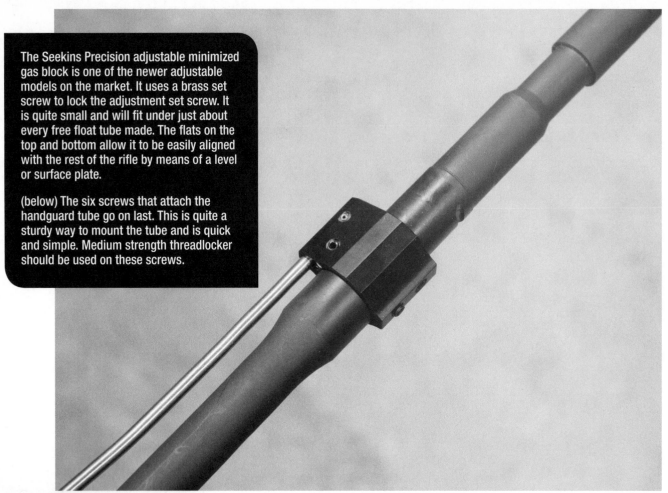

The Seekins Precision adjustable minimized gas block is one of the newer adjustable models on the market. It uses a brass set screw to lock the adjustment set screw. It is quite small and will fit under just about every free float tube made. The flats on the top and bottom allow it to be easily aligned with the rest of the rifle by means of a level or surface plate.

(below) The six screws that attach the handguard tube go on last. This is quite a sturdy way to mount the tube and is quick and simple. Medium strength threadlocker should be used on these screws.

right. There is a noticeable difference in diameter, left to right. Use a short thick punch to get them started and then a longer punch to finish pushing them out to the right. The front sight tower may be quite tightly attached still, so a little twisting and possibly a little propane heat on the tower rings may be in order.

Once it is off the gas block collar of the barrel, it should easily slide off the muzzle, assuming you have removed whatever muzzle device might be present. It can however be on tightly and require a little heat to expand the rings. Take care to not kink the gas tube if you left it in place. If you twist the assembly too far with the gas tube installed, you will likely damage the tube. It's supposed to have a bend in it but not more than it started with. Honestly, it's best to remove the tube before you play with the block, but not necessarily mandatory.

Now the barrel should be clear of stuff. If by chance there is something still on the barrel, now would be the time to remove it. Since we are assuming a standard rifle upper here, there should not be anything else there. Here is where you take your handy dandy action wrench to remove the barrel retainer nut just like we did in the last chapter. Once that is done, you are ready to install your new handguard. Let's for the sake of argument say that it is a JP Enterprises Modular handguard. This is one of the less common styles of handguard, using both inner and outer retainer nuts. The outer nut is screwed onto the receiver, often with thread locking compound to hold it in place in alignment while the inner nut is tightened against the barrel extension. The same amount of torque is used to secure the nut as a normal nut, around 30–100 ft/lbs of torque, and if you don't know what that feels like, then you should borrow a torque wrench from your buddy in the auto shop.

In the case of this JP handguard, the body of the unit is a simple extruded tube with slots cut in it for ventilation. The rear end of the tube is counterbored to accept the outer handguard nut and has six holes around it to fasten it to the nut. However, since we are replacing a carbine length standard handguard with a rifle-length free-floating handguard, we now have to install a minimized gas block first, since it is going to be fully inside the confines of the tube and virtually impossible to install correctly with the tube emplaced. If you are going to install accessory rails to this tube, this too should be done before the tube is attached.

This JP tube uses six flat head screws to hold the tube to the nut. The tube can inadvertently be installed upside down, so don't do that. With these six screws attached, you are pretty much ready to go, as long as you remembered to install the gas tube and gas block.

Of course, you no longer have a front sight. Perhaps you decided that you don't really want one and you are going to use only optics. Ok, so you're one of those... people. Well, I guess that's okay, and you can stop here, since your super optic mega scope will take care of everything. If you aren't one of those...people, then you can still mount a front sight to the front end of the handguard tube. JP sells partial or full sized rails for that purpose. Flip up sights can still be used effectively with optics, and particularly offset sights are a good choice for rifles with high magnification scopes used as the primary sighting device. We'll talk more about that later.

CHANGING OUT: EXAMPLE 2

For this example, we'll look at one of the more obscure models to appear, and that is the Hera Arms handguard. It is made in Germany and is much more commonly used there than in the states. It might surprise you to learn that AR style rifles are quite popular in Europe with those folks who happen to be competitive shooters. We simply don't see much of the stuff they make for that pur-

The Hera Arms free-float tube is manufactured to be a very sturdy, and rather heavy for its type, handguard model. It attaches by means of a clamp system similar to the previously covered Midwest Industries handguard. Unlike the MI tube, the Hera tube uses three smaller screws and uses a steel backer plate (compared to the MI two larger screws and no plate). The tube walls are thicker than most domestic tubes.

pose, partly because we have a glut load of choices here already, partly because Europeans look at things a little differently and the parts show it, and partly because we're arrogant Americans and they're arrogant Europeans.

The Hera Arms handguard is free-floating and attaches similarly to the MI tube mentioned earlier. Removal of the standard handguard and barrel retaining nut is necessary, as is the front sight/ gas block, and muzzle attachment. Here is where the similarities diverge. The new retainer nut is a heavy steel cylinder that has wrench flats on it instead of the teeth or series of small holes found on American retainer nuts. A groove is also present for two set screws in the handguard itself. The primary means of retention is a screwed clamp system very much like the MI tube, but with three smaller screws rather than the two large machine screws of the MI. The nut is wrenched on (clearly, the Europeans are not quite as obsessed with the idea of super tight barrel retainer nuts as Americans), and the tube is then placed over it with the rails on top aligning with the receiver. The clamp is tightened with the set screws tightened down into the alignment groove in the retention nut. Of course if you were using a minimized gas block you would have installed that prior to the handguard tube.

This handguard is extremely sturdy and rigid. The tube wall is much thicker than comparable domestic walls and the retainer nut is at least twice the weight of domestic nuts. This tube is not meant to be lightweight, but it does appear to have been Germaneered to never break.

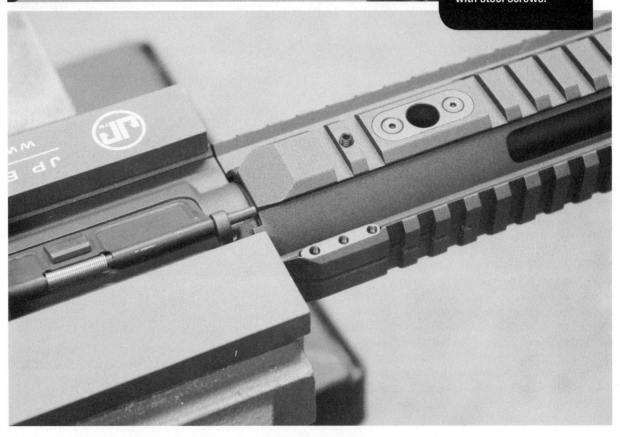

(left) As you can see, the Hera barrel retaining nut looks nothing like a standard model. This big steel nut contributes to the heavier weight.

(below) The steel backer plate helps prevent cross threading in the screw holes. Aluminum screw holes don't always play well with steel screws.

OTHER OPTIONS

It would be remiss of me to not mention the two-piece non-free-floating options for handguards. Just about every company that makes replacement free-floating handguards, and a couple more, also makes non-free-floating enhancements. For example, MagPul makes the M.O.E. handguard that straight up replaces the standard two piece handguard. It has a less than round profile and incorporates mounting points for rails that are included and can be purchased separately. Multiple colors are available, and indeed, many manufacturers are using the M.O.E. parts, whether they be handguards, stocks, or grips, as OEM equipment from the factory.

Four-railed handguard replacements probably represent the original idea here, since the M-16A4 uses the Knight's Armament handguards in place of the standard plastic pieces. These are simply aluminum railed tubes that are cut into two pieces and mount the exact same way as the standard tubes. You might occasionally see an AR on TV or the movies that has no handguard, particularly the pistols. This is really not practical as the gas tube needs some protection and the only way to do that is to mount a handguard of some sort.

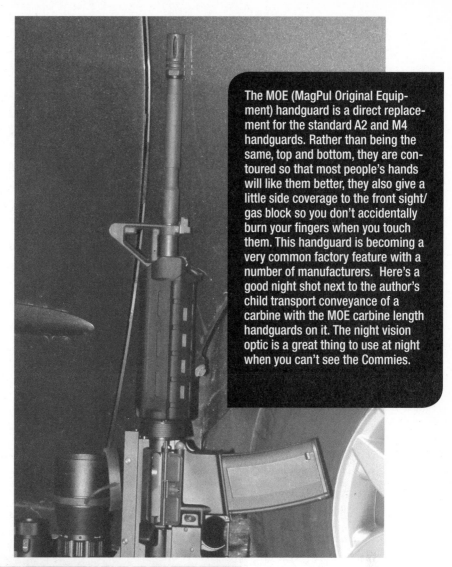

The MOE (MagPul Original Equipment) handguard is a direct replacement for the standard A2 and M4 handguards. Rather than being the same, top and bottom, they are contoured so that most people's hands will like them better, they also give a little side coverage to the front sight/gas block so you don't accidentally burn your fingers when you touch them. This handguard is becoming a very common factory feature with a number of manufacturers. Here's a good night shot next to the author's child transport conveyance of a carbine with the MOE carbine length handguards on it. The night vision optic is a great thing to use at night when you can't see the Commies.

I've seen this on several movies, Escape From New York being one of them. Stupid. Don't shoot a gun like this. You can but after a few rounds you will be sorry. Actors don't know crap and the prop guys know it.

(left) Pretending to be Dick, I don't have much room to use on the handguard to lay it down or lean it on a surface.

(below) Pretending to be Jack, I have a huge area to use for outside support, literally the full length of barrel with the extended free floating handguard. Jack is less exposed with better concealment.

Half the time this is just the guys who actually know something about guns (the set armorers) playing pranks on the big-shot actors. It's similar to the red dots and scopes mounted backwards on rifles (watch "Mr. & Mrs. Smith" and "Tears of the Sun" for good examples of that) and guys having different guns from one shot to the next all within the same scene. I've seen "military" units in shows running around with rifles sans sights or magazines. Let me tell you, that kind of crap is painful to watch. It makes a dude think that the gun guys on set are having a real ball just screwing around with the rest of the cast and crew.

Anyway, these types of handguard replacements tend to be less expensive than the free-floating models and might be a great way to personalize your gun and add some accessorizability to your gun on the cheap. They are also much more readily available. While some of the more premium models of handguard upgrades tend to be upwards of $200 and usually restricted to internet sales, the two piece replacements like these are often found in department stores like Fleet Farm and Gander Mountain.

A NOTE ON HANDGUARD LENGTH

It's important to point out that one would be well advised to choose the longest handguard that one is comfortable using. A long free-floating handguard enables the user to rest the rifle on that handguard without fear of altering the point of impact. A theoretical handguard as long as the rifle's barrel (actually not that theoretical, lots of guns have them) allows the shooter to rest the gun along its entire barrel length. This is so much more superior to the M4 carbine length handguard that it is difficult to express properly. But I'll try by using an anecdote. Dick has an M4-style rifle with the short crappy normal handguards. His sworn enemy Jack has the exact same rifle but he replaced the standard piece of crap normal handguards with a free-floated extended length (15") handguard (necessitating a minimized gas block, of course). From magazine to muzzle, Jack can lay that rifle down on something (a wall) to steady his aim, but Dick has only about the first seven inches, less than half the rifle's barrel length, to do the same thing. Incidentally, since Jack can mount his front sight waaaay down the barrel, literally at the muzzle, he also has a longer sight radius and a more inherently accurate gun. Furthermore, both of them sling up hard; Jack's is on the handguard, but Dick is still using the normal sling swivel attached to his front sight tower. Between the pulling from the sling and the contact with the wall he's steadying on, Dick's point of bullet impact is not staying consistent with his point of aim. But Jack has no stresses on his barrel at all, despite the

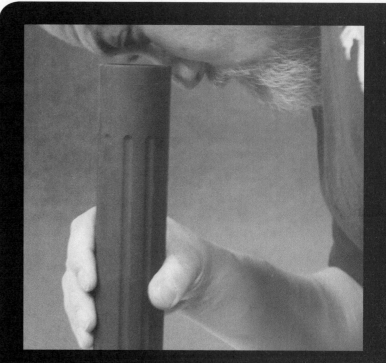

Guys with short barreled rifles often get handguard tubes that are much longer than the barrel. This is so Mr. SBR can also be Mr. Silencer and have the handguard partially cover the silencer. The concept works well and also protects the hands from getting burned on the uber-hot silencer after a mag dump. I don't have one, so I'm simulating in a non-compensational simulated simulation of an SBR in a compensation inspired simulation.

fact that he is steadying on an identical wall to the one that Dick is using and despite the fact the he is slinging up so tight that the handguard is visibly being pulled off center to the barrel. On top of this, neither one is slinging tightly universally, so every time Dick or Jack breathes, the sling tension changes slightly and this has an effect on Dick's shooting, but not on Jack's. So, in a nutshell, when the shooting starts, Dick can't hit Jack, but Jack can most assuredly hit Dick.

A purely secondary but entirely pleasant aspect of a full barrel-length handguard is that Jack doesn't accidentally burn the top two layers of his precious skin off when he grabs the barrel after a mag dump or two. He grabs a slightly warm handguard while the palm of Dick's hand becomes a giant blister.

The Operating System:

Gas Blocks, Bolts and Bolt Carriers, Pistons

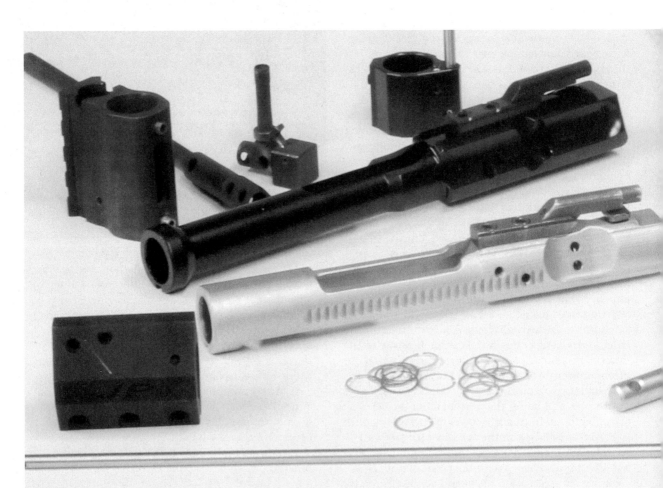

You may have heard that ARs are "gas operated" right? So what does that mean? I'd wager that if you are purchasing your first AR or if you aren't a "gun person," you don't know what that means and that is totally completely okay. I don't really know how my car works or how my wife works, and I still have them, but that is a common trait shared by a lot of people. However, I can get a little edumacated on the process and, for the record, understanding how the operating system works can make maintaining and accessorizing the gun easier and less confusing. We already sort of covered it in an earlier chapter, but let's summarize it again because it's so important to understanding the mechanism of operation of standard AR rifles, as well as some of the interesting options for upgrading that we will see in the ARverse. Let's start by saying that you do not add any kind of "gas" to the system manually. NO GASOLINE, DIESEL, OR PROPANE!

The term "gas operated" means that some of the propellant gases pushing the bullet out of the barrel are tapped off to operate the system. This is one means of making a firearm semi-automatic, meaning every time you pull the trigger, the gun fires and reloads itself. Fully automatic guns, or machine guns, fire two or more shots per trigger pull, also reloading themselves. Bolt action, hinge action, and pump action guns fire one shot per trigger pull, but require the shooter to manually reload, or operate the gun (indeed, DPMS even made a couple pump action ARs for several years). Any of these may have magazines that hold multiple rounds, and full and semi-auto guns must. The others can be single shot, where there is no magazine holding cartridges, and the gun must be operated and loaded manually each time.

Semi and full automatic guns do not have to be gas operated. They can be blowback, recoil, or inertia operated as well, or even combinations of the above. Let's skip all that detail for now, and you can look all of those up on Wikipedia. Suffice it to say that the gun operates itself by tapping propellant gas from the bore and uses that gas to make the guts move around (sort of like my guts). Or more specifically, initiates the bolt carrier movement which unlocks the bolt; the momentum of this bolt carrier assembly then carrying the assembly the rest of the way back. In this overall picture, they pretty much all work the same way, be they ARs, AKs, FALs, or M14s. For that matter, so do all the gas operated hunting rifles.

This is where we have to understand a very im-

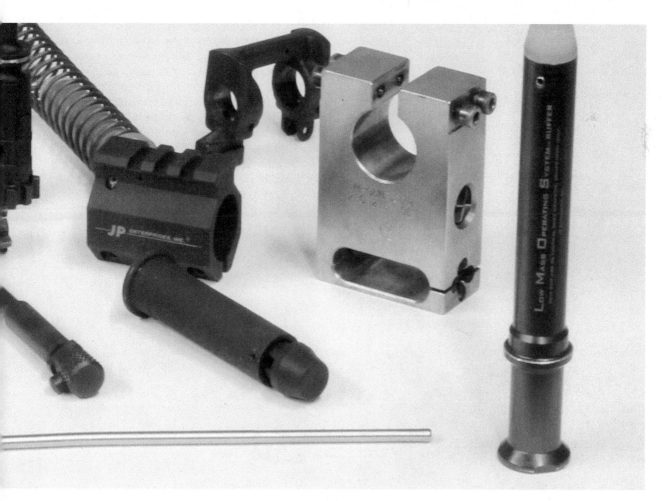

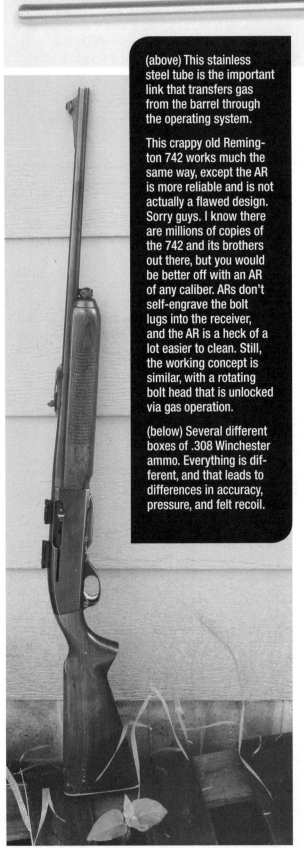

(above) This stainless steel tube is the important link that transfers gas from the barrel through the operating system.

This crappy old Remington 742 works much the same way, except the AR is more reliable and is not actually a flawed design. Sorry guys. I know there are millions of copies of the 742 and its brothers out there, but you would be better off with an AR of any caliber. ARs don't self-engrave the bolt lugs into the receiver, and the AR is a heck of a lot easier to clean. Still, the working concept is similar, with a rotating bolt head that is unlocked via gas operation.

(below) Several different boxes of .308 Winchester ammo. Everything is different, and that leads to differences in accuracy, pressure, and felt recoil.

portant thing. No ammunition is made the same as the rest. You can pick up a box of .308 Winchester off the shelf and it will perform differently from every other box of .308 Win. Each ammo manufacturer makes their cartridges to fit within a window of operational pressure designated by SAAMI, but within that window they can do whatever they want. Two different boxes from two different manufacturers, though of apparently the same design and characteristics, will shoot differently from the same barrel. Furthermore, the same ammo from the same manufacturer will vary depending on the manufactured lot. Available for purchase at the retail storefront is 308 Win. ammo with bullet weights that run from 110 grains to 180 grains, a significant difference, yet all are expected to function. For this reason, rifle manufacturers build their rifles so that an excess of gas is bled from the bore during firing to ensure the reliable cycling of the rifle. If not enough gas is introduced to the system, the gun will fail to cycle, either failing to fully extract or eject the fired cartridge case, or fail to move sufficiently to the rear to pick up a fresh cartridge from the magazine. So a little extra is built in to accommodate as much of the known existing ammunition as possible. Because it never fails that some dude will purchase a $4,000 rifle and then proceed to try and save a buck (or mollify the wife) by buying and shooting the cheapest ammunition that he could possibly find. The super cheap stuff as we'll find in the ammo chapter may not be consistently manufactured and may well cause problems with his rifle. Of course he will then blame

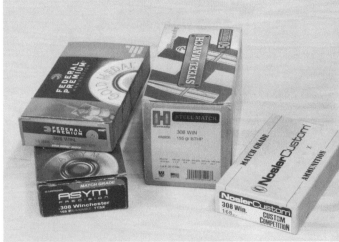

this on the rifle, not the crummy ammo. I apologize for the little rant here, but having worked for a manufacturer I can say from experience that this unreasonableness occurs on a frequent basis.

BOLTS

I'm covering bolts in this chapter because it really is the best place to cover them. The bolt carriers are part of the operating system of the rifles, are central to it in fact. Since the bolt is directly attached to the carrier, then well…

There have been attempts to make a "better" bolt than the mil-spec type that is used for virtually all AR-15s, and the derivation of such for the larger frame guns (since there is no mil-spec for the .308 bolts; most follow either the AR-10 or the SR-25 patterns).

One of the common major alterations is the use of some sort of plating or other surface finish to enhance the natural lubricity of the bolt. The most likely to be found is the old reliable hard chrome. Salt Nitriding (Melonite, Tenifer, QPQ, etc.) and Nickel/Boron are becoming more popular but are still far less common than chrome. Titanium Nitride

plating, which makes a bright golden color, is also seen on occasion. These are nowhere near as common as the black oxide or parkerizing finish of a normal bolt, but neither are they difficult to find. The advantages are real. The greatest advantage is that they are much easier to clean than the parkerized bolts and have a greater surface hardness, while retaining the natural toughness of the underlying substrate steel. Theoretically the engagement between the bolt and barrel extension lugs is smoother, but I'd welcome someone showing that to me with science rather than anecdote. The other advantage

If you decide to reload, you can create ammunition perfectly suited to your rifle, from matching bullet to rifling twist, to reducing felt recoil by using lower pressure powders, to using the bullet that your particular barrel seems to like the best. Furthermore, you can shoot more because the components are cheaper than the cartridges, and most of us have more time than money, and those that have more money than time just buy factory only or don't shoot at all.

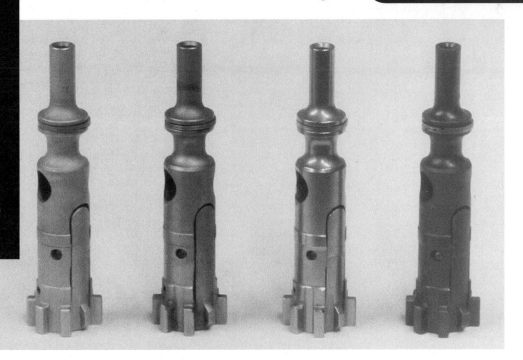

As we see in this image, the bolt can be purchased in one of several alternate finishes. Hard chrome is the classic and is silver, usually matte in appearance. The gold colored bolt has been plated with Titanium Nitride. The bolt with the high polish is plated with Nickel-Boron. Finally, the black bolt is simply the unplated standard Magnesium Phosphate (parkerized) finish.

is not functional. It's bling. The silver or gold or buffed yellow appearance of these platings can enhance the cosmetics of the rifle, particularly when such a surface finish is also applied to the bolt carrier, as it usually is. I tend to support the idea of

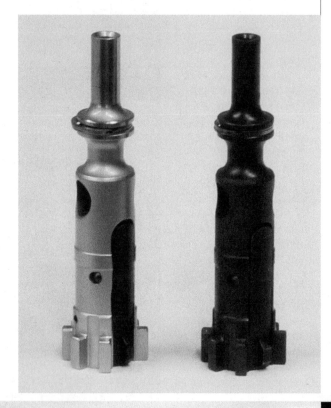

personalizing your gun as much as possible, and the use of an alternate finish like these on your bolt and bolt carrier can help do that.

A second alteration is the use of a different steel to make the bolt. The original steel used is still used now and the mil-spec purists will birth cows in support of keeping the mil-spec here, but sooner or later everyone must bow to progress. The big problem is that progress can be very expensive. In the last five to ten years alternate steels have been introduced for use in the AR series of guns. The original steel for those tech heads out there is Carpenter 158 and is an excellent material for the purpose. Newer stuff includes AISI 8620, SAE 9310, and a few others. These newer alloys can arguably be considered better than the 158, but tend to be more expensive. 8620 is the material often used to make the carriers and there are 8620 bolts, but rumors suggest that these bolts do not perform as long as the 158 and 9310 bolts. 9310 is probably the most common alternate material, and the companies that use it claim higher bolt life, from 50% to 10,000% greater service life. Cost is usually two to three times the cost of a standard mil-spec bolt.

A third alteration that has been attempted with some success is to alter the original design of the bolt's extractor (and the bolt, too, to use it) so that it is enhanced in some way. For example, several companies have modified the extractor hook area to give the cartridge head more support on the bolt face, which tends to also give better extractor hook purchase on the case, but this also has the tendency to thin the extractor and make it easier to bend or break it. Other examples might add a second extractor spring to more strongly allow the hook to grip the case rim.

Still, probably 95% of bolts are of the traditional design and finish and make excellent choices. If you want to upgrade to make it easier to clean or for longer expected work life, then getting these products will not hurt you anywhere but your pocketbook.

Bolts will have gas rings, just like the rings on a piston in an engine that act as gas seals. The bolts will not work without these

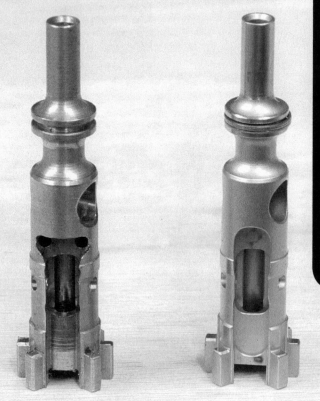

(top) A JP Enhancedbolt is a good example of the use of more modern steels in AR bolts. It stands next to a standard mil-spec bolt.

(botom) This is a newer bolt design, to which I know not the provenance. It is unfinished, and I picked it out of a guy's nonfunctioning seconds box. But anyway, it makes a good illustration; it utilizes a modified extractor with two springs to increase extractor tension for better case extraction.

rings (there have been the odd examples that did) and the gaps in the rings should not be in alignment. If the gaps are aligned you may leak just enough gas to prevent the rifle from operating, but there must be a number of confluent other issues to see this occur. The three gas rings will wear out, particularly if the bolt/bolt carrier fit is a tight one, though they may remain serviceable for the life of the bolt itself. Attempts to make better rings have resulted in single rings or two piece sets that wrap around like a key chain ring, leaving no gap that the gas can potentially use to escape the system early. These work sometimes, but when they do, they are great. Basically, if the bolt/carrier fit is tight, you can sometimes use these alternate rings to loosen the fit and make the bolt easier to move in the carrier.

Bolt/carrier fit, if too stiff, can inhibit the movement of the assembly when the gun is fired, making it seem undergassed, basically putting extra resistance in the system when the carrier is trying to unlock the bolt. Feel free to experiment with these types of rings. They are more expensive, but not prohibitively so, and their use will prevent malfunctions due to gas ring alignment, if such a thing will occur in your gun. Ideally speaking, the bolt/carrier fit should show very minor resistance, not requiring more than the slightest effort to push the bolt in or pull it out, yet also preventing collapse of the carrier onto the bolt when the assembly is extended all the way and set upright on the bolt face.

(left) The gas rings are vital to a DI rifle. They are there to form a seal so enough gas stays in the carrier to initiate its movement. Old or damaged gas rings will compromise performance. You might want to keep a few spares handy.

(below) You will probably be doing just fine using the standard three-piece gas ring set up that comes with nearly every rifle. However, at times, the use of a one-piece ring can make a performance increase in the gun. Here is the JP one-piece ring, which has squared, knife-sharp edges on it. It is similar to the extant MacFarland ring but has fewer, sharper-edged coils.

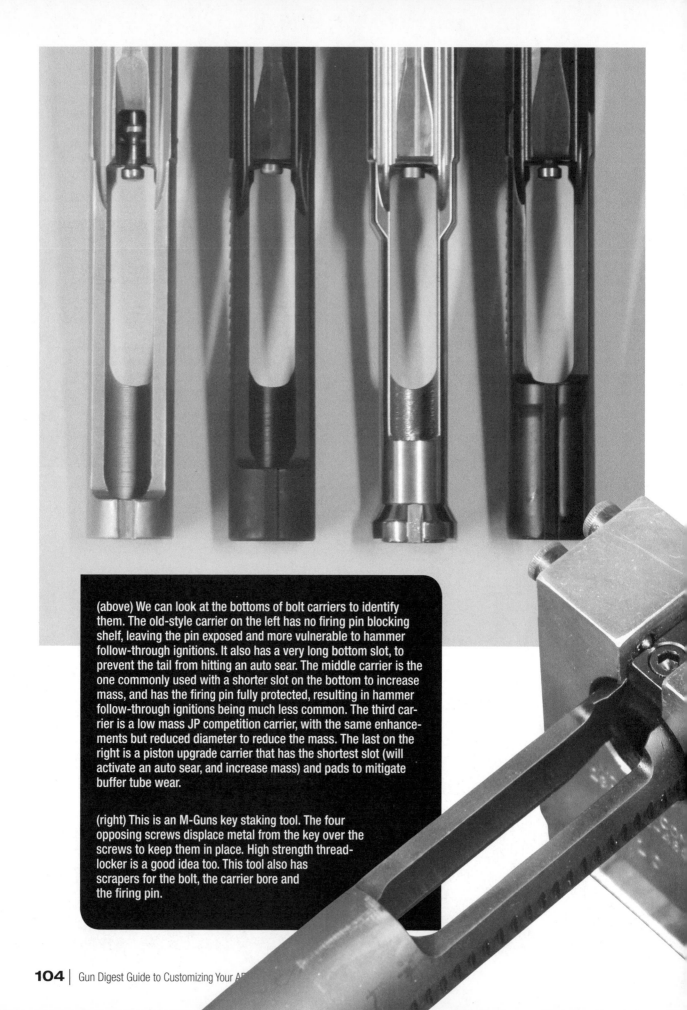

(above) We can look at the bottoms of bolt carriers to identify them. The old-style carrier on the left has no firing pin blocking shelf, leaving the pin exposed and more vulnerable to hammer follow-through ignitions. It also has a very long bottom slot, to prevent the tail from hitting an auto sear. The middle carrier is the one commonly used with a shorter slot on the bottom to increase mass, and has the firing pin fully protected, resulting in hammer follow-through ignitions being much less common. The third carrier is a low mass JP competition carrier, with the same enhancements but reduced diameter to reduce the mass. The last on the right is a piston upgrade carrier that has the shortest slot (will activate an auto sear, and increase mass) and pads to mitigate buffer tube wear.

(right) This is an M-Guns key staking tool. The four opposing screws displace metal from the key over the screws to keep them in place. High strength threadlocker is a good idea too. This tool also has scrapers for the bolt, the carrier bore and the firing pin.

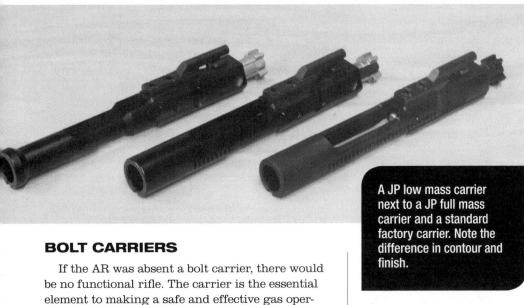

BOLT CARRIERS

If the AR was absent a bolt carrier, there would be no functional rifle. The carrier is the essential element to making a safe and effective gas operated AR. Without the movement of the bolt carrier the bolt would stay locked in place. Without the carrier to carry the bolt, the bolt would float in nothingness, searching in vain for a purpose. The buffer spring and buffer push against the rear of the carrier to strip rounds from the magazine and to close the bolt, so that absent the carrier this return cycle would have to function completely differently. Finally, the interior of the bolt carrier forms the cylinder for the piston design of the bolt tail.

Most bolt carriers, as mentioned before, are machined from AISI 8620, a tough steel ideal for bolt carriers. These carriers are then typically sandblasted and given a parkerized finish. This is good and works well. The insides are generally ground to size and then hard chrome plated. This chrome plated interior cylinder is what the bolt fits into and against which the bolt's gas rings slide across. With the exception of having a reduced rear shelf that cannot activate an auto sear, the commercial carriers are pretty much the same as the mil-spec carriers.

Enhanced bolt carriers are becoming fairly common, particularly in the competitive arena. One of the first ideas was to reduce the weight of the bolt carrier and buffer so that there was less reciprocating mass smacking into the buttstock, thus reducing felt recoil. This really only works in conjunction with an adjustable gas block and for

The WMD Guns Nib-X carrier and bolt are Nickel-Boron plated and extremely highly polished. These things can be used for a mirror to shave that soul patch off your chin.

the most part has been pursued only by one or two companies. The effect is dramatic however, so in sports that require fast follow up shots, such as in practical or 3-gun events, these guns will perform very well. On the other hand, the service rifle matches tend to see the shooters shooting comparably heavy bullets and the movement has been to the other direction. Several companies make extra mass bolt carriers for use with these rifles. The theory is that since you are firing heavier bullets at theoretically higher pressures, a heavy carrier will be a better choice. There is a fair amount of argument over this matter, so if you are buying your first gun or building a new gun for the first time, I'd recommend sticking to a traditional carrier.

There are other benefits to the enhanced carriers on the market. Most have greater surface area on the engagement surfaces that touch the inside of the receiver and this reduces the wear as a result. There will be wear marks on any gun that is shot to any moderate degree, but the effects will be less with the carriers with greater engagement surface area. I've seen upper receivers that looked like Wolverine stuck a middle claw into it and dug a groove half the way back in the inside wall of the receiver. It took a lot of rounds to do that, but it happened, and it was as ugly as the Wolverine when he's drawn by Frank Miller. There are some bolt carri-

ers that downright look like jewelry compared to a mil-spec carrier, and that special surface finish does help to reduce wear in the upper receiver, particularly when combined with a high-lubricity plating or surface treatment. The two that jump out in my mind are the Nickel/Boron carriers as made by WMD Guns and the QPQ treated carriers made by JP Enterprises. Both are very slick and have a highly polished surface as well.

If you assemble a carrier, you should stake the gas key screws. You can do it with a punch, but if you have access to a special tool designed for that purpose, you should use it. You can get them from several companies such as Brownells, who makes their own.

GAS BLOCKS

The gas block is the transfer point from the bore to the gas tube. It wraps around the barrel like a loving embrace of cold steel to fully (hopefully) seal the interface between the barrel's gas port and the corresponding larger gas port in the gas block itself. This is usually done by means of set screws in the bottom of the block or by means of clamping screws, if the gas block has a split in the bottom. The tighter the fit, the better, as gas leaks will result in residue escaping from the interface

It should be clear from this photo that one gas block will fit under the handguard and the other won't. Better handguards require smaller gas blocks. The lone gas block is designed to be used with handguards that terminate before the gas port.

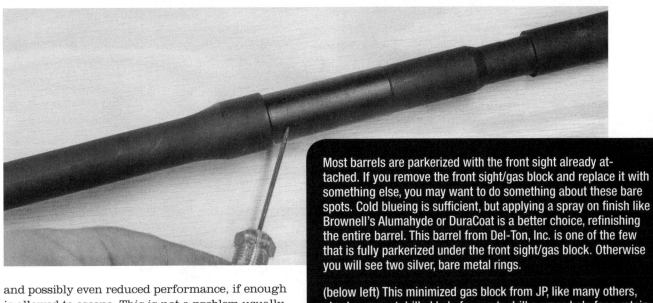

and possibly even reduced performance, if enough is allowed to escape. This is not a problem usually encountered. Where we usually encounter different gas blocks or the need for different gas blocks is when we need to replace the block to accommodate a different or longer handguard than what the rifle was manufactured with. As we covered in the superbly composed handguard and barrel chapters, if you have a carbine length gas system but want a longer, more useful handguard, such as a rifle or extended length, you will have to use a gas block that fits fully under the handguard with clearance to spare.

With the exception of the stock A2 tower/gas block, they should be pretty easy to remove and replace. Guns that have been shot a lot will tend to have a bit of residue built up under the gas block and may be difficult to remove. The easiest way to

fix that problem is to heat up the gas block with a propane torch. This will expand the block or straps enough that it will be easier to remove, particularly if the block is made of aluminum. Once it has been removed, all traces of the residue, thread locker, or whatever should be removed as well. A stiff nylon bristled brush, particularly if the barrel was heated, should be sufficient to remove this grossness. If not, it can prevent a good seal from forming when the new block is tightened down.

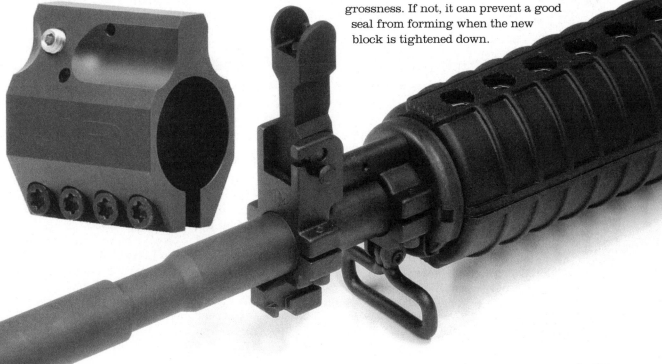

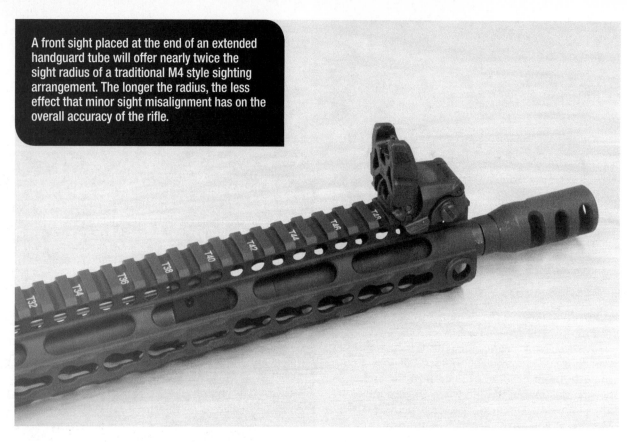

A front sight placed at the end of an extended handguard tube will offer nearly twice the sight radius of a traditional M4 style sighting arrangement. The longer the radius, the less effect that minor sight misalignment has on the overall accuracy of the rifle.

There is no need to remove the gas block from the barrel unless you are changing it out for something else. You do not need to clean under it when performing maintenance.

Minimized gas blocks tend to be, well, minimal, with only enough material to guarantee structural integrity. Often they are also shorter than normal blocks, covering only two thirds of the gas collar on the barrel. This is an attempt to reduce the weight as well, since there only needs to be enough meat there to hold the gas tube and keep the thing on the barrel. These gas blocks are ideally pinned on as well to completely prevent the block from migrating down the barrel toward the muzzle should the screws loosen somehow. This is why the mil-spec A2 front sight uses tapered cross pins rather than screws.

If you like, you can have folding front sights on your gas block. The usual approach is to have a fully external gas block that has Picatinny rails on the top of it, as most piston gas blocks tend to have. Then you can mount your handy-dandy folding back-up sight right on the gas block, and in the case of long handguards paired with minimized gas blocks, the folding front sight can be placed on the handguard tube itself. Some fellas will even mount a full barrel length handguard tube with a fixed front sight on the very end of it to maximize sight radius with their iron sights. This way a 16" barrel will have the same distance between sights as the 20" rifle, almost doubling it.

ADJUSTABLE GAS BLOCKS

This was pioneered by JP Enterprises but other brands have started to catch on. The usual approach is to install a small set screw through the right side wall of the gas block so that the screw will penetrate the vertical interface between the gas block's gas port and the entry point for that port into the gas tube. By restricting this hole, the gas can be regulated. If you want to introduce less gas into the system, you can do so by slightly closing the hole by screwing the set screw further into the gas block, even all the way if you want to go single shot for a while. In this way you can tune your gas system so that only sufficient gas is used in the rifle to operate it. In essence, you are taking away the unneeded excess gas that all guns have had built into them. Care should be taken when changing ammunition that the gas system be re-tuned. On the other hand, most users of adjustable gas systems will set the gas block to let into the gas tube sufficient gas to operate with the lowest pressured ammo that they expect to use. Should the shooter own a sound suppressor, then an adjustable gas block is a godsend, since the suppressors tend to create a significant amount of backpressure, meaning that you don't need as big a gas port as you would with the suppressor off.

You may encounter gross adjustment gas blocks. This simply means that there are only a few settings available for adjustment. Usually these are Normal, Open, Restricted, and Off. Or

This Adams Arms piston gas block has a three point adjustment and is typical of such types of gas blocks.

(below) The typical set screw gas adjustment.

settings are commonly found on the gas blocks associated with piston upgrades, but they will pop up on occasion with the DI systems too. That brings us to…

something like that. You can never get these people to name things consistently. The "Normal" setting is designed for "normal" use and this is what 99% of people will use all the time. The "Open" setting is for guns that are so fouled that only by introducing extra gas into the operating system will they function. "Restricted" is also known as Suppressed, since that is the state that most of the guns that use this setting will be into. Introducing less gas into the operating system means that the gun can take advantage the extra backpressure inherent in suppressor use and keep the banging around in the receiver to a normal level. Without this restricted setting (reduced flow) felt recoil is enhanced, and a significant amount of hot gas is typically blown around and out of the receiver. If you are shooting a suppressed gun, make darn sure you have glasses on. The "Off" setting is literally that: Off. The gun is a single shot and must be manually operated in order to cycle the action. These

PISTON UPGRADES

There is almost certainly no greater conflict that arises in the AR world than when you start discussing the merits of the piston upgrade. As you well remember, the standard operating system introduces propellant gases directly into the bolt carrier and thus the guts of the receiver every time it shoots. Depending on the ammo, this can make the gun quite dirty back at the after end. The proponents of the piston upgrade are usually adherents first and foremost to other rifles, most particularly the M14/M1A. The truth of the matter is that the problems associated with this DI operating system are easily surmounted by a proper maintenance and cleaning regimen.

This is not to say that using a piston upgrade is without benefit. There are tangible benefits, but the second argument is whether those soon-to-be-mentioned benefits are enough to justify the increase in cost. Piston upgrades run around $300 or so. This can increase the cost of a low-priced gun by 50% and the average by about 30%. It's significant. While many companies now offer AR models from the factory with some piston system or other, the vast majority do not for two simple reasons. One: cost. Two: "that's not the way it's supposed to be."

So what are the benefits to a rifle with a piston system? Remember, the vast majority of gas operated rifles and shotguns use a piston system, so it's not unusual to expect it to be in a rifle, quite the opposite actually. When you have a piston you generally can disregard any concern about the rifle getting fouling in the receiver area. It is extremely minimal. The gas, instead of venting in and around the receiver, is vented around the gas block, typically under the handguards. You don't need to clean that area, and if and when it gets really dirty, there is no detriment, with one important exception which we'll mention in a minute. Lubrication tends to get blown around in DI receivers but not in the piston systems.

While both bolts are identical, the one used in a piston system to the right adds a spring around the bolt tail, and subtracts the gas piston rings.

(below) A typical piston specific carrier, this one from Adams Arms, placed next to a standard carrier. Note the absence of the gas key on the piston carrier, replaced by a machined anvil.

"open" position for ease of insertion into the upper receiver.

However, there are detriments as well. There's no free lunch and there are always trade-offs. One of the reasons for increased expense is the complete redesign of the bolt carrier necessary for operation. The bolt carrier no longer needs a gas key and instead, in most cases, the key is replaced by an anvil machined right into the bolt carrier. This alone makes the fabrication of the carrier significantly more expensive and we haven't even mentioned the anti-tilt pads. Since the DI system is fully in line with the barrel, the carrier stays fully aligned with the barrel bore. By adding an offset piston and operating rod above the barrel, rotation is caused, literally the front of the carrier rising up as the rear of the carrier drops. This can cause damage to the front of the buffer tube as the bolt carrier enters it upon moving to the rear. Now this is not really a big deal as long as you keep an eye on the wear. Buffer tubes are inexpensive and easy

The lube tends to stay where it is much better and so you don't need to add more quite as frequently as a DI gun might require. So in theory, a piston-equipped gun is more reliable over a longer period of time. Furthermore, on guns with short barrels, the pistons seem to work quite a bit better and are not as ammo-sensitive as short barreled DI guns. It is related to the port and chamber pressure stuff we mentioned in an earlier chapter. If you have a short barreled gun, and/or a suppressed gun, the pistons are good choices.

You won't have to worry about gas rings or gas tube cracking either. Neither part is necessary. Most piston upgrades also add a small spring to the tail of the bolt. This spring is not a required item, but it serves to keep the bolt forward, in the

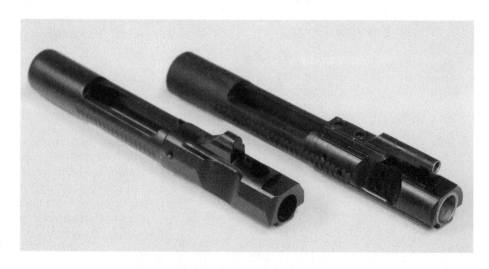

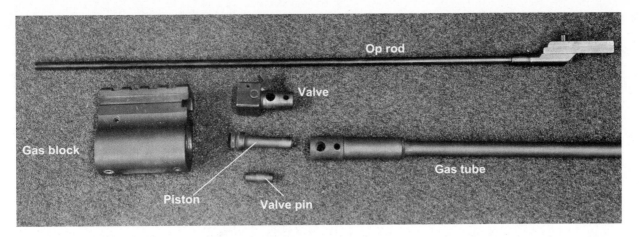

Op rod

Valve

Gas block

Gas tube

Piston

Valve pin

to replace. But the piston system carriers typically will have small pads on the bottom rear end of the carrier designed to ease the carrier's entry into the buffer tube to minimize the damage incurred. These pads work well. Carrier tilt is something that most piston equipped guns will exhibit with few exceptions. Having the bolt thrust off center in an AR is unnatural to the system, since it was designed as a completely in-line system.

Another funny symptom to observe is that the gun will still get quite dirty. Most of the piston systems have an actual reciprocating piston in the gas block that will get very fouled. This is one reason the "Open" settings are on most piston gas blocks.

If the piston gets jammed up from excessive fouling, you are in as deep doo-doo as if your gun was jammed by gunk in the receiver or barrel extension. There is a myth that

you don't have to clean piston guns as much. But you do, you just clean out the gas block rather than the receiver and bolt carrier.

The biggest reason for the AR's inherent accuracy is that it uses a simple gas tube with nothing banging about above the barrel. Remember that accuracy is reduced whenever any outside stress is imparted to the barrel when firing. The piston operated guns will demonstrate slightly poorer accuracy than a standard DI gun. But not much, as it also seems that the rest of the system is pretty tolerant of such an addition and you can still expect well under 2 MOA accuracy with any of the systems (so I hear, anyway).

The final detriment is only a deal for some people. You will add several ounces to a pound to your gun. If you had an aluminum gas blocked DI rifle and replaced it with a piston upgrade, then you will feel this acutely. The steel gas block is much heavier than the aluminum block, and then you add in the operating rod as well and you may increase the weight of the rifle by 10 – 15%. Really not that big a deal, but if you had a super lightweight, then this upgrade is counterproductive. It's like putting a winter jacket on. You gain weight and it's a little harder to move, but you aren't going to fall over either.

(top) This early PWS upgrade has a small piston inside the gas block that strikes the operating rod attached to the carrier, replacing the gas key. PWS has since gone to long stroke style pistons that make the piston and op rod one integral unit.

(below) The Adams Arms system utilizes a cupped operating rod that slips over the rear projecting gas block tube. There is no removable piston, unless you consider the operating rod the piston.

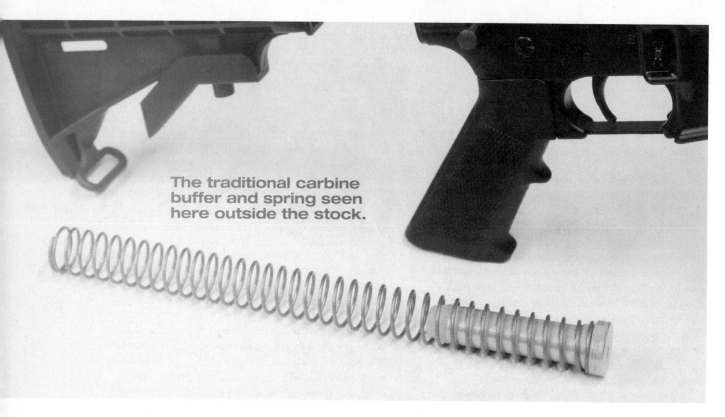

The traditional carbine buffer and spring seen here outside the stock.

It should be noted for the tech heads that there are two types of piston systems that will be encountered regularly: short stroke and long stroke. Long stroke systems are typified by a piston that is attached to the bolt carrier itself, like the upgrades from Primary Weapons Systems, or seen on AK type rifles. Short stroke systems tend to use a small piston housed in the gas block in conjunction with a long operating rod. This is typical of the upgraded rifles available from Ruger, Patriot Ordnance Factory, and Heckler & Koch. There are sort of hybrid types that have no piston proper but simply use a cupped operating rod that fits over a short stubby gas tube coming out of the gas block. In reality this fat stubby tube is the piston and the cup is the cylinder, but it can also be considered a forward op rod equipped DI. For that matter, Stoner considered his design a gas piston system that did not use an operating rod. Semantics. The piston upgrades made by Adams Arms and Osprey Defense function in this manner. The benefit to these is you don't even have to clean the piston, since there really isn't one.

BUFFERS AND BUFFER SPRINGS

The buffer spring is essentially the main spring, or recoil spring, of the AR platform. It is the spring that forces the action closed again after extraction and ejection. A strong buffer spring is critical to feeding, as a weak spring in partnership with a frustratingly tight bolt/carrier fit can actually cause failures to fully feed. When using

reduced mass carriers, extra strength springs are recommended, as less mass in the carrier means less effective force imparted to stripping cartridges from the magazine. F=ma. Force equals mass times acceleration. If the mass is reduced you have to make the mass faster to impart the same amount

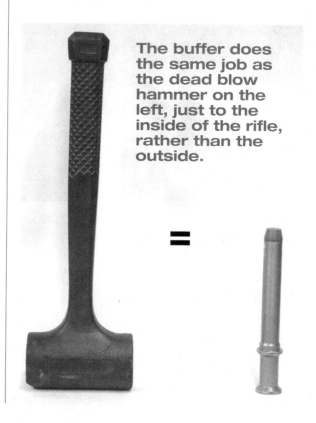

The buffer does the same job as the dead blow hammer on the left, just to the inside of the rifle, rather than the outside.

of force. Heavier springs and buffers are also often used to slow down the cyclic rate, which makes the stress imparted to the extractor much more manageable. 9mm rifles have and must use very heavy carriers, very heavy buffers, and often, much heavier-than-normal springs in order to inhibit extraction until the chamber pressure is sufficiently reduced.

Buffers are around for one purpose. They are designed to impart a "dead blow" effect to the carrier assembly when it slams closed on a cartridge. The bolt carrier has a tendency to bounce. It is a steel object that forcefully hits the barrel extension (another steel object). As you know, when you hit two hard things together like hammers (as opposed to a hard object like a hammer and a soft object like your thumb) they will bounce. If the trigger is pulled when the bolt carrier is in a bouncy state, the hammer will fall but will not hit the firing pin and the gun will not fire. You will have to recock it manually. Inside the buffer is a bunch of open space, some of which is filled with weights. When the carrier hits the barrel extension, the weights keep going forward, so that a fraction of a second after the carrier stops, the weights hit the front wall of the buffer, and correspondingly the carrier, and prevent or significantly reduce the bounce. They function just like the dead blow plastic hammer that has lead shot in it. You use it to hit something soft that needs to be convinced to move. You can't use a steel hammer and its weightiness or you'll mess up the surface of the object to be moved, like a two by four board. So you hit it with something soft and heavy like the dead blow hammer and all the force of the impact is conveyed to the board without damaging it.

Extra heavy buffers, like those used in 9mm rifles, and the heavy carbine buffers will often use tungsten weights rather than the standard steel weights. The low mass buffers used alongside the low mass bolt carriers will use something even less massive, like aluminum for weights.

Buffers and springs, in large part, exist in only two forms. The standard, or rifle, version is meant for use in fixed stock rifles, like those equipped with the standard old fashioned A1 or A2 type stocks, or with the new popular fixed styles like the MagPul PRS and MOE stocks, or ACE ARFX skeletonized stocks. The most common nowadays is the carbine buffer and carbine spring. Both are shorter than the standard rifle variants, the buffer being a bit lighter and several inches shorter, and the spring having fewer coils and an inch or two shorter as well. There are also pistol springs and buffers, but since the AR pistols are still nowhere near as common as the carbines and rifles, you will generally have to look for them to find them.

The standard rifle buffer and spring alongside the carbine buffer and spring for the AR-15s. Note the shorter spring and buffer length in the carbine. The .308 versions demonstrate even greater dimorphism.

The larger .308 sized ARs will also have their own sets of carbine and rifle spring and buffer sets and these must not be mixed, under threat of pain of potential injury, with the smaller frame AR parts.

COMBINATION UNITS

Combination units are the name I'm giving to buffer/spring assemblies that seek to make one part from two, or that incorporate some sort of spring or hydraulic dampening system in the buffer itself. The reasons for this are worthy and the results have generally been quite good. I'm however going to start with the bad news here and get it out of the way. This is because the good news is a lot better than the bad news is bad and I just want to get it over with.

(below) This is the rate-reducing buffer for carbines. If you are having extraction problems because of early extraction, try one of these to slow down the cycle.

(opposite) The Silent Captured Spring System is the new self-contained buffer system that replaces both buffer and spring. It would be wise to remove the buffer detent and spring from your lower if you purchase one of these. You won't need them anymore, and getting the assembly in and out with the detent in place is a real pain in the butt. From left to right are the .223 model, the .308 model, and the 9mm model. The 9mm model uses Tungsten weights while the others use steel.

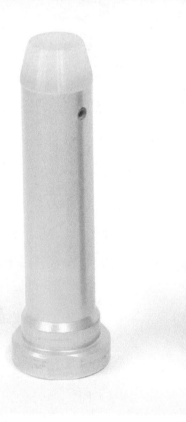

The biggest disadvantage is the old reliable high price point. A standard buffer and spring will run you, even at MSRP rates, $30 or less. So when a buffer spring wears out or if you lose or somehow dufus-damage your buffer, you will not need to save too long to purchase a replacement unit or set. The other thing is that the early hydraulic style combination units worked super well in normal temperatures but would leak when it got cold. Then it was "no workie."

Okay, now the good stuff. When these things are in your rifle they tend to slow down the cyclic rate. This makes it much easier on the extractor when it's trying to pull that fired case from the chamber. They are often heavier than the standard buffer and this works to slow down the system a little. Secondly, and this is why they exist at all, these buffers use the incorporated hydraulic or spring system to reduce felt recoil. Finally, it is one part rather than two.

The usual pattern works like this. Rather than the buffer slamming against the back of the stock, they hit and then give a little as the spring or cylinder is compressed, softening the impact. The felt recoil impulse is reduced considerably. Now there are those who might say, "Come on! It's just a .223. What recoil?!?!" The .223 may have little recoil, but that doesn't mean it has none, nor is there no reason to not try to eliminate it anyway. It is always supremely amusing to me to shoot a shot, using a high magnification optic, and have recoil so slight that I don't even half blink when firing, and the recoil disruption and vibration is so low that I can easily see the impact through the scope. That is just COOL! You will not likely get to that point without several recoil mitigating features in combination, but it is worth the extra dough you put into the parts and makes the shooting much more pleasurable.

A great example of these buffers is the MGI Rate Reducing Buffer. This is a spring model that has the standard buffer pad at the back but that pad had a spring in front of it. The body is made of steel to make it a bit heavier as well. It simply replaces the standard buffer assembly and is made in both carbine and rifle variants.

One of the most unusual models is the SCS (Silent Captured Spring) system from JP Enterprises. It is available for small frame, large frame, and 9mm models of rifle. This unit does incorporate the buffer and spring into one unit, though in a completely redesigned format. Its name does describe it pretty well. The spring is a small diameter coil surrounding a guide rod that forms the basis of the assembly. At the rear, the guide rod connects to a plate with a buffer pad on the front of it, and at the front end is a weight assembly that has steel or tungsten weights. The front end is pushed to the rear when cycled, the spring compressed and then expanded to push the weight and carrier assembly back into battery. You can further tune your rifle with the extra spring packs sold separately, and in conjunction with an adjustable gas system will completely change the recoil impulse of the AR. It literally feels like you are shooting a very low recoiling bolt action rifle.

One of the more mundane and common complaints about the AR system is the noise the buffer and spring make when the gun is fired. It is audible even over the report of the shot, and the grating grinding "sproing" that is created inside the stock has irritated many people. It is literally worse than fingernails across a chalkboard (is anyone old enough anymore to remember that sound?). It doesn't affect function. Most people get used to it and when they shoot a rifle with an SCS they often think the rifle didn't actually fire correctly. It just feels wrong, mostly because they have gotten used to the "sproing" and all of a sudden it isn't there. Furthermore, the insides of the buffer tubes are often rough with machine marks that also grate on all the coils of the standard springs. This is no longer a problem and the weight assembly has enough surface area that this roughness is rendered inconsequential. There was an early full length hydraulic buffer that had a similar effect to the SCS but is no longer made. It was the one that leaked when it got too cold.

Anyway, whichever of these units you decide to use, it will run you between $75 and $150 to get one, but you will likely find that you won't want to go without.

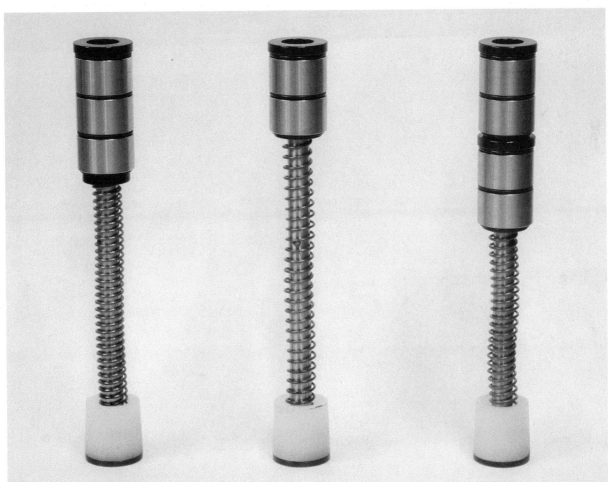

The JP SCS system can be modified. Spring kits are available that will strengthen the spring rates of the springs, if you should desire to tune the SCS to your rifle.

Muzzle Devices:

Comps, Flash Hiders, Brakes and Suppressors

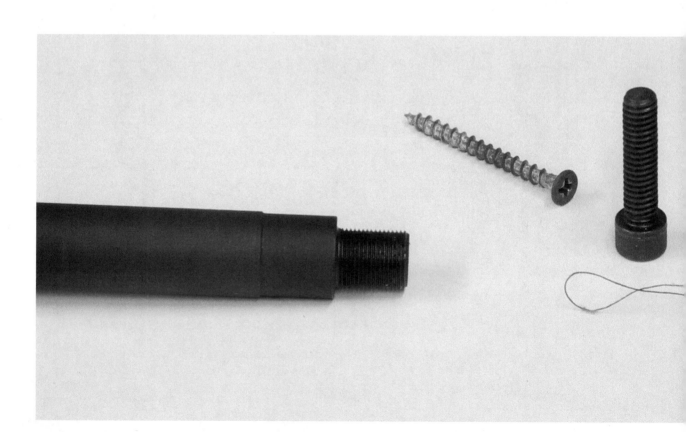

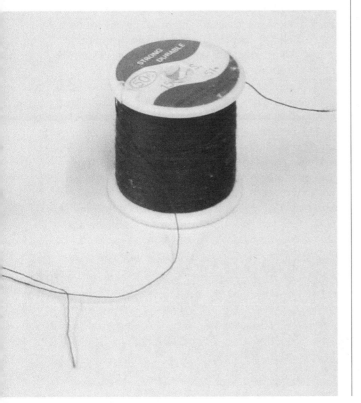

The sound suppressor is one of the most useful additions to a firearm, especially a quick attach like this one. However, they are strictly regulated. iStock photo.

and compensators are generally acceptable and it is the height of inconsistency that these states of affairs are present.

The biggest drawback to shooting is the noise it produces. In most other countries where firearms can be owned by the general population, for hunting or sport, the use of sound suppressors is just considered to be good manners. Suppressors, or cans as they are known colloquially, are unregulated (not the guns) and not only keep the noise down for everyone else, but also prevent hearing damage by reducing the gun's report to a much less harmful

The contents of this chapter, in my humble opinion, encompass some of the cooler and most performance-enhancing articles of modern manufacturing that you can add to your gun. Ironically, muzzle attachments are one of the parts that are most regulated out of existence in certain states. Since 1934, the use of sound suppressors (silencers) has been heavily regulated. In solidly Liberal/Progressive/Democrat states the use of flash hiders has been largely made illegal as well. Muzzle brakes

level, particularly if the bullet is traveling under the speed of sound. Flash hiders are extremely useful on shorter-barreled guns because they greatly reduce muzzle flash in low light. This muzzle flash can kill your night vision, and as much fun as big globular flashes are, they are generally not desirable. Both, particularly the cans (which also reduce flash so very well) are of high utility but are apparently "evil," and only terrorists or criminals would use them (according to the powers-that-be in those states).

On the other hand, the one thing that makes it harder to shoot rapidly and accurately at the same time is recoil. Muzzle brakes and compensators greatly mitigate recoil so that you can make accurate follow-up shots at a quicker rate, and apparently they are okay for mere peasants to own. They make hellish amounts of noise, and shooting any rifle with one of these gadgets without hearing protection will actually physically hurt and cause cumulative permanent hearing damage. It seems that the powers-that-be have clung to the incredibly false Hollywood stereotype of quiet equals bad, but loud equals good. Quite contrary to reason, I would say. Anyway, let's look at these in turn and specifically cover the goods and bads and some specific examples.

SOUND SUPPRESSORS

I'm not going to get too deep into this category. Part of the reason is simply that comparatively (but growing in number) few people actually jump through the hoops to purchase a silencer. Essentially, you have to fill out an ATF form/application and pay a one-time tax of $200 to get a tax stamp. This form requires fingerprinting and approval by your local Chief Law Enforcement Officer. It is then mailed in and at the time of this writing takes around a year to clear the paper shufflers. All it really amounts to is the same background check that you fill out every time you purchase a gun from a dealer, just more involved and with the addition of the LEO approval and prints. The local chief does not have to sign it, even though he bears no culpability if he signed a form for an item used in a crime. Generally this is a political opportunity for the average anti-gun non-elected official to act all anti-gun on us. So you may be effectively banned from ownership of any item affected by the National Firearms Act, simply because your local chief or sheriff does not like guns. So be prepared for that. There have been options to bypass the signature, but the Obama administration seems to have executive ordered a stop to that (unconstitutionally, by the way).

However, if your local CLEO is a reasonable guy and signs the form, you send it in and wait. When you get your tax stamp back you go to your local Class III dealer and pay for and pick up your silencer (or machine gun, or destructive device, or short barreled rifle, etc…), go home, shoot it and have lots of safe, freedom-loving fun.

Sound suppressors are awesome. I hate wearing ear protection. Muffs are bulky and uncomfortable, and while I mind the plugs less, it's still annoying to have to wear them when I shouldn't have to. Suppressors used for .22 rimfire guns are truly a hoot to shoot. A pop is all you hear and the gun's action cycles louder than the gunshot itself.

This is a silencer, and is made in almost the same way and almost the same design. It is designed to soften the sounds made by an automobile engine. The concept is the same with firearms, but you have to get special approval first.

Centerfire pistols with cans act much the same way, but with a deeper fully "choof" sound, as long as the bullet is traveling sub-sonically. When the pistol bullet, or pretty much any rifle bullet, goes faster than sound, it will create a sonic boom that cannot be dampened by a sound suppressor.

See, there are two events that contribute to a firearm's gunshot sound. The first is the sonic boom created by the bullet traveling faster than the speed of sound, just like a fighter jet, but on a much smaller scale. The greater contributor is the instant expansion of the gas pushing the bullet out the barrel. This is the greater portion of the gunshot sound and is what the silencers work very hard to minimize.

A sound suppressor is called a can because that is basically what it is. A large diameter outer tube is mated to a sequence of baffles housed inside it. The baffles and large internal diameter form expansion chambers for the gas behind the bullet and also serve to rapidly disrupt and cool the gas. The gas follows the bullet out the barrel as it would without a can being present, but it is much cooler, and traveling much more slowly when it does. This makes a lot of the sound that we would hear go away. You can't do anything about the sonic boom

Several companies make solid aluminum fake suppressors for decoration, like this GemTech Outback II. These things are kind of fun and give the gun a fun look. The GSG-9 .22 rifle next to it has a suppressor-looking shroud that surrounds the barrel. This is a popular feature on guns that have long skinny-looking barrels sticking out of short forends, like this MP5 clone.

GEMTECH
BOISE, ID
D10-47162
OUTBACK-IID .22LR

the bullet makes, but suppressing the muzzle blast allows many guns to be fired safely without hearing protection. Rimfire pistols and rifles and most centerfire pistols can be fired in this fashion, without muffs or plugs. Centerfire rifles will still often need light hearing protection. Understand this: silencers or sound suppressors do not make guns silent! This is the biggest travesty of the entertainment industry. In movies and shows, all you hear is a "thwip" or small pop, even from large rifles, and this is complete fabrication. They still make noise, it's just that the noise is much softer than when unsuppressed, they're not completely silent.

Thirty-plus states graciously allow the peasantry to own sound suppressors, and I bet you can guess which ones they are. If you live in one of them, get one. Let's flood these states with them. If you live elsewhere, here's a good reason to add to the other good reasons to move, like high taxes, crummy schools, and busybody dumbass politicians. And lastly, for the record, there have been fewer than one legally owned silencers used in a crime in the U.S. since the NFA was passed in 1934. I'd say that is an acceptable record. For more info on silencers, cans, sound suppressors, look elsewhere. There's plenty of good info available from multiple sources. The best might come from your local gun business, since they might actually sell the things in the first place.

FLASH HIDERS

Flash hiders or flash suppressors reduce the muzzle flash caused by still-burning powder exiting the barrel behind the bullet. Some powders have flash retardants in them, so a smaller signature will be seen. Others are naturally bright and

using ammo with these powders will create quite the bloom when fired. Furthermore, rifles with muzzle brakes attached tend to flash brightly, but in a more directional manner.

Here's an example. I once conducted an experiment to see how effective a couple of these were. Now this wasn't a truly scientific experiment but it still was pretty definitive. I shot my 16" carbine nekkid muzzle, with a standard A2 flash hider, and with a Yankee Hill Machine Phantom 5C2 flash hider. I did this around 8pm in the autumn, dark enough that there was little ambient light. The ammo used was Winchester 5.56 (Q3131A for a part number if you care), made in Israel for Olin Industries (owns Winchester name for ammo), known for producing a bright flash.

The first shot with the nekkid muzzle produced an orange basketball sized globular flash. It was bright and did in fact disrupt the night vision I had at the time. I followed this up with the mil-spec A2 flash hider on the muzzle. The result when fired was a small orange flash about the size of the average Clementine orange. Then I fired with the Phantom and I was duly impressed. There was no flash visible to me or the observers (my extended family) but there was a single spark that traveled a few feet from the muzzle before extinguishing. A. Spark. Anyone within several hundred meters would have seen the nekkid muzzle flash, and within at least a hundred meters would have seen the A2 flash. I doubt anyone within as little as twenty feet would have seen the spark and they would have had to have been looking directly at me to even catch a glimpse of it. The Phantom, at least that model, is a superb flash suppressor and it is even pretty affordable. You can get one for under thirty bucks and there are several models

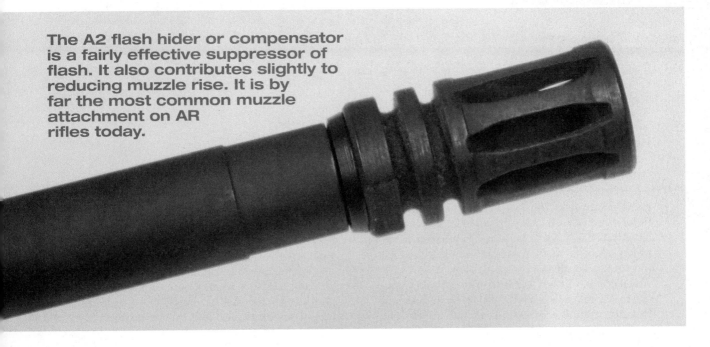

The A2 flash hider or compensator is a fairly effective suppressor of flash. It also contributes slightly to reducing muzzle rise. It is by far the most common muzzle attachment on AR rifles today.

that have closed bottoms so you don't kick up dust when firing prone. They work just as well as the standard models. They are similar to the A2 flash hider which also has five open ports on the top and sides, but has a closed bottom. They have the added minor benefit that they combat muzzle rise slightly like dedicated muzzle compensators.

Back when I tried this, the only options were the mil-spec A1 (six evenly spaced ports), A2, the Phantom, and the Vortex (Smith Industries) and the copies thereof. Now, you'll get a headache trying to figure something out and you will ultimately probably decide based purely on the aesthetics of the device. There are a number of well-functioning flash hiders on the market now, though the best seem to be variants of the Phantom or the Vortex. The Vortex has long tines similar to the Phantom, but the tines are not connected at the end. This allows the tines to vibrate like a tuning fork when the gun is fired and this is the mechanism to

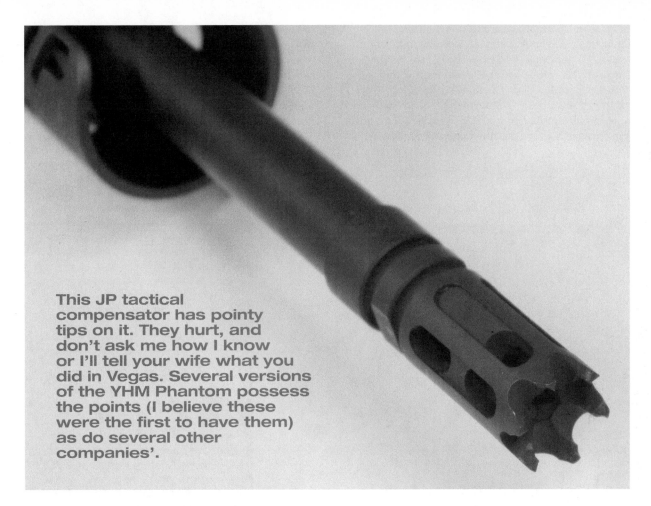

This JP tactical compensator has pointy tips on it. They hurt, and don't ask me how I know or I'll tell your wife what you did in Vegas. Several versions of the YHM Phantom possess the points (I believe these were the first to have them) as do several other companies'.

disperse the flash. These types of flash hiders are arguably the most effective designs, but also tend to approach $50 in cost. You also have to watch where your muzzle goes (you already do anyway, right) or you might get stuff stuck in between the tines.

The place you might be glad to have a flash hider is in the self-defense role, in the home, at night, in the dark. Of course you will hopefully never actually encounter this but it's better to be prepared, and I am, after all, trying to be as informative as possible. Multiple assailants are common in muggings and in armed robberies and home invasions. It has been shown that many of these perps are high and not thinking at their top notch levels, hence the number of criminals that have been warned to leave at the muzzle of a gun yet didn't, and found out first-hand what a "Darwin award" is. Hence the utility of a carbine with lots of rounds and good self-defense rounds to boot. Criminals like the dark, which is why they break in at night. If you are unable or unwilling to improve the lighting, a large muzzle flash will temporarily disable what night vision you might have and theoretically leave you at a disadvantage against secondary or tertiary threats. Having a flash hider on your firearm at this point would be a

good idea, and would greatly mitigate or eliminate that potentiality.

What's more fun about some of these flash hiders is that they incorporate what has become known as a "pain compliance device." Just as some soldiers might sharpen their issue flash hiders in order to "nudge" people into moving smartly, the points and sharpened tines on some of these things are downright scary, and good on them for it. I would however not recommend actually using them in that fashion or you might as well kiss your house goodbye. They may be "pain compliance devices" but they are most definitely not "litigation avoidance devices."

COMPENSATORS

The term compensator is almost always ascribed to a muzzle device that is designed to reduce muzzle rise, not necessarily recoil. Indeed, if the device pushes the muzzle down, more recoil force is often transmitted straight back, enhancing felt recoil while keeping the muzzle movement minimal. It is true however that compensators and muzzle brakes can be combined effectively in the same unit and we'll talk about those in the following section on muzzle brakes. The vast majority of compensators are designed with a common element of holes or slots on the top. These slots may extend somewhat to the side but then they become more like brakes. When the bullet exits the barrel and passes through the compensator the expanding gas behind the bullet exits through these holes before exiting the "muzzle" of the comp. This produces a jet of gas that is going straight up or up and to the rear, acting as a counterforce to the rise of the muzzle. The higher the pressure of the gas behind the bullet the more effective the comp.

As mentioned already, the A2 flash hider also acts as a compensator, where the older A1 flash hider did not. Many companies, in particular YHM, make compensator or brake versions of their flash hiders that look virtually identical.

(left) The Vais compensator can sometimes be found on ARs but it is usually seen on traditional hunting rifles. The large series of holes vent gas 90 degrees to the bore axis, all the way around. This particular brake requires non-standard threads. Be aware of things such as thread pitches when you order your muzzle devices from retailers.

(below) Placing the A1 and A2 units side by side you will notice that the A1 has six equally-spaced slender ports. The A2 has a fully closed bottom with five closely spaced slender ports going from 9 to 12 to 3 o'clock. This prevents dust from being kicked up when firing and also gives some muzzle rise mitigation, while retaining good flash suppression. A closed end would make the compensation better but make the flash suppression much worse.

MUZZLE BRAKES

Brakes are designed a bit differently and are typified by the inclusion of baffles in the design. They work by using the expanding gas, as the compensator does, but in a different manner. These are designed to reduce felt recoil, not necessarily muzzle rise. To do this they have what amounts to virtual expansion chambers formed by the baffles. When the expanding gas following the bullet hits the rear face of the baffles, the gas literally pushes the baffles, the brake, and the rifle it is attached to, forward. The gas then vents out the large holes on the side of the brake. Most brakes also incorporate a few holes on the top to vent some of the gas up, giving them very good muzzle compensation in addition to the braking. You will see these in variations of two basic designs. The first is simply a hollow cylinder, bored out with dozens of holes all the way round the outside of the comp. These are reasonably effective as long as there is a front face to deflect some of the gas out, and are typified by the Williams muzzle brakes. The second type is much larger and will have the large flat baffles and large side vent ports and most of these work incredibly well. The JP Enterprises, Dreadnought Industries and other similar models are very popular in the varminting and sporting realms because of the ease of follow-up shooting.

A very important note must be made. Compensators and muzzle brakes are so loud that you must have hearing protection. Do not shoot these guns indoors if you can help it. The concussion on these can be quite powerful and much of it is directed to the side or rear. Do not teach new shooters, especially women (who seem to be particularly sensitive to concussive effects) to shoot with centerfire rifles equipped with these muzzle devices. On the other hand if you are at the range and you have a couple stupid couch commando tough guys next to you (you know the type, too tough to wear sissy hearing protection, and smells like he hasn't showered in an week) you can get rid of him quickly by getting out your compensated rifle and ripping off five or six shots one right after the other. He will quickly want to be elsewhere.

(right) This close-up shows the baffles typical in muzzle brakes. This JP Bennie Cooley Tactical Comp also retains four small compensation ports above and just behind both baffles. The increased length of most comps and several flash hiders allows them to be used for permanent attachment to short barrels to bring them up to the 16+" legal length.

(below) One of the originals. The JP Recoil Eliminator is huge and works extremely well. However, it often looks out of place on barrels because of its large profile. The tactical models on the right are more common.

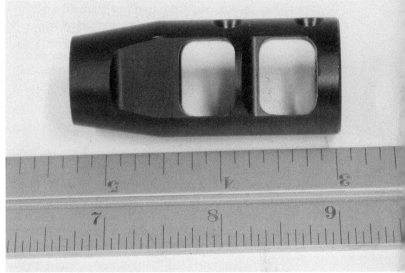

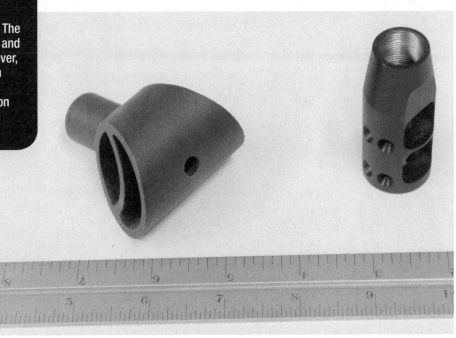

BAYONETS

Bayonets really are yet another muzzle attachment. We just don't commonly use them in the civilian world. You kind of get the impression that mounted and fixed bayonets were used in all kinds of assaults. I mean, why else would the anti-gun zealots be so against their presence on rifles, as if it was a critical public safety issue? I think the mainstream media is stuffing the reports of rampant drive-by bayonetting in the heartland of America. Oh, yeah, right, that doesn't actually happen. But bayonet lugs look evil, therefore apparently otherwise-law-abiding citizens are mind-banged into committing drive-by bayonettings in rural Minnesota. Right, that doesn't happen either. Wow, it's almost as if bayonet lugs are just a stupid little piece of steel sticking out from the barrel. Well, since it has no practical use, we should probably ban it. I've got an idea. Let's ban everything that has no practical use, like say, 15-round magazines, large soft drinks, brightly colored paint, processed sugar, trans-fat, or salt. Wait, that's already underway. Huh. Yeah. Just because it has no practical purpose (or sporting purpose) should not mean an automatic banning. Besides, bayonets are frelling cool.

OTHER STUFF

Some competition guns have what are known as "bloop tubes" to lengthen the barrel for attachment of a front sight, giving the rifle a much longer sight radius (more accurate). Some guns simply have a plain muzzle or have a thread protector cap to prevent damage to the muzzle threads. I've even seen a golf ball launcher that threads on and fires golf balls into the next county using blanks.

Whatever the case, 99.9% of muzzle devices use some form of thread to attach them to the barrel. Apparently barrel threads are also evil, but I won't go into another rant. One per chapter is probably sufficient. Let's just remove everything useful on a gun.

One final item that is becoming more and more common is the permanently-attached muzzle device. There is a very valid reason for this. Why put something on that you can't get off later? The answer is so that you can have a shorter than normally legal barrel. If you have a 16" barrel (legal minimum) you add a flash hider and get a 17 ½" barrel. Some people want a shorter barrel without having to go through the NFA to get it. The only legal solution is to have a barrel and muzzle attachment that overall, slightly exceed 16". The muzzle device must be permanently fixed to the gun. The usual means is to attach the device to the upper, drill a hole, insert a pin, and weld the hole closed. This will prevent the device from coming off. Another way might be to use silver braze on the threads. However you do it, it must be impossible to remove using common tools. High heat or machining is not considered normal tools, and unfortunately there really isn't much in the way of a list of ways to do it properly. Pinning and welding is acceptable and really ought to be the way you do it. Plus, it isn't all that hard to remove using a lathe or mill later on if you want to change out the comp. Just make sure to not put the upper without the muzzle device on the lower or you will be creating an unregistered short barreled rifle, according to the ATF.

The standard threads are ½-28" for .223 and 5/8-24" for the large stuff like 6.8, 6.5, and .308. Some alternate threads were used during the Clinton Assault Weapons ban, like 5/8-28" and others, but you won't likely find too many of those. 9mm barrels tend to use ½-36" threads.

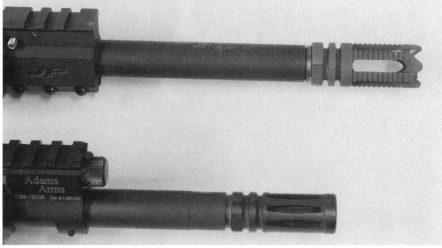

(left top) The Miculek comp is another typical muzzle brake with large baffles. Rather than top holes the rear baffle chamber exhausts up as well as to the side to gain the compensation benefits.

(left) A shorter than legal barrel can be made legal by permanently affixing a muzzle device to make the required 16". The device should be attached and aligned, and then pinned on. You can see here the spot where the pin was inserted and welded over, then cold blued.

(left below) The VDI A2 flash hider above is pinned to a 14½" barrel, while the standard A2 is below. Except for being a bit longer to used as a pin-on, the VDI is the same as the A2. This product allows the shooter who likes the A2 look to still have it, even on a shorter than 16" barrel.

(bottom) A 14½" barrel with a pinned on extended flash hider below a 16" barrel with unpinned extended flash hider. 1½" is a lot.

CHAPTER 10

Optics and Sights:

Red Dots, Riflescopes, Mounts and Oh, yeah… Sights Too

By far the most common optic used today is the traditional magnifying riflescope. The origins of this optic stretch far back into the hazy past, all the way back to Robin Hood if you believe the Kevin Costner movie. Back in the day when the really smart people were coming up with all that astronomy garbage and rotating planets and revolving asteroids and heliocentric systems and such the telescope was invented. The desire to see far away objects has ever been a quest to the human being and the telescope made it possible. Magnifying riflescopes have been used on rifles in the US at least as far back as the American Civil War, when comparatively crude devices as long as the barrels were mounted on rifles that weighed heavily, sometimes thirty pounds or more. However, riflescopes did not become a common accessory until much later, well into the 20th century. While we still have and use fixed magnifying optics, which are pretty basic in comparison to the variables, variable scopes are the types that see the most use and are the most purchased. It is really convenient to be able to start with a wide field of view, low magnification to find the target, and

This is a typical scope marking, showing the magnifying power of the scope, or in this case, the range of the power adjustment, and the size of the objective lens (the one toward the muzzle).

(below) This Vortex PST scope is a great buy for a long range high power variable scope. It sells for under $1000 and has a lifetime warrantee, like all Vortex Optics.

then that scope is a variable and the two numbers divided by the hyphen are the minimum and maximum magnification possible for that optic. The "x" means "by" like in a two by four board. The number after the "x" is the diameter of the objective lens, which is the lens at the front of the scope. Why that lens you ask? It is the primary determiner of how much light enters the scope. Theoretically, the larger the objective lens, the greater the amount of light that enters the scope tube, and the brighter the image. In practice, this is limited by the tube diameter and anti-reflective coatings that are applied to the lenses. Furthermore, the greater light transmission is not physically realized unless the magnification is much higher than most scopes are capable of displaying. Higher magnifications require thicker lenses, or larger diameter lenses, and the larger lenses stop less light than thicker lenses.

The reason most hunting scopes have a 40mm objective is that anything bigger on an average one-inch diameter tube riflescope starts showing diminishing returns. For normal purposes, we want the line of sight as close to the bore line as possible. With an AR you simply aren't going to

then max out the power to the highest setting for precision shooting. Single power optics have made a small resurgence in the form of tactical optics such as the Trijicon ACOG, and the plain fixed multiplier scopes that are often mounted behind red dot scopes. But the variable power still remains the uber-optic.

Riflescopes are described in a similar way to this: 4-16x40mm. The first number is the magnification. If there is a hyphen and a second number

get that and, in fact, it's a negative gain because the scope mounted less than two or inches above the bore would be virtually impossible to look through. It makes the ballistic calculations a little more complicated, but they are still pretty easy to compute. There are a lot of 50mm or larger tactical scopes, and it is a strength of the AR that the required scope mounting height allows some truly huge and capable optics. Get what you want, but just be aware that you don't gain much using a larger diameter objective unless the tube is larger

(below) Nikon makes a line of riflescopes designed for AR work. This is the 1-4 model. They are great, but could use some caps on the turrets to prevent unintentional rotation.

(bottom) Burris is one of the companies that makes an amalgamated optic/laser rangefinder unit. It's not just a rangefinder, but contains an entire usable ballistic computer.

(opposite) The Burris Eliminator tells you how far to hold your shot over to hit, based on the atmospheric info you put into it and the laser's read on the range.

and your high magnification starts creeping higher than 20. Bigger scopes weigh more, cost more, and are well, bigger.

The standard tube size is one inch. Most optics in the hunting realm are still an inch in diameter, but the 30mm tubes are starting to find appeal. In the AR world, 30mm and 34mm scopes are all the rage and are very common. Competitively, very few shooters use optics that are less than 30mm in tube diameter and the 34 and 35mm tubes are becoming as prevalent as the one-inch tubes. It used to be that the only size scope tube available was a one-inch-diameter tube with larger bells on either end. In the last ten to twenty years the 30mm tube has become very common. The larger tube allows greater internal light transmission, allowing larger objective lenses to be more effective, theoretically more internal adjustment range, and a few other minor enhancements. On defensive guns, the greatest representation of optics is held by the red dot or similar fixed 1x (one power) optics. These are ideal for close range (as self-defense pretty much is defined) as we will see later in the chapter.

Scopes used on tactical rifles tend to the lower powers like fixed 3x or 1-4x20mm and stuff like that. The 1x scopes are great because they are basically unpowered red dots with a crosshair, until you crank them up and then you have a four power scope, like on the Nikon M-223 1-4x. Versa-tile and handy, they allow precision work up to several hundred yards but will not serve for much more, since shooting stuff farther away requires the image be bigger so you can see it, much less hit it.

There are some new models that incorporate rangefinding lasers in them. They are big, somewhat bulky and relatively heavy, though the newest version of the Burris Eliminator is lighter than it looks. This model uses a Horus Vision reticle with illuminating dots. You put the ambient atmospheric data into the scope, range the target and the scope will tell you where to aim. Pretty cool.

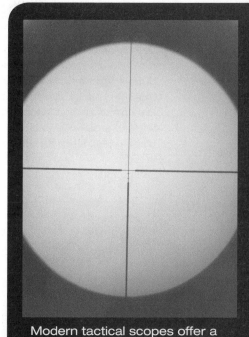

Modern tactical scopes offer a bevy of different aiming reticles to the consumer. The point of these reticles is to make distance shots quicker and easier for the shooter, particularly if the range is not known precisely. Generally, all of these are useful, although some are much more useful than others. Unless you get really into the ballistics of long range shooting and learning how to use the more complicated reticles, such as the series of Horus Vision types, you should stick with the "bullet drop" types that are sort of calibrated to certain specific rounds. I say "sort of" because atmospheric effects will alter these results somewhat, but if you are shooting under 300-400 yards the compensation offered by the bullet drop reticles will be reasonably precise, as long as you use the bullets that the scope manuals specify that the readings are actually good for. For example if the reticle is designed for 55 gr. FMJ bullets, you can get away with using 55 gr. V-Max bullets, but a 75 gr. match bullet may not behave enough like the 55 gr. bullets to mirror their trajectories.

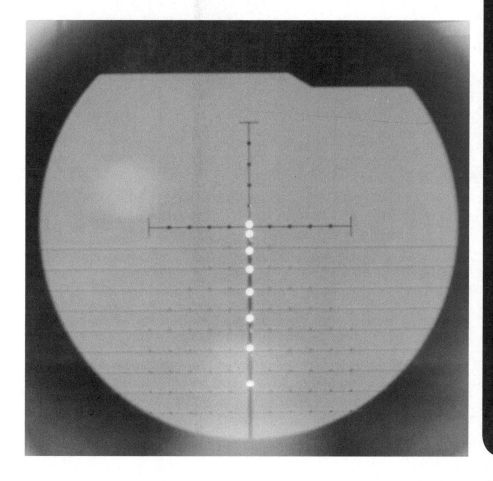

MOUNTING THE TRADITIONAL RIFLESCOPE

It's pretty important that the riflescope that you purchase be appropriately mounted to the rifle. Since pretty much every modern centerfire hunting rifle is designed for use with a riflescope, there are on the market the means to mount them in all sorts of shapes and sizes. We'll go over just one of these types, since it's pretty much the only method on ARs.

The Picatinny rail is very similar to the Weaver

(below) See here how the handguard rail acts as a continuation of the receiver rail. The only real interruptions are the small gap that should be between the handguard and receiver, and the lack of a slot at the front of the receiver.

(bottom) The C-More Scout mount is a great way to place a red dot on your carry handle equipped rifle, though in this case it's sitting on a detachable carry handle. You can still use the iron sights, and for the most part, users of this style of mount will "co-witness" the dot to the irons.

(opposite) The Scout mount has to be fit to most rifles. This bright area must fit around the gas tube, in between the receiver and delta ring. To that extent it must often be thinned in this area to fit properly. Note the rub mark indicating further removal of material is necessary.

Matching your red dot to your sights, so that when you look through your sights you see the dot sitting right on top of the front sight tower, is called cowitnessing. It can also refer to simply being able to see your iron sights through your red dot, and in fact is generally referring to both at the same time. If your iron sights are already zeroed, it is pretty easy to zero your red dot. Simply set the red dot on top of the sight. The sights, if they are folding, can then be moved out of the way when using the red dot sight.

mount used on traditional rifles. Its cross section is very close, differing only in some dimensioning. Weaver and Picatinny equipment will often be cross- compatible, but not always. Weaver cross slots may have only two or as many as the manufacturer desired and they do not have to be evenly spaced. The Picatinny rail, also known as the 1913 rail, was developed by .gov and is a much more versatile interface, being used just as much for other stuff like bipods, grips, lights, and "lasers" as for optics. The main visual and practical difference is that the cross slots on the Picatinny system are regular and identical, filling the entire rail/mount. Indeed, the majority of free-floating handguards have a Pic rail along the top that acts as a continuation of the receiver rail. You wind up with essentially one uninterrupted rail from rear sight to front sight.

While most ARs will still mount an optic in the traditional location above the receiver, some use the type of mount that is really just a forward relocation from the standard point. The "scout" mount basically moves the optics mounting rail forward over the rear half of the barrel, using an extended eye relief, low magnification optic. This set up is often found on rifles that to not readily accept a mount over the receiver, such as rifles with the standard A2 or A1 upper receiver with fixed carry handle.

The scout mount most often is seen with a red

dot type of optic, to which it is well suited, and is a very quick-acquisition arrangement that leaves the shooter's field of view completely unobstructed. The optic is attached to a rather long dog-legged mount that mounts to the carry handle, with the optic sitting over the handguard, but not touching it. These were common a decade ago, but are rarely seen now since the vast majority of AR owners get a rifle with the top rail on the upper receiver. Otherwise if this style of mounting is desired, canted mounts that attach to the receiver are commonly available, as is the mounting of the optic directly to the handguard rail. This latter method however is not recommended, since outside forces (i.e. your hand) will act on the handguard and mess up your zero.

ONE-PIECE INTEGRATED SCOPE MOUNTS

Also known as tactical mounts, one-piece mounts that integrate the rings and bases into one unit are the mounts of choice for increasing numbers of shooters. Except for a few models, these are used almost exclusively with "tactical" rifles based on the AR series and others, and for the record, this is the type of scope mounting equipment that you should use for a traditional style riflescope. Two separated rings are an obsolete feature on an AR and inherently less useful. A Picatinny top rail

is required to use these mounts, as they all are designed for that rail accordingly, but virtually all ARs have this now. The basic pattern is a single machined piece that incorporates both a large footprint clamping base and stems that rise to form the bottom halves of the two scope rings. The top straps of the rings are then screwed down onto the base with the scope in between.

Virtually all of the one-piece mounts have some sort of forward offset built into them. This is so

(left) A traditional Weaver base scope ring with a much larger beefier Picatinny rail based ring.

(below and bottom) The American Defense Industries uses a locking lever that also adjusts to perfectly fit your receiver. Unlike most rings, the ADI uses vertical left and right straps rather than top and bottom. This makes it marginally harder to mount the optic, but it does keep the width of the rings to a minimum.

(above) The Burris PEPR mount is immensely popular, very tough and rigid, and can come with locking levers or the more standard retaining hex nuts. It also is shipped, when alone, with railed or plain ring top straps. The Burris Skulltac scope combo is a great deal. While I'm not that big on the whole Skull thing usually, this thing is attractive and works well with the Urban MirageFlage DuraCoat camo on this rifle. The combo comes with the 1-4 variable tactical scope, a FastFire III micro-red dot, and the PEPR mount to attach them to. These combos street-sell for under $700.

JP Enterprises' Flat Top Scope Mount has been around as long as anyone's single piece scope mount, and may have been the first to incorporate the forward offset necessary for traditional riflescope mounting on small frame ARs. It is available only as a screwed on clamp, no QR levers.

the longer scopes can be mounted in these mounts and still have the footprint of the mount be left entirely on the receiver. There are major advantages to this type of scope mount. These mounts are very rigid and usually somewhat bulky, and as a result are unlikely to break, bend, or flex, and also act as a limited armoring for the scopes themselves. Furthermore, this also allows the majority of these mounts to be removed and then remounted with negligible or no change in zero. This makes them handy for guns that need to be cleaned often (because they are shot often). There is a third, minor, advantage in that these mounts, being machined in one piece (the base anyway) and almost always to very exacting tolerances, means that you will not have to concern yourself with having to lap these ring/bases. Generally wider scope ring thicknesses also reduce the chances of crimping on the scope due to over-tightening. The thicker rings with greater surface area also means greater holding power with the same relatively low torque on the screws.

These mounts are all designed with the height necessary to bring a scope into alignment with the eyes of the average shooter when mounted on a rifle that has the barrel in line with the shoulder. This means most have been envisioned to be mounted atop of AR-15 rifles and carbines, where the axis of the scope is around two and a half to three inches above the bore. They will vary, so be prepared for this. As a result, these mounts are seldom seen on traditional bolt action and other hunting rifles that have stocks that drop below the bore axis. Bolt action rifles that use the newer aluminum chassis will often use mounts like this, but that's about it.

Many, actually most, of these one-piece mounts have quick release levers of some sort so they can be quickly and easily removed. It's a useful but not vital to have that feature, and these levers will raise the cost of the mounts a bit. A few really good mounts will have locks on the levers, like the American Defense and Burris P.E.P.R. scope mounts for example. The lock is just a small button integrated into the lever that requires an inward push along with the outward pull on the lever itself. This particular lock is also tension adjustable for precision fitting on the particular rail that it is being mounted upon, as the overall width of the rail is not the critical fitting dimension of the Picatinny rail, and has a wider tolerance than the other angled surfaces.

Several examples of this type of mount also have the ability to mount a secondary red dot optic on top of the rings. The two most common examples are probably the AR-P.E.P.R. mount from Burris and the Flat-Top Scope Mount from JP Enterprises. A top strap with the proper mounting interface, or Picatinny rail replaces the standard top strap and the micro-red dot is mounted on this top strap. In a similar way to the see through scope mounts, the shooter can then make a small adjustment of his head, raising it slightly to make use of the secondary optic in very short order. While you do lose the cheek weld doing this, most of the micro-red dot optics like the FastFire III and JPoint that pair with these mounts are parallax corrected so that your dot does not have to be in the center of the picture for you to hit the target. A little shaking or displacement will not cause the shot to suffer.

Mounts of this type still should not be hulked when it comes to the screw torqueing. The torque specs on most of these mounts are going to be in the same range as the scope base ring screws on more conventional hardware.

MODERN TACTICAL RIFLESCOPES

We just discussed how there are a number of one piece scope mounts that are designed to be mounted on flat-top Picatinny rail-equipped rifles, like AR-15s, SIG556s, and others. We should not neglect to address those particular optics that are housed in such mounts, as they are an entire study in ballistic technology, optics technology, and ergonomic technology all wrapped into one long extended experiment.

Many tactical riflescopes resemble their more mundane brethren in appearance but many deviate when it comes to the components and materials therein. Very few hunting riflescopes for example, have first focal plane reticles. The reticle is the crosshair, but rarely in these scopes is it anything like the traditional crosshair. Modern optics have reticles placed on one of two planes, the first, or you guessed it, the second. When placed on the second focal plane, the reticle is fixed in size. No matter which magnification your variable scope is set to, the reticle will always be the same size in when looking through the scope. With first or front focal plane reticles, the reticle will zoom with the zoom in magnification.

Let's say you are aiming at some piece of crap truck on your back yard and the door is exactly as tall as the lines on your traditional duplex crosshair where they get thicker, a little ways out from the intersection. On this scope, if you zoom in from 3x to 9x the truck will get bigger and now the door handle will fill the same image area, but the door now fills the entire picture and the crosshairs have stayed the same size. This is a second plane scope.

First focal plane scopes are a little different. Instead of duplex lines, you might have dots or hashes that run all the way up and down, left and right from the intersection. As before, the truck door fills the area in the center of the scope, one hash above to one hash below the intersection. Now zoom it up to max, in this case from 6x to 24x. Not only does the truck door expand to fill the picture because of the zoom, but the crosshairs and reticle grow with it at the exact same ratio.

Any scope with any sort of deviation in the reticle that allows an imaginary line to be drawn between two points can be used for determining range, whether it was really designed to do that or not. However, on a second focal plane reticle it will only be possible at one specific magnification, unless you want to have to memorize a whole bunch of formulae. Some guys like to do that, so let loose dudes, let loose. For the rest of us we can get a scope with a front or first focal plane reticle that allows us to range at any magnification, since the distance between the two points will always be x at 100 yards, or 200 yards, or whatever you determine it to be.

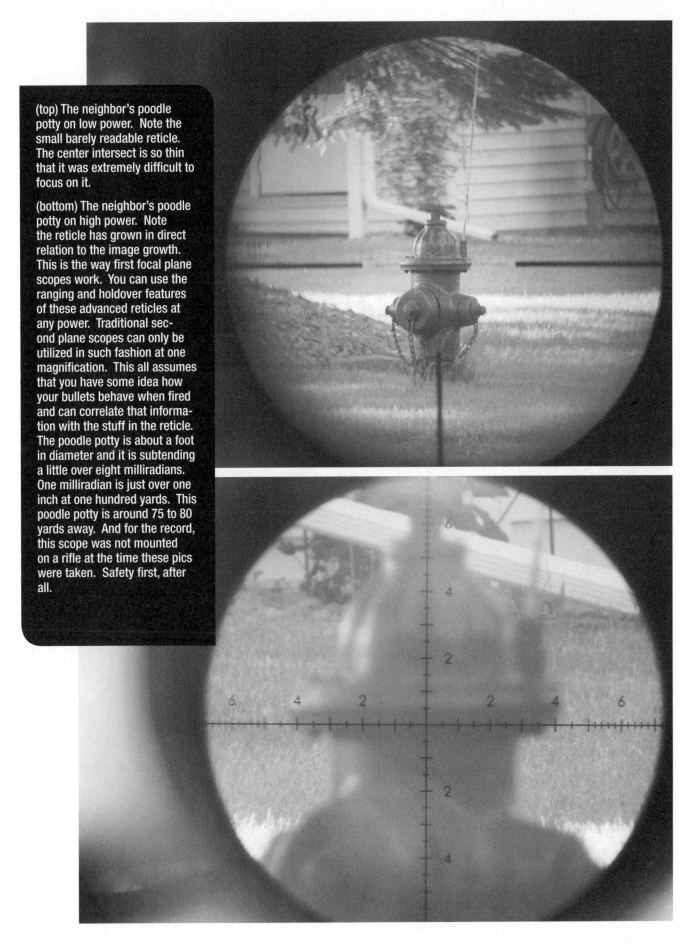

(top) The neighbor's poodle potty on low power. Note the small barely readable reticle. The center intersect is so thin that it was extremely difficult to focus on it.

(bottom) The neighbor's poodle potty on high power. Note the reticle has grown in direct relation to the image growth. This is the way first focal plane scopes work. You can use the ranging and holdover features of these advanced reticles at any power. Traditional second plane scopes can only be utilized in such fashion at one magnification. This all assumes that you have some idea how your bullets behave when fired and can correlate that information with the stuff in the reticle. The poodle potty is about a foot in diameter and it is subtending a little over eight milliradians. One milliradian is just over one inch at one hundred yards. This poodle potty is around 75 to 80 yards away. And for the record, this scope was not mounted on a rifle at the time these pics were taken. Safety first, after all.

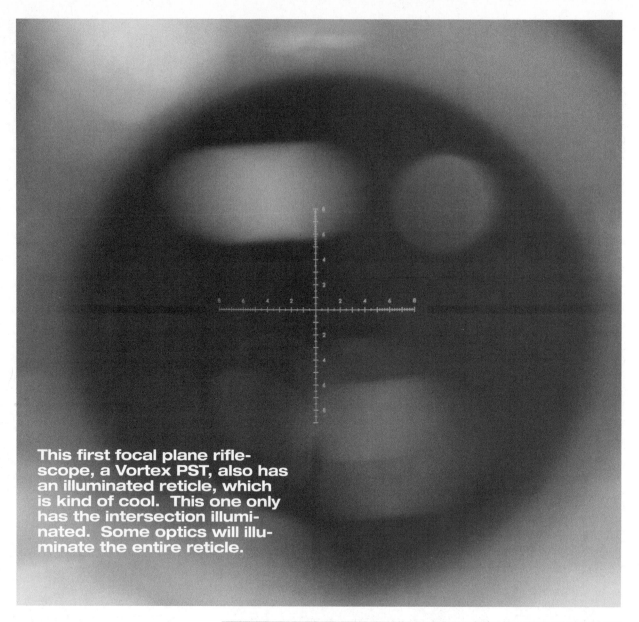

This first focal plane riflescope, a Vortex PST, also has an illuminated reticle, which is kind of cool. This one only has the intersection illuminated. Some optics will illuminate the entire reticle.

The reason the long range shooters, tactical competition shooters, or real life shooters use these scopes is that they will often have to engage targets at completely unknown distances, distances so far out that they have to have the scope maxed out to even see the target. You might think it's easy-peasy to hit a 12" white painted steel target, but it's not when that steel target is 684 yards away in a 15mph. crosswind. Notice the yardage. I gave you a freebie. You're lucky if the situation even tells you where the target is much less the exact yardage. You can get into some real challenging shooting and I

Most illuminated scopes will use one of these common CR2032 watch batteries to power them. Most of them.

heartily encourage new shooters to try out some long-range competition shooting if they have the chance. It can be very discouraging at first, because I will tell you right now that you will miss that 684 yard 12" target on that first shot unless you are really, really lucky. But with some practice, knowledge of the science, and a halfway good gun you can achieve some pretty good practical long-range marksmanship. But traditional riflescopes won't cut it and you will have to buy one of the more expensive and more capable tactical scopes.

As well, reticle illumination is much more common in tactical riflescopes than in traditional models. It isn't completely absent, as it is very handy in the dusk and dawn times of hunting. But since all the other cool features are in the tac scopes, there is no point in leaving out illumination, and a much higher percentage of tac scopes will have illumination. Be warned that, like on lasers and lights, the batteries will be exhausted at just the wrong time, so change them frequently whether they need the change or not.

RED DOTS

Now we enter a category as vast and varied as the traditional riflescope. The original idea behind the red dot scope was to have a single illuminated aiming point, sort of like a crosshairs in a riflescope, but at zero magnification, with a wide field of view. There are a lot of different sized dots, different colored dots (don't have to be red, but most are, and the originals were), not dots at all but circles, triangles, whatever, powered and unpowered, small and large.

The basic theoretical red dot sight is encapsulated in a smallish housing roughly 30-50 mm in diameter and three or four inches long. And black. Black is still the new black. A diode inside the back of the housing shines a beam forward that reflects off the front lens assembly back through the rear lens into the shooter's ocular sensory

(above) This is a great place to start for red dot sights. This Bushnell TRS-25 runs at about $100 and has a Pic rail interface on the bottom, though you might have to get the set with the riser (another $20) to mount on your flattop receiver.

(left) The TRS-25 mounted on the author's scratchbuild, a 5.56 from everywhere. This model's color closely matches the Burned Bronze Cerakote on the rifle and they make a good pair for close range de-Commiefying work.

(left) Eotech Holosights are also very popular. This is a basic 512 model that sells for around $400 and uses AA batteries, for those of you not yet into the Lithium age.

(below) The "standard" Aimpoint Red dot optic looks like this CompM3. This is the civilian counterpart to the M68 CCO.

(below) The JPoint from JP Enterprises is very lightweight (housing is plastic) and has been used for years as a secondary optic. It is suitable for pistols and long guns alike.

(bottom) This micro-red dot from Sightmark represents a good quality, low price model of micro. It also has a fun little sun shade overhang, and it's green rather than red.

This Meprolight reflex sight uses no power source except what can be taken from the wild outdoors. Sort of. It works during the day with fiber-optics, with light from the sun. At night, it illuminates using Tritium, derived from seawater.

apparatus. Adjustments are present to move that dot around the inside of the optic so that you can adjust the point of impact. There is generally no magnification. The dot covers a certain-sized circle at 100 yards. 4 MOA dots are common that cover a four-inch circle at that range. In a way, the dot size can allow some basic rough ranging ability, but the dot size can be variable and often is of different sizes for different tasks. Larger dots are better at short ranges where precision is secondary to speed, and smaller dots, as small as 1 MOA or less, are used past 100 yards with good precision. Intensity settings on the theoretical red dot scope are user adjustable so that you can set it high for bright sunlight or quite low for those times when you are protecting your home in the dead of night. This theoretical model will also have a clamp mounting system integral to the housing so that it can be slapped down on a Picatinny or Weaver mounting rail. The theoretical model, since it is basic, is also cheap and can be found for under $50. There are all kinds of models available.

Let's expand out from there. You can go up to the $100 range and find something with a little

more in the way of flexibility. A Bushnell TRS-25 red dot scope is a nicely made, compact optic with familiar looks. There is a downside: it is going to need a Picatinny rail riser. UTG makes a super and super priced riser, that looks like it was meant to be used with the TRS-25, for about ten bucks. Remember, an AR optic needs to be high up in order to raise it to the correct usable height. Up to this point, the battery life of these red dots mentioned is in the dozens of hours, using a watch battery as a power source, usually a CR2032 button. This battery is common (get it at any department store) and inexpensive.

The next tier of red dots gets expensive. This is because we are entering into the tactical realm of this particular universe. The previously mentioned types are generally hunting use or relatively low impact resistant, but are still commonly used as entry points on ARs and related rifles. Tactical, competition, and military/LEO shooters have a much more demanding agenda with red dots, just like with riflescopes. Likely the most well-known red dot optic at this level is the Aimpoint. This is the small scope seen on many rifles carried by

Night vision is fun. Fortunately the cost of night vision has dropped considerably in the last ten years or so. The easiest and cheapest to find are first generation, with the most expensive (and lightest and best performing) being the third gen + or fourth gen, depending on who made it. Being able to see in the dark has been one of mankind's deepest desires and modern night vision technology makes it possible. This is a modern first generation scope from ATN. It weighs a bit but it does amplify existing light nicely and has good enough resolution to not drive you nutty looking through it. If you really want to spend money, get a thermal imaging sight. Since most new AR owners don't have the means to drop $8000 on a thermal imager, that's all I'm going to say about it here. This ATN scope costs around $400, no worse than a number of quality riflescopes.

our military and is known there as the M68 Close Combat Optic. This model is based on the Aimpoint CompM2 red dot scope. In use it is much like the theoretical baseline model but with some under-the-surface enhancements. Battery life has been extended to the tens of thousands of hours. You can leave these things on at full power for well over a year. The housings are reinforced and overall, the durability of the Aimpoint red dots is an order of magnitude above the previous tier of red dot optics. The CompM2 is pretty much obsolete now and they are a couple generations past it. But it is still in production and still well sold nationwide.

A different but still common alternative to the Aimpoint has been the EoTech Holosight. First of all it's not round. It's more squarish and boxy. If you are into squarish and boxy then boy, is the Holosight for you. Rather than using a red diode, the Holosight uses a "laser." I point that out simply to be a know-it-all. It doesn't really matter in the grand scheme of things. The effect is the same in that you have a dot, or in this case a circle dot that appears to proj-

ect onto the target but never leaves the confines of the optic body. Rather than using dials to adjust intensity, it has buttons either on the rear or the side of the housing that activate and adjust up and down accordingly. The fun part about this model is that is uses the common AA battery, or the becoming common CR123 battery. Formerly used solely in cameras, the CR123 is regularly used in optics and tactical lights so that it is much more common. This is unlike the 1/3N battery that earlier Aimpoints used and you had to dig up online or at Radio Shack.

There are a host of Holosight models (same with Aimpoint) that you can choose from, based on requirements and cost. This tier of red dots ranges from $300 to over $600. Fortunately most now come with integral Picatinny mounts from the factory, so you don't have to pay extra for mounting hardware. They even come in something other than black, with several models available in a desert tan color. There are different reticles available too, the craziest one being on the Brownells model that looks like a biohazard symbol.

Micro-red dots are also increasingly common, and as the name would suggest, are quite small. These include the JP JPoint, Burris FastFire, Docter Optics red dot, Trijicon RMR, and others. They are small, very lightweight, use button batteries and last a long time, and often are constantly on, with no on/off switch, using a light sensor to self-regulate brightness. Prices come within a wide range. These optics are generally used not as primary sighting devices but as secondaries, mounted offset on the receiver or handguard, or to the primary scope's mounting system and used only when use of the primary would not be optimal.

The final (at least for now) tier of red dots is rarely red and there are only a few models to choose from. Most of these are passively powered, either by the great firebox in the sky or by radioactivity and usually by both. Models like the Trijicon Tri-power and the Meprolight optics use Tritium to make a visible reticle in subdued light and fiberoptic technology to illuminate the rest of the time, and they do so in a way that self regulates to ambient conditions. In a way, what goes in comes out again in a perfectly visible, perfectly intense reticle. Meprolight calls it an Electro-optical sight, but the idea is that you don't have to do anything to the sight. You don't have to turn it on. You don't have to play with settings. Nothing. But this convenience comes at a higher price tag.

It's pretty clear that red dot sights are in a very real manner similar to the traditional magnifying optics in one crucial aspect: price. You get what you pay for. If you only want to spend $100 you will get a unit that is somewhat bulky or has relatively short battery life, works well, but is made in the PRC. If you want to spend $300 or more, you will get a more streamlined or lightweight unit that has battery life measured in the hundreds or thousands of hours, works really well, and is made in the USA, Japan, Israel, Germany, or Sweden, with a lifetime warrantee.

BACK TO BORESIGHTING

There is a little thing called boresighting that must be done to a freshly mounted optic. "Why?" you ask? Well, I'll tell you. Normally, if you just slap the bases onto the gun's receiver, then slap the rings down on the bases, and then slap the scope down into the rings, go to the range, slap it down on the bench, and try it out at fifty or a hundred yards, there's a good chance that you will wind up wasting a good box of ammo trying to sight in the scope. Boresighting got its name from the idea that you set up (or down) the gun so it won't move and then you look down the barrel bore from the

back end. Pick something to look at. Maybe it's the doorknob on the other side of the room. Perhaps it's the headlight on your beat up Chevy at the end of the driveway. Then you look down the scope and adjust it so the cross hairs are on the same point as the item you centered down the barrel. Even if you are using a one-piece scope mount, you will still need to do this.

It's most important to get the left/right correct. The vertical alignment can and will be off a little. With some experience, and a little knowledge of ballistics, you can get the vertical boresighting down so well that the rifle will shoot vertically within an inch of where you boresighted it, and right on horizontally. This is zeroed from the shop for all intents and purposes. "So," you ask, "how exactly do you do it?" I've already told you the old fashioned way, but that is less precise than using a purpose built collimator. Another way, similar to

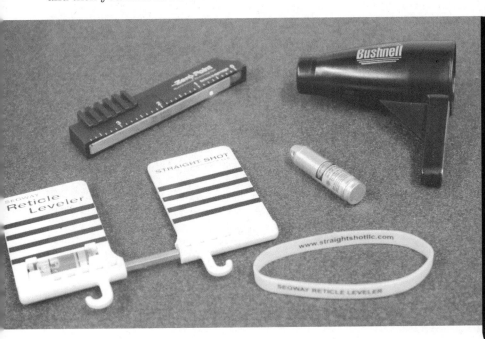

(left) Save your ammo and sight in with only a couple shots by boresighting your optic after you mount it. If you don't take it to a gun-smith, you will need these tools.

(below) The laser bore-sighters are very popular and can be used for just about anything. Rotate the boresighter in the barrel to make sure that the laser is properly aligned. If the laser is misaligned in its' hous-ing, the dot will scribe a circle on the target to some degree. Then bore sight to the center of the circle.

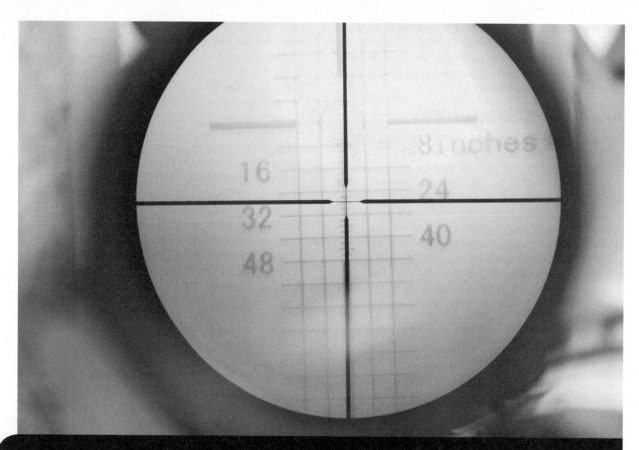

This is the grid you see when you look down one of the optical boresighters. Simply line up the crosshairs with the "0-0" intersection on the grid.

(below) In the author's opinion, this ZeroPoint from Leupold is the most versatile optical boresighter on the market. It has a magnet and is self-illuminated. Centering it is important as it has a much smaller view window than other optical models. However, it is head and shoulders above the arbor type optical boresighters, which are next to useless when boresighting an AR. There is too much distance between the optic and the bore.

the old fashioned look-down-the-barrel method is to use a "laser" insert, either in the chamber or in the muzzle, to project a "laser" beam from the barrel onto the wall, or even better, a grid or target on the wall. The scope is then adjusted so that the reticle centers on the projected dot.

There is a possible weak point in the laser boresighting method. The laser may not be perfectly aligned in its housing. With a chamber model, if the dot is visible to any degree, use it. With muzzle variants, particularly the under-forty dollar models, rotate the laser in the muzzle a full 360 degrees. If it light scribes a circle on the wall, boresight to the center of the circle. If you can do this whole process at the range at a certain distance, like 25 to 100 yards, then this will be a perfect boresight, and you just compensate a few clicks for the bullet drop. For example, a .223 bullet will drop about one inch at 100 yards, so set the scope's vertical adjustment so that you are aiming through the scope an inch or so below the dot that is projected at 100 yards. Of course the point of boresighting is simply to get the shots on the average paper target, say a 12"x12" square. If the shots are on target, then you can easily adjust the crosshairs to move the point of impact.

The most commonly-used means of boresighting are the various models of optical collimators. You can get them so they clamp to a barrel mandrel that slides down the muzzle end of the barrel. These are usually an inch and a half to two inches above the barrel. Do not use these with an AR style rifle. They simply cannot rise tall enough to work as well as they can with traditional rifles because of the low bore axis of the AR rifle. The other models are those that use a rare earth magnet to affix the unit to the muzzle. I prefer these models because you can then vary the height according to the height over bore of the scope, since not even all the one piece scope mounts are the same height. Some guys will say that doesn't really matter, but I disagree. I want the vertical and the horizontal as close as possible, and if the boresighter isn't high enough, you won't even be able to use it. These magnetic models work with standard and stainless steel just as well. Most are passive, using only ambient backlighting to light

the collimator, but the very compact Leupold model has an internal power source as well. You will want to make sure that the magnetic models are centered left to right on the end of the barrel.

Possibly the most frustrating aspect of mounting a scope is getting the reticles level to the gun. Some rings when you torque them will cause the scope to rotate slightly (or a lot) so you have to take that into account. I've found that just barely snugging one set of one ring and then doing the

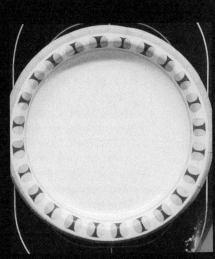

Let's just say for giggles that you are shooting at a paper plate, the most common pick up target in America, next to aluminum cans and propane tanks. You just mounted your scope and you don't realize that the scope, at 100 yards, is off by an entire foot up and to the right. You will never hit that paper plate at 100 yards. Had you started at 25 yards, the bullet would only impact three inches up and to the right of the center of the plate where you Sharpied a dot. You can then do the multiplication and find that you need to adjust down and to the left about 12 inches, and if your scope is in ½ MOA adjustments you would then go 24 clicks down and 24 to the left. You will wind up an inch or two below and to the left of the target at 100 yards but the following adjustments will be easy as pie. You will spend lots fewer rounds when you start your zeroing close in, and then moving out when you are dang close to the dot.

You can use one of these little cheap levels to level the rifle and then level the optic to the rifle. Confirm that the reticle is also level to the gun by visually checking. Using the Segway reticle leveler from Brownells is the best way to visually match the reticle to the rifle. Simply match lines from the reticle to the lines on the Segway evenly.

same to the other ring will fully immobilize the scope, allowing the other two pairs to be tightened normally, followed by the first two pairs. This is assuming that each ring has four strap screws. I can tell you that most of the rings you might purchase from sporting goods stores that are mounted on traditional rifles will do this to you. Very few of the rings from one-piece scope mounts for Picatinny rails will do this. Then alternate screws side by side and diagonally to tighten.

The reason we want the scope to be level is that when we make corrections, particularly at ranges greater than, say, 200 yards, we want those corrections to be accurately reflected in the shots. Let's exaggerate and give an example. Let's say our scope is canted by ten degrees to the left or counterclockwise, and when you shoot for zero, the first shot is three inches directly to the right of the bullseye. You adjust the windage to account for those three inches, and you shoot again. Congratulations! Instead of making a hole right smack in the center, you just made another hole one quarter inch to the right of the center and an inch low. The adjustments will not work correctly and precisely if they are not level to the gun and the gun is not level to the ground. When you are mounting a scope, you can only account for the scope to gun arrangement, so we try to level the reticle to a flat on the gun, say the flat on the top of the receiver rail. Then, the scope is leveled so that the reticle, or the horizontal crosshair line, is level to the gun. You can do this often enough by using bubble levels, utilizing the scope adjustment turrets. Be it known that I have boresighted a lot of scopes and

some of the reticles are not square with the flats on the turret caps. Remove the caps and use the turrets themselves.

Here is a little leveling tip. The vast majority of scopes are not properly leveled. When the reticle is perfectly leveled to the gun, it will not look level to your eye. This is caused by the compound angle your eye and face display when you are cheek to stock and looking down the scope tube. It's an optical delusion. If you are a righty, you will be looking up and to the left with your right eye and this will make the reticle appear to be slightly rotated to the counterclockwise. If you then mount the rifle on the other side with a left handed hold and look through with your left eye, the reticle will then look ever so slightly misaligned clockwise. Most people, including some gunsmiths, align the reticle so that it looks perfectly squared when they have the rifle mounted, and because of this optical illusion, is actually slightly rotated clockwise (if you are a righty). So if the crosshairs look ever so slightly rotated counterclockwise with your right eye, but the reverse when using your left eye, you are right on.

(below) The line shows the length from the optic lens to the middle of the eyebox. The eyebox is three dimensional, having some length width and height, a literal box that your eye must be in somewhere to use the optic. Some scopes have huge eyeboxes, some have very small ones. It's still ideal to be in the center.

(opposite) A lot of guys touch nose to charging handle. Nothing wrong with that, but your scope will generally need to be mounted further forward than you might think.

To compensate for or just remove the possibility of scope reticle misalignment, you can use the Segway Reticle Leveler available from Brownells. This is a wonderful product that allows you to square that reticle off based on the reticle itself and the scope mounting rail which is screwed to or integral with the receiver. It's also cheap, around twenty bucks.

Looking through the scope and through the collimator you will see a grid that represents a target at 100 yards, gridded off usually into two-inch demarcations. To do it quickly and easily, use your scope turrets to move the crosshair intersection to match the same intersection in the boresighter. To compensate slightly for bullet drop to get the closest possible boresight to zero, then set the scope crosshairs to subtend the boresighter grid two inches lower than the center intersection. This is a bit of a generalization, but making that little adjustment has gained me some happy customers who were very satisfied with having to shoot only two rounds to establish their hunting zeroes.

Finally, when boresighting is completed, the gun needs to be shot first at 25 to 50 yards to ensure that the shot is somewhere on the paper. Then go out to 100 or whatever you want for your zero. If you start at 100 or farther out and your boresight was a dismal failure, you may not even be on the paper. I always tell customers to start at short range for a couple shots then move out to their desired zero range.

OPTIC IDIOSYNCRACIES
Eye relief

Through all of this you need to make sure you have the scope set properly for distance from your eye. We've all (well, at least in my admittedly limited circle of friends) seen people with the cuts on their eyebrow from the scope's ocular bell hitting their mug on recoil. This means the scope was too close to their face and/or they were not holding the stock firmly against their shoulders when they made the shot. It's one of those things that's incredibly amusing when it doesn't happen to you or your daughter. Scopes with magnification have a limited "eye-box" in which your shooting eye must be placed in order to see the full field of view in the scope tube. If you are not in the eye-box you will see a hazy black ring flipping around the periphery of a too small image, or the scope will gray out entirely, particularly on high magnifications. The bigger the eye-box is, the better, as it makes the scope a little more forgiving during use. It is literally an imaginary invisible box. Anyway, the scope needs to be mounted so that your eye is in the middle of that box when you are cheek welded to the stock. The box will sometimes vary in size based on what power a variable power scope is set to, so setting the scope to the middle or highest magnification is the best idea. The box will be biggest on the lowest magnification setting.

On AR-15s, most of the one piece scope mounts have a sharp forward offset to place the rear of the scope just above the charging handle or pistol

grip, while keeping the footprint of the mount entirely on the receiver, as I mentioned earlier. This is especially necessary for the guys who choke up on the stocks so that their noses are smearing snot all over the charging handle. Man, that is so not cool for your neck, or my rifle, dude. Still, this forward offset is necessary for proper eye relief, particularly for those nose-to-charging-handle dudes.

Parallax

Without getting into too much boring detail, parallax is the effect of the crosshairs moving off the point of impact when your eye moves out of the centerline of the scope, or the scope axis (the image is essentially not on the same focal plane as the reticle). Most commercial scopes are parallax corrected at 100 yards. Other scopes have manual parallax adjustments and many shooters consider this knob to be more of a focus ring, and it sort of is, since you set it by focusing your eye on the image and then turning the knob so that the reticle also is focused onto the image plane at which you are looking. This is the knob or dial that has measurements from like, 50 yards to infinity. If this is set correctly, you can be off center in the scope and still hit the target at the given yardage. Better yet, maintain a good cheek weld and keep your eye in line with the scope axis. The more expensive red dots are also parallax free or corrected, the cheaper

(opposite top) This knob is the parallax adjustment for this scope. This is a handy thing to have, but is usually limited to existing on higher magnification, variable scopes.

(opposite bottom) This thing that no one ever seems to mess with is the diopter adjustment. Effectively, it's a secondary focus that you set and then leave the heck alone.

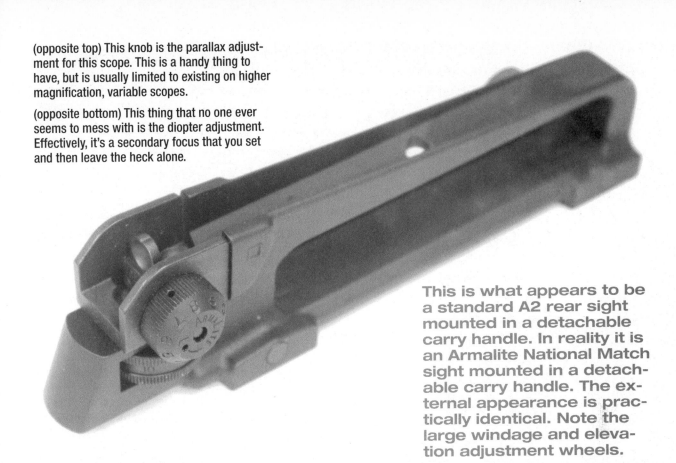

This is what appears to be a standard A2 rear sight mounted in a detachable carry handle. In reality it is an Armalite National Match sight mounted in a detachable carry handle. The external appearance is practically identical. Note the large windage and elevation adjustment wheels.

ones generally are not. So, in a nutshell, parallax is very much an important property of optics to be aware of, but you can minimize or eliminate any bad effects by keeping your eye placement correct.

Diopter adjustment

There is a little focus ring on magnifying scopes on the ocular lens at the very rear of the scope to help you adjust the scope to your crummy eyesight. When looking at a distant object through the scope (with parallax adjustment set accordingly, if you have it), turn the diopter ring until the image is perfectly clear. There will be a lock ring. Lock that down and leave it there forever. It is also poor etiquette to then use

someone's scope and mess up their diopter adjustment, so don't do it. These adjustments will be obvious and marked with a "0" + and – something. Many scopes just say "Focus" here anyway.

IRON SIGHTS

The majority of factory rifles, or at least half of them, are still shipped with the standard Iron sights. A great many rifles will have the A-frame front sight but will be shipped without rear sights for two reasons. The first is to keep the cost down. The second is that there are so many options that the end user will probably rather get what he wants rather than using what he might get on the factory rifle. Otherwise, the carry handle sights, either as part of the receiver or a detachable model, are likely the most commonly shipped and the most commonly used rear sight on ARs.

The basic model of this carry handle sight, known as the A1, was simply a windage adjustable flip sight with two apertures. The model used today, the A2, still has a flip aperture but utilizes a much larger, easier to manipulate windage knob, and incorporates an elevation adjustment to allow more fine shooting at longer ranges.

The A2 sight can be rather precise, depending on the skill of the shooter, and that is just, considering the military wanted it so that each infantryman could also be a an accurate rifleman, not just

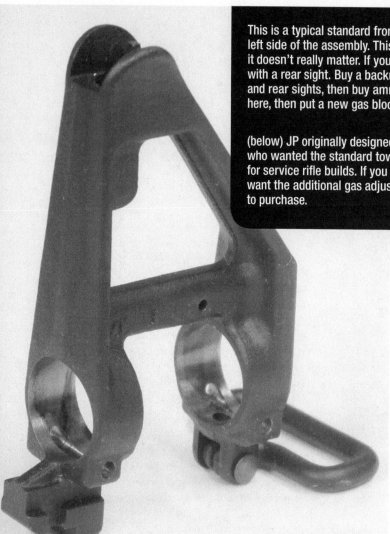

This is a typical standard front sight tower. A close inspection will reveal an "F" on the left side of the assembly. This is for sticklers an important mark but for newer owners it doesn't really matter. If your gun came with such a front sight, it likely did not come with a rear sight. Buy a backup iron and go shoot it. If the gun came with both front and rear sights, then buy ammo and go shoot it. If you are going to take it off, as I did here, then put a new gas block on it, scope it, buy some ammo and go shoot it.

(below) JP originally designed their replacement front sight tower to sell to people who wanted the standard tower but with gas adjustment, and to those who wanted it for service rifle builds. If you like the standard A2 style front sight, and many do, and want the additional gas adjustability and way friggin better appearance, this is the unit to purchase.

ing prairie dogs or something, just by taking the handle off and attaching a riflescope. As I'm sure I mentioned earlier, the flat top receiver adds great flexibility to the rifle system because of its Picatinny rail system.

The standard front sight is also adjustable for elevation, but is meant to only be adjusted when you are setting your initial zero. Then you leave it and only adjust the rear sight elevation when needed. However, there are a number of alternatives for the front sight and in some cases for the rear sight aperture as well. For example, several companies of-

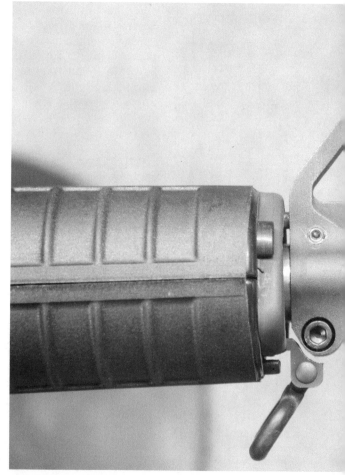

some conscript with a machinegun (the concept most other nations adopt). There are upgrades to this sight that competition shooters will install in place of the standard sight assembly. This upgrade usually incorporates a much smaller aperture, which may also be shrouded, and finer click adjustments in the windage and elevation. I will warn you though that changing out the A2 rear sight can be fraught with despair, as it is common to kink destroy the elevation spring and/or lose one of the small steel ball bearings used for detents. I'd advise you either to purchase one already assembled or take yours to a gunsmith to retrofit.

It is not typical to use a detachable carry handle for competition, rather most service rifle shooters will go with the traditional carry handle upper. Some (like me) like the flexibility that having a flat top receiver grants, so putting a National Match sight onto a detachable carry handle, while somewhat abnormal, is the best choice for me, since I can now use this very accurate rifle for shoot-

This is the Trijicon Tritium inserts that the Tritium conscious will substitute for your standard front sight post and rear sight aperture. These are quite bright at night and would serve the home defense-minded AR owner well.

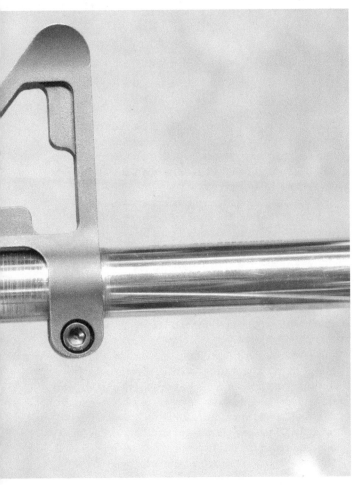

fer sight upgrades with some sort of illumination, such as Tritium, to make them easier to see at night. Trijicon is the most obvious provider of these upgrades.

KNS makes a wonderful set of front sight posts of different widths and tips for your shooting pleasure. It should be noted however, that the round-topped posts are not generally acceptable in competitions. In particular, the smallest round-topped front sight post seems to be a perfect bullseye front sight as at whatever range you shoot at, it will perfectly cover the black center of the NRA targets for that range.

BACKUP SIGHTS

It is to backup iron sights that we will direct the most attention, though they are simply a category of iron sights. Since most owners eventually go to an optic for their primary sighting device, whether it is a big riflescope or a small red dot, the iron sights are then relegated to secondary use status. This is why there are so many models of flip sights on the market. The sights if left up can interfere with the view through the scope (recall the co-witnessing concept). Whether they actually interfere is subject to the shooter's opinion, but regardless, the standard front sight is visible, if only as a blur when looking through a scope.

If you can quickly remove the sights from your field of view, then that field is fully unobstructed and you have a potential distraction eliminated. The options are three. You can have no iron sights at all. You can remove them and reinstall them willy-nilly (sucky option), or you can use some sort of flip sights, offset sights, or combination thereof. Flip sights allow you to rotate the sights down 90 degrees to lie flat. When you need them again simply press the button or manually flip them up and they are quickly usable. If they are offset to the side, then you simply roll the rifle on the shoulder to move the optic out of line and the sights into play. Offset sights can give the illusion of bulk or catch on things just as easily as sights on top so that is something to consider, however the offset sight has two large advantages.

The first advantage is rapid deployment, assuming the sights are not flipped down, or the

sights are indeed fixed. Rolling the rifle on the shoulder takes a fraction of the time it takes to activate a spring button or manually lift the sights into position. The second advantage is that if something happens so that you cannot see through the optic, you will not be able to use your sights either, if they are co-witnessed. This is why there are a number of quick detach clamps and such for optics mounts, so that if anything happens to the optic, the shooter can get them off as quickly as possible. Or, you could just mount your irons offset so that if the optic is unusable, you simply rotate the rifle on your shoulder.

Much of this boils down to personal preference. I prefer offsets, but many others do not and that is okay. Let's look at a couple of options for sights. Again, there are simply way too many options to cover, so I'll examine the ones that I like and with which I have the greatest experience.

MagPul MBUS

The MagPul sights were the first mass-produced, low profile, folding plastic backup sights that I played with, and I still play with them now. They are inexpensive, a set costs less than $100. They are easy to install and are very well made. Depressing the housing down causes them to spring up. To push them back down, simply push them back down until they lock flat. The only real word of warning that I can give you concerning these sights, and other plastic sights, is that if you mount them on a gas block, you will probably melt the front sight housing. The gas block can get hot. Stick to mounting them on the handguards if you can. You have to do a few mag dumps to get the gas block hot enough to melt the plastic, but it can happen.

The original plastic models are still all the rage, but MagPul now has all steel models called the Pro series as well.

Diamondhead

The Diamondhead sights are a recent offering. They pretty much follow the standard stuff when it comes to flip up sights that other quality alumi-

num sight manufacturers like Troy, Samson, and MI follow but with one glaring exception. Neither the aperture nor the sight guard wings are round. The Diamondhead sights square off the aperture to a diamond shape (okay, it's still square, but for some reason when we rotate a square onto one point, people say it's diamond shaped; whatever, dude). When you look through them, your brain wants to line the points up nice and straight so you wind up creating imaginary lines in the sight picture, which makes centering the front sight post in the aperture more instinctive. I can say definitively that I can bring my rifle in line on target faster with the Diamondhead sights than with a standard round aperture. Others can't wrap their minds around a square hole for a sight aperture and it drives them nuts looking through it. Yet another example of personal preference having an impact not just because of cosmetics but because of function, and every human being is unique. Diamondhead makes aluminum sights and they have begun producing plastic, cheaper versions as well, that work just the same as the originals.

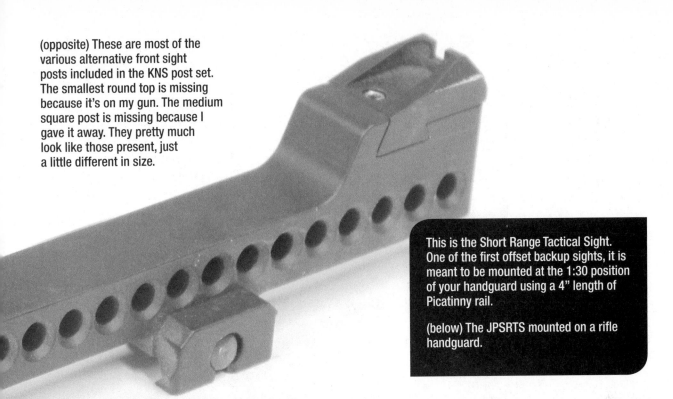

(opposite) These are most of the various alternative front sight posts included in the KNS post set. The smallest round top is missing because it's on my gun. The medium square post is missing because I gave it away. They pretty much look like those present, just a little different in size.

This is the Short Range Tactical Sight. One of the first offset backup sights, it is meant to be mounted at the 1:30 position of your handguard using a 4" length of Picatinny rail.

(below) The JPSRTS mounted on a rifle handguard.

Note how the shooter here has merely rotated the rifle on his shoulder to bring the BUIS into play.

JP Offset rails and SRTS

JP has for close to 20 years offered a product called the Short Range Tactical Sight. This was and still is very popular on the 3-gun fields and was probably the earliest offset backup sight available. It consists of an assembly into which both front and rear open sights are mounted and is clamped to a four-inch Picatinny rail segment. This segment is installed in the 45-degree angle location slots on the JP handguards, or anyone else that has a slot or screw holes in that position. The sight radius is rather short though and so it really is short ranged.

The Offset rails are clamped onto the top rail on the handguard, or handguard and receiver, and are meant to have back up sights mounted to them. The difference between these and most other companies' similar offerings is that these are designed to keep the aperture at the same height over the barrel as the center axis of the scope, so that you do not have to adjust your cheek weld when you rotate the rifle, just rotate the rifle and the sights will be lined up. Other examples tend to be lower so that you have to really squish your cheek down, or they tend to be laterally off bore axis when

deployed. The down side is that these rails do stick out a bit and can hook branches or clothing pretty easily. This is a minor price to pay for the rapid deployment and constant height offered by this combination.

Both are certainly useful for gaming but are equally handy for hunting and other engagements. It is useful to be able to quickly transition to backups should your optic no longer be usable, for any number of reasons.

XS XTI sight set

This set incorporates the back up and offset sight ideas as well as incorporating XS Sight Systems' big dot front sight concept. The front sight is a large white dot, with a Tritium vial in the center. The rear sight is a shallow V into which the front sight is centered. It works well and the sights are very low profile, so low that I can't squish my cheeks down far enough to use them, but that is a personal preference. There are plenty of skinny guys with high cheekbones who can utilize the XTI set with perfect fit.

I've spent a lot less time on sights in this book than one might expect. Mostly, it is to reflect the fact that ARs seldom stay primary sighted with optics for long. Just about everyone acquires some sort of optic and I encourage them to do so, as this will help them discover the accuracy potential of the AR. Secondly, there are libraries of books and online information on how to shoot accurately with open sights and optics that the reader can reference at his or her convenience. Sights are not unimportant to an AR, but optics have definitely eclipsed the iron sight on America's rifle and have done so for some time.

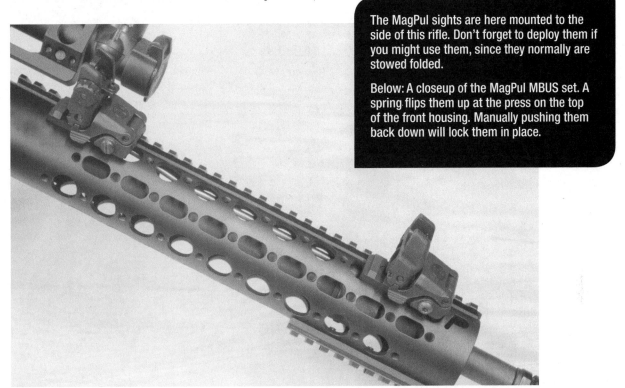

The MagPul sights are here mounted to the side of this rifle. Don't forget to deploy them if you might use them, since they normally are stowed folded.

Below: A closeup of the MagPul MBUS set. A spring flips them up at the press on the top of the front housing. Manually pushing them back down will lock them in place.

(above) Note that the protective wings on the Diamondhead sight are squared off and approximately will strike an imaginary line right across the top of the front sight post. Similar wings on the rear sight and the same design rear aperture make sight alignment with Diamondhead sights very quick and precise.

These are the JP offset mounts which keep the back up sight on the same planes vertically and horizontally when the rifle is rotated out of optic alignment, and in this case is mounted directly to the piston gas block.

(left) The XS Sights Xpress Threat Interdiction sights are small but carry a big name. The big white dot in front is placed on top of the line in the center of the shallow V of the rear sight. This too is a fast sight to acquire, as long as you do not have fat cheeks.

There's no reason you can't put fixed sights on your long handguard. Here is an extra length handguard rifle with fixed iron sights, front and back. The rear sight assembly, from UTG is essentially the back third of a detachable carry handle. The front is reminiscent of a standard gas block, made by DPMS.

Lights and Lasers

A handy accessory for any gun is a flashlight, or tactical light. Lights are particularly useful with HD guns. Most recorded home invasions occur at night when people are sleeping with the lights off or low. Proper identification of the silhouette passing before you on the stairwell is essential. The light switch may not be in convenient reach and you don't want to shoot what you can't identify. Kind of like you don't want to shoot at something when you don't know what's behind it. I heard a very sad story a couple years ago of several families that were out shooting recreationally on the back forty. They weren't paying as good attention as they should have on the kids pres-

ent and one of them wandered unseen behind one of the targets. When they noticed he was missing, they finally found him behind one of the targets. Don't let this happen to you. Make sure you identify what you are about to shoot at. In the home, in the dark, that means a tac light.

Lights have been companions to firearms for generations. It simply makes sense to be able to identify the danger. Only recently in the most modern generation have we gotten to the point that the two can be combined into one unit because of better power technology, attachment technology, and better miniaturization.

Investigating suspicious noises in the shed is easier if your light is mounted to your rifle. Please don't shoot anything by accident, like your lawn mower. This 550 lumen Nextorch T3A tac light completely washes out the door of the shed. Imagine being in the spotlight. The flare launcher is underslung the barrel for backup auxiliary lighting. And at this range, firestarting.

This is a good place to have a tactical light. It's dark, but the light from the clock radio is actually backlighting the potential home invasion victim.

Light is your friend and your enemy's enemy. Soldiers could be snuck up on by the enemy in the darkness, so when the soldiers got the bad feeling about this moment, or heard something suspi-cious, they called for starlight shells, giant flares that il-luminated the night so that the enemy could be seen in their sneakiness and shot. Darkness continues to be the friend of the criminal. Most home invasions, burglar-ies, and violent as-saults occur at night or in low lighting for a reason. The crimi-nal does not want to be spotted before he is ready to act.

In this chapter we are going to cover the tactical light. Also known as a weaponlight, the tac light is a great non-lethal weapon all on its own. It used to be the only choices were the models from Surefire, prob-ably the first company to mass market the super

A pistol with a light is great for checking out the stairways.

bright high luminosity tac light. Soon there were comparable models from any number of sources, and now I can't even begin to count the brands that exist to fill this market. Be aware that the majority of the tac lights on the market, cheap or expensive are made in China, and this is what makes them affordable. The few that are made in the US are very-very expensive, but are said to be of extremely high quality. I have to be honest and admit that I don't know that for sure. What I do know is that the new gun owner has no business spending $400 on a palm-sized tactical light. Get a Surefire, Streamlight, or NexTorch to start with and if that doesn't seem adequate, then by all means move up. We are going to go over a few of the more common options, and options that won't break the bank too badly.

Perhaps I should define what a tactical light is. I'm not sure if there is an official canonized definition, but I will put one forth. A tactical light, whether attached to or separate from a firearm, is a device that projects a bright beam designed to over-illuminate the objective, acting supplemental-ly as a distraction and stunning tool. Getting into luminosity and lux and candlepower or whatever each light says it is rated by can be a sales trap and gimmick, as all that stuff is subjective and can be manipulated like raw statistics on dope. If

YES!

NO!*

(*If Oriental man in house is home invader, then YES! It works very effectively on Orientals.)

technology started humming and the vast majority now have super bright LEDs that are every bit as bright, even brighter than the Xenon and Krypton bulbs. The LEDs don't get quite as hot as the Xenon bulbs, but they will still cook when left on for a while.

This style of small light is very capable of being used as a non-lethal weapon, particularly if it has the strobe feature. Strobe lights are very disorienting. Since shining a light with the luminosity of a supernova into someone's face has been shown to be an effective deterrent even when used without a gun. When it flashes ten to twenty times per second it's that much more unnerving and can give you the time to either run away or to better identify the potential adversary when he is temporarily but very effectively blinded.

Oh, by the way, you may think it is fun

A lot of folks went the cheap way for a tactical light. This is an old Surefire Nitrolon hand light that is stuck in a mount and slapped on the gun. This light's bulb is susceptible to shock damage, but with the .223 recoil, I never had any problems. Most lights are LEDs now.

you shine it in your own eyes and your reaction is the same as if you looked directly into the sun, then it's a tactical light. The extra brightness is a means to an end. The brighter the light, the better and more focused you will see the target, and the harder it will be to for he/she/it to see you clearly.

The early models had Xenon bulbs that made them quite bright and Surefire even went to the extent of patenting reflectors and lenses that removed the bulb shadows from the beams. Then

to shine somebody to show them how bright your new toy is. Leaving aside the fact that the light better not be mounted on the gun when you do this, this activity is downright rude and low class. I still feel awful sorry for the time I did this without even really thinking about it and strobed my friend into an instant migraine. Just don't do it. Shine it on the ground or the wall or whatever, just away from someone's face. They are often referred to as non-lethal weapons for a reason.

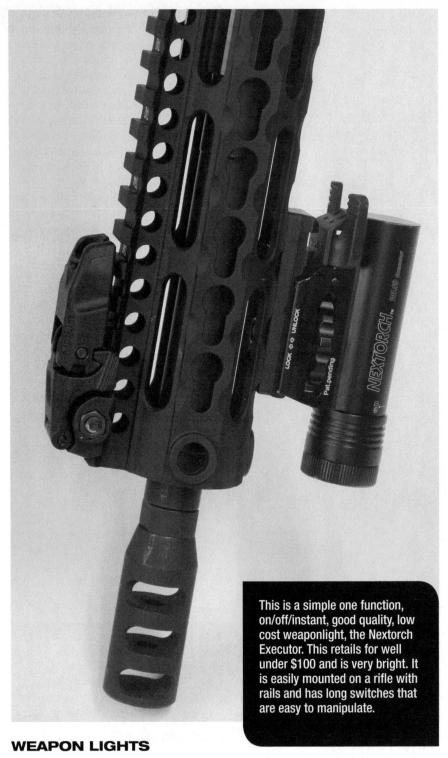

This is a simple one function, on/off/instant, good quality, low cost weaponlight, the Nextorch Executor. This retails for well under $100 and is very bright. It is easily mounted on a rifle with rails and has long switches that are easy to manipulate.

WEAPON LIGHTS

Weapon lights are probably as common or more so on pistols as they are on rifles like ARs.

Rifles will mount just about any weaponlight most easily if they have a stretch of Picatinny rail. Of course the endless varieties of railed handguards available for AR-15s make that easy, but there are a number of clamp on, screw on, or slip on rails that can be added to just about anything. In fact, the lights made for mounting on pistols are often used on ARs because of the small size and low weight inherent to the pistol lights. Rifle weapon lights tend to be much brighter however, but also much larger and heavier. Decide on your own what you need. The majority of weapon lights are now built with LEDs rather than incandescent bulbs, like the Xenon or Krypton models. The incandescents must be shock absorbed, making them more expensive, while the LED models do not. Plus the LEDs tend to run longer and somewhat cooler.

With the light mounted on the gun, it should be placed so that it can be easily and instinctively activated with the support hand. This might require a remote switch, and a number of the lights can accept such a device, but many do not have a remote switch that does not have to be purchased separately. The point is that you should not have to fumble about trying to activate your light when you need it most. When you need it most is when you are jacked up on adrenaline, about ready to pee your pants, and you can't figure out how to disengage your gun's safety because you are so keyed up you can't remember how to do it. Stress can mess you up, and most weapon lights have gross (as in large) buttons or lever to activate them. However it's done, the point is to make the activation instinctive and not something that requires concentration.

Anyway, if you really want to spend some money and have some wicked cool tactical lights, they are available and can be purchased in most outdoor sporting goods stores. But as I said before, if you are a new gun owner, you would be best served by sticking to something under $400. This means you will most likely want to start with one of the many fabulous pistol lights on the market. Most pistol lights are going to be much less than that. Then

(continued on page 177)

REFINISHING AT HOME

It used to be that if your firearm's finish was scratched, damaged, scuffed beyond your ability to endure, or you just didn't like it, you could have your local friendly gunsmith refinish the thing. You can still do that.

Or…you could do it yourself. Most AR receivers and other aluminum parts are black hard coat anodized, and the barrels, when they are chrome-moly barrels, are parkerized.

It turns out that parkerizing, especially the zinc phosphate variety, is the best surface treatment for the spray-on finishes that we cover in this chapter. Anodizing on aluminum is also excellent as a substrate surface finish. This is because both are chemically bonded to the part, and are essentially a transformed outer skin. This skin is also quite porous, especially the parkerizing. When you paint it, the paint actually intercalates into the pores and forms a better bond than if the surface finish was not there and you were just painting untreated metal. You do not need to blast off the anodizing or parkerizing, despite what some Internet gunsmith wannabes might say.

In the last twenty years, we have in a way, gone full circle. Back in the day, guns used to be painted all the time with enamels (and often still are, DuraBake is an enamel) because it was easier and cheaper than blueing. Now we sort of do the same thing for two reasons.

The first reason is the same as before: to rust-proof the gun and make it more resistant to environmental assaults. Steel can't rust if the oxygen can't get to it. Whether it is

DuraCoat, Cerakote, KG Guncote, Alumahyde, or whatever, the spray-on finishes completely protect the metal from corrosion and, depending on the product, from a number of solvents and acids as well.

These coatings also vary in hardness, scratch and abrasion resistance, flexibility, and ease of application. So I'm going to go over in a fair amount of detail the two most commonly-used gun industry-specific spray-on coatings, DuraCoat and Cerakote.

The second reason is purely cosmetic. Remember that this book is about personalizing and taking care of your ARs. You want them to be unique and different from the other guy's. You may not consciously recognize this but it is indeed there. These coatings will allow the final touch, the icing, to be put on the cake to make it entirely yours. Yeah, Jim across the street might have the exact same model gun, down to the scope and rings, but his isn't purple and gray camouflaged. Is it?! These products come in so many colors it makes your head spin, and even then you can still mix those to make colors that don't come from the factory. In fact, I do a lot of this kind of refinishing as part of my business, and at least a quarter of the paint jobs are done with special mixing involved. I do what I want.

If you want a flat green gun, entirely, down to the last pin, you can do that. If you want a Saddam Hussein Gold colored AK, you can do that. If you want purple hearts on a pink stock, you can do that. If you want a funky camo pattern, or a real camo pattern, you can do that.

BOTH OF THEM...

Both DuraCoat and Cerakote require essentially the same preparation to the metal parts. Get it out of your head that you can get a good result by painting the gun in assembly. You can't. If you want to Krylon-Kamo your gun in assembly then you go right ahead and do it. These are not that product and they require a full disassembly of the gun, followed by a complete degreasing of the parts that you are going to be painting.

For example, an AR needs to be completely taken apart, down to the last pin, spring, and screw. Let's say you are only painting the handguard and the two receivers, and leaving the rest of the gun alone. These parts should be ideally immersed into some kind of degreaser, and at the very least hosed down with it if you don't have enough for a bath. It should be left in the degreaser for at least several minutes. Good degreasers would be lacquer thinner or acetone. LCW (DuraCoat) offers a solvent called Trustrip that works real well. This stuff comes in containers and in aerosol cans.

When removed from the degreaser, let it evaporate from the parts. If you want anything masked, like receiver threads or the inside of the upper, then now is the time to do it. You may then want to preheat the part to see if more oil sweats out of the pores of the metal. If nothing happens then you are ready to paint. If oil seeps out, then repeat the

(top) An immersion degreaser bucket is better than sprays. Dunk. Leave it. Swish it. Pull it and let the solvent evaporate.

(above) If an immersion degreaser is not practical, then you can spray degrease with something like LCW's Trustrip.

degreasing procedure as necessary.

Most companies tell you to hang the parts by wire, but I hate doing that. It's clumsy and uncontrolled. An AR-15 upper receiver bore is one inch in diameter. Get a wood dowel that is 1" by 12-18" long. Run it all the way through the receiver so that one end sticks out the back of the receiver about an inch. Wrap masking tape around the receiver threads at the front where the barrel nut screws on, so that

(left) This is the way most application is done. It's clumsy, but it works.

The same concept of fixturing is used on the lower receiver. Use the design to your benefit. In this case, a ¼-28 bolt was glued to a ½" wood dowel. The bolt is screwed into the pistol grip screw hole.

(above) The better way to apply surface treatments. Fixture it up. No matter the shape of the part, there is usually a way to fixture it.

(right) Badge Crescendo 175 airbrush. Not too expensive, but a very good airbrush kit.

the tape is also wrapping the wooden dowel. You now have a very useful fixture that is easy to use, fully supports the part and when it is painted, can simply be held in a bench vise until the paint is cured. If you are baking the part then you may have to hang it after all, or you could take a small piece of two-by-four board and drill a 1"-diameter hole in it and insert the fixture dowel into the hole like a peg. This can then be moved in and out of the oven, assuming the oven is tall enough. It may be necessary to shorten the dowel.

The lower receiver can be held in a similar fashion. Wrap enough tape around a 1" dowel so that you can screw the taped end into the threads at the rear of the lower receiver. You don't need to get paint on these threads any more than the threads of the upper receiver, and no one will know the difference later.

Both DuraCoat and Cerakote are best applied with an HVLP gun. Most of you don't have one, nor will you want to buy a nice one, so you can get by with a good airbrush. It'll just take longer to paint the gun. Both products are binary, consisting of the base pigment and a hardener that is added just before the application of the product. Ratios are dif-ferent but that is a semantic we don't need to cover. It is fun to note, though, that more hardener makes a more glossy appearance in the coating when done, and less hardener makes a flatter appearance.

The pigment and the hardener are mixed in the airbrush jar and then applied to the parts. They will go on fairly wet looking if you are doing it right, but not too wet as you don't want to have to deal with runs. A good plan is to put on multiple thin coats. Enough coats are necessary to fully cover the original color of the work piece and give a solid uniform color to all the pieces of the gun. Both companies say that you want a coating that is a half thousandth to a full thousandth of an inch thick. Well if you are like me, you have no way of determining exactly what that is by eye. Just paint it fully and uniformly. It should look like the solid color you painted on, with no black or whatever showing through, but should not have that thick, soft, "painted on" appearance.

When application is complete, you can drop the residual paint in the wastebasket. It will dry and the solvents will evaporate. There is a limit to this. Don't dump a jar full of paint in the trash. But a tablespoon or two is okay. The air-brush can be disassembled and cleaned with acetone or

A spray booth is a good thing to contain the overspray. This booth has two very good exhaust fans to evacuate the air.

lacquer thinner. It also doesn't hurt to spray the solvent through the brush for a second of two to make cleaning the nozzle easier.

Needless to say, you should have sufficient ventilation for a project like this. Don't do it in your basement. Do it in the garage, with both the front and back doors open. Wear a respirator, and if you have a spray booth, even better.

DURACOAT

DuraCoat is the easier of the two to apply for several reasons. First, you don't have to bake it. Standard DuraCoat will cure over a period of time at room temperature. After only a few minutes you can handle it. Do not f-ing play with it or reassemble it for at least a month. The cure time is fairly long, but it does cure, and it continues to harden for quite some time. If you can manage leaving it alone for a year, it will be extremely durable and tough, however the protection is still excellent after that first month. Put it in a closet and leave it there.

Secondly, the air from the airbrush or HVLP will flash off a great deal of solvent, so you can make an application pass, followed by a pass with just air, and keep doing this until the part is completely painted. If you do this in a slow and controlled fashion you need not stop, just fill in the spaces and uniform the thing with slow alternating passes of DuraCoat and air. You can do the same thing by putting it in an oven on low temperature, if you have a bunch of stuff to paint and want to make more efficient use of time. This property also makes it the easiest to create a camo pattern with. You can pump out a camouflaged rifle in very short order with DuraCoat.

DuraCoat can be purchased in different sized containers, including paint cans. It is mixed with a hardener and sprayed.

AR home build with Spikes Tactical
Havok flare launcher in Urban camo.

Third, DuraCoat is very tolerant of residual oils that you didn't quite get off. Also, and I found this out first-hand, if your air compressor is spitting oil or water out with the air, because your tank and filters hadn't been emptied in a while, you will see little fisheyes on the part. Just leave them alone until the stuff has flashed off. Let it sit for ten or twenty minutes. Then take a rag, or Q-tip and wipe it off. The DuraCoat literally will get under the oil spot or water. Wiping it will leave a slight blemish that you can then fix with a new coat.

Fourth, if you mess something up, like putting a finger print on the part just to see if you could, you can just let the part flash off for ten or twenty minutes and then sand off the stupid fingerprint and repaint over the fix. This cannot be done with any of the other products since you would have to finish the baking cure first. DuraCoat is very fixable. It is also very flexible and will deform with the part if the part is dented, rather than chipping, as long as you thoroughly degreased the part.

DuraCoat can be obtained in standard form and also in a form called SL that includes PTFE (Teflon) in the mix. This gives it some self-lubricating properties and greater point impact and abrasion resistance.

CERAKOTE

Cerakote is very hard. It has ceramic particles in its matrix and this, when cured, forms a very abrasion-resistant coating. Cerakote tends to go on thinner than DuraCoat, but with a denser deposition. It will look wet, but will flash off if you put it in the oven for a few minutes. The oven must be hot. Normal baking temp is 250 degrees F for two hours, though a slow, low heat cure can also be used for woods and plastics. You can, if you are good, apply Cerakote in one coat and bake it, but you have to be really good and have a good eye and good finger and hand/eye coordination with the airbrush. I still recommend applying a thin coat, baking it for five or ten minutes to flash off the shine, and then putting another coat on it, making sure that everything is uniformly covered.

Do not, under any circumstances, touch the painted part with anything whatsoever. It will look dry after ten or fifteen minutes in the oven but, it. Is. Not. Dry. You will then have to wait till the stuff is cured, and hope you can make a touch up. NIC Industries, the manufacturer of Cerakote, says not to even do that. Strip the paint and start over. If you got a dust mote or something, wait till the Cerakote is cured and out of the oven and cooled off. You will be able to flick that crap off the part, with likely little or no blemish remaining.

Like DuraCoat, Cerakote is available in various sizes, with a significant savings per ounce in the larger size jars.

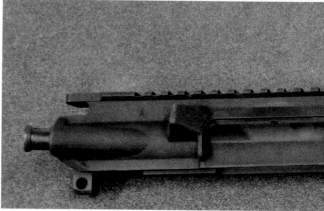

A piston upper using a JP tube and Adams Arms Piston upgrade. Cerakote Burned Bronze color.

A DPMS free float tube with Tungsten Gray Cerakote.

Cerakote's greatest advantage is abrasion resistance, and this makes it ideal for handguns that will see lots of holster wear. The down side to Cerakote is that it is the most expensive of the do-it-yourself spray on applications. For the most part this, and its hardness properties, has made it much more popular as an OEM finish for gun manufacturers, than for home application. Still a small 4 ounce bottle will paint three or four pistols and for 35 bucks, that ain't bad either.

AEROSOL PRODUCTS

There are other quality spray-on products that work well if you don't have an airbrush. Brownells has a great assortment. They offer Teflon/Moly paint, Alumahyde, DuraBake, and Gun-Kote, as well as the standard DuraCoat and Cerakote. All are superb finishes, some are baked and some are not, so you can use them on just about anything.

The aerosols generally require some preheating. You can do this in an oven or with a heat gun, like you would use when stripping paint. Do not use open flame like from a blowtorch or propane torch to preheat as they will leave residue and ash on the parts. The cans all have fanning nozzles so that you can easily make wide coverage passes, and if a nozzle clogs up, you can buy them by the dozen from Brownells as well. If you want to camouflage the gun with some funky pattern you saw online or on your father's brother's nephew's cousin's former roommate's gun, you can get stencils to do so.

Aerosols work well too but require baking and/or preheating. LCW makes DuraBake, an enamel, and Brownells offers their Teflon/Moly spray on coat. Both make a very good finish that requires no cure time.

Patterns can be added to guns by a good free-hand ability or by the use of stencils.

RICK BYLO "AR15 pistol. Matrix Aerospace upper and lower, Carbon Fiber quad rail, 8" 1/7 twist barrel, PSA BCG, Extended ambidextrous CHARGINGHANDLE, Ambidextrous Phase 5 Tactical extended bolt catch, Troy ambidextrous mag release, UTG tactical sniper pistol grip, SIG SAUER wrist brace, Dura Coat Aged Bronze finish, Burris E1 Fullfield 3x9 scope, Bipod, Custom MuzzleBrakes Tactical low concussion muzzlebrake, Extended takedown pins."

(right) **BOB BOUCHARD** "PVS-14 3rd gen night vision with Surefire FA556AR silencer. It also has the Surefire M952 LED IR weapon light, GG&G mounts with Eotech 552 weapons sight, Larue FUG & Vtac sling. Cost to build is over $6,000 dollars."

DAVID BOOKSTABER "Noveske .300BLK upper with 16" bbl, pistol-length gas, GEMTECH Sandstorm suppressor, Leupold Mk4 scope in LaRue QD base, Double Star lower with Timney 3.5lb single-stage trigger, JPSCS-15 Silent Spring System, Magpul UBR stock and MOE+ grip."

JEFF ELLIOT "Medium range 5.56x45 upper. Specialized Tactical Systems VLTOR upper receiver, Primary Weapons Systems long stroke gas piston system, 10.5 Daniel Defense cold forged chrome lined barrel, Micro Slick FA Bolt Carrier Group, YHM Phantom 556 suppressor w/ QD flash hider, BCM Gunfighter Mod 3 charging Handle, Eotech XPS2, Bobro vertical grip, Streamlight ProTac HL offset mount, Magpul XTM rail covers."

ANDREW "DREW" DE PASS "AR Blackout...5.56 Bushy lower with MagPul B.A.D. Lever and UTG Ergo Pistol Grip mated to R- Guns' 16" National Match H-Bar upper with extended charging handle/latch, free float handguard and faux-suppressor end cap. Unit is topped off with a Burris FullField Tac-30 riflescope and Fastfire III red-dot sight."

WALT KULECK "AN/PVS-4 looks very odd on the long-range 5.56 rifle."

MIKE WARREN "300 BLK w/ Nikon 300Blk."

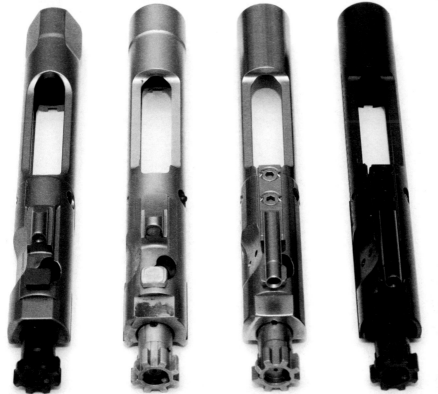

(left)
DAVID BOOKSTABER
"BCG material, Phosphate, nickel-boron (NiB), hard chrome, nickel-teflon (NP3). And last two are for piston guns, first two are for DI guns."

(left) TIM DAHLIA "A girl's AR15. Pink on black, Dura Coat color matched for Hogue grip, polished stainless and aluminum acents for BLING! Chromed bolt, pink sling with polished buckle from grandpa's Springfireld 03A3. Engraved with owner's name on magwell, Matching ammo box with pink strap with lettering 'I shoot like a girl.'"

(above) GARY PRICE ".300 Black Out with a 10" integral suppressor on a 16" ported barrel, Jard trigger, side charge operating handle, Magpul furniture, Harris bi-pod."

RICHARD TRASK "Red Jacket KMP Advanced. Leupold Mark AR for a scope mounted on a Warne, ARMS 71L flip up sights mounted on a 45 degree offset for backup."

EARL BARTOLOME "Budget build, Aero lower, Blackthorne rifle kit, Omega Tactical free float quad rail, Magpul MBUS sights."

ANDREW POOLE "Arms of Glory lower, Windham Weaponry parts kit, YHM Black Diamond Specter XL upper, YHM Phantom muzzle brake, Bushnell AR optic with the BTR-1 radical on a Buriss PEPR mount. Irons are a Magpul MBUS rear and a YHM front. I had to switch to the MBUS to get the room I needed to mount my optics where I wanted them."

From the readers of gundigest.com

CUSTOM AR PHOTO GALLERY

R. WEIBEL "Adcor piston AR-15 built by Delphi tactical in Raeford NC. 16" with Giselle trigger, Magpul furniture and an Eotech sight."

(below) JOE FRENDO "Top AR-15 has an 18" Noveske barrel with a Jard adjustable trigger, Young Manufacturing Match BCG, LaRue Tactical Handguard - Free float, Black Rain Ordnance Upper and Lower., Magpul PRS stock. Optics are a Leupold Mark-AR scope 6-18X, Noveske ambi-safety, Magpul BAD lever, Harris Bi-Pod. Bottom AR-15 has a 16" Noveske barrel with a Wilson Combat SS trigger, Young Manufacturing Match BCG, LaRue Tactical Handguard - Free float, Black Rain Ordnance Upper and Lower, Magpul UBR stock. Optics are a EOTECH hologram site, Noveske ambi-safety, Magpul BAD lever."

(continued from page 160)

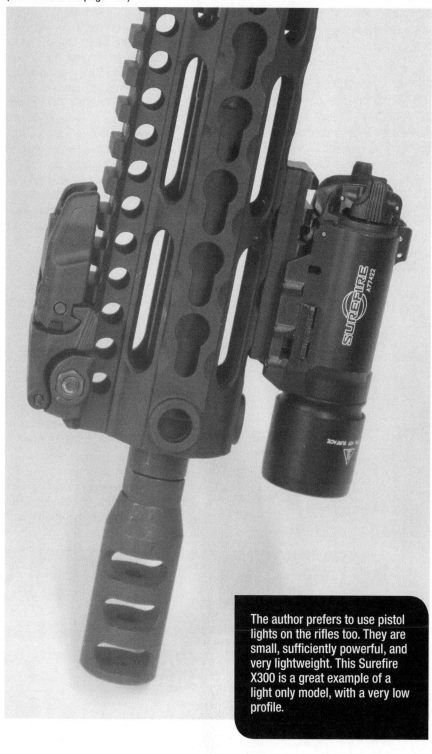

The author prefers to use pistol lights on the rifles too. They are small, sufficiently powerful, and very lightweight. This Surefire X300 is a great example of a light only model, with a very low profile.

aiming device. I am not aware of any ARs on the market that are factory supplied with lasers. Lasers are imprecise when used alone, but are excellent supplements for existing iron sights, and can be extremely helpful when learning to shoot the gun, since the dot bouncing around can give great visual feedback on shooting technique. Green lasers are less common and more expensive than red lasers, but are much easier to see, since the green wavelengths are in the center of the range of human visible light and red is at the lower end. Green lasers are great for daytime use and red for everything else. At night, green lasers appear so bright that they can actually display a visible beam in addition to the terminal dot, while the red lasers can wash out in the sunlight at quite close ranges or if the user is colorblind.

There is a bit of a dispute on how a laser should be zeroed. It is, in my opinion that the best place to mount a laser is directly below the bore of the rifle, parallel in all ways with the bore. When it is directly below, and zeroed for a particular distance, then you will only have to compensate for bullet drop, and you won't have to concern yourself with windage. If your laser is mounted below the barrel, say three inches, then all you have to do is find out how far out the bullet will be when it drops three inches. Let's say it's 50 yards. Anything below 50 yards will see the bullet striking high within three inches of the point of laser aim. Beyond that, the bullet will strike lower. But beyond 50 yards, you are no longer in imminent danger according to virtually any standard of self-defense in any state. The military and police applications differ here, but this book isn't written for them, it's for the average gun owner. Laser

you will find some examples of units that intuitively combine tactical lights with aiming "lasers," and that is the subject to tackle next.

LASERS

Frankly, in this author's opinion, these should only be used in conjunction with a gun that already has sights, and the "laser" should be set so that it is a point shooting device, not a precision

(continued from page 161)

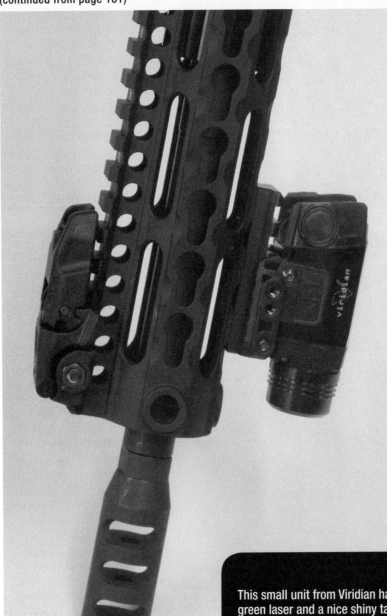

At some point downrange, the bullet will intersect the same vertical plane as the dot as its trajectory comes back to earth, but much farther to the right. This, in the end, composes a lot of variables to remember and you really don't need another set to try to remember.

It's much easier to simply set the laser as close to parallel with the bore as you possibly can. In this anecdotal case you will know the bullet will always strike a half inch to the left of the dot, and an inch or more below the dot, increasing as the range increases. Again, out to reasonable self-defense ranges you only need to know one thing: how low will it go? At normal self-defense range, that will be one inch and one inch only. And finally, having recommended all this, at normal self-defense range (under 10 yards), this all won't make a lick of difference anyway, since one inch off in any direction, if the gun is zeroed with the laser and is fired at center mass of the target, you will hit center mass.

Except when your sights are completely unusable, lasers are not a replacement for your sights, but a supplement. They make an

This small unit from Viridian has a green laser and a nice shiny tactical light all in one.

(right) As you can see here, the rather powerful light and laser are both slightly offset from center of the unit, but both are small and compact subunits that allow the entire package to have a small profile, as befits an assembly designed for pistol use. There is no reason that you can't use a pistol light on a rifle.

for the average gun owner. Laser aiming at anything on a human body between the eyebrows and groin with a maximum of three inches of vertical deviation is going to result in a hit.

Now let's say your laser is offset to the side and below the barrel. Let's say the laser is about one inch above the bore and a half inch to the right of the bore. If you zero the laser at ten yards, the bullet will hit the dot at that range. Up to ten yards, the bullet will strike below and to the left of the dot. Past ten yards the bullet will strike above and to the right of the dot.

You can see here the apparent difference between red and green lasers during the day and during the night. Both lasers are aimed at the same area about a foot apart. The sunlight will wash out the red beam in only a few yards. At night (photo was taken at 11:00pm, with extended exposure) the green laser is almost too bright, and it leaves a visible trace.

excellent point shooting aiming device if you are in a big hurry, and when you are using night vision. It's easy to line up the dot with whatever needs a hole in it. Unlike regular sights, lasers have batteries that can and do expire at the worst possible moment. Laser (and light) owners would do well to replace the batteries on a regular basis, whether the batteries appear to need replacement or not.

"They" say that lights and especially lasers can make a good intimidation tool. Certainly, bright lights have a very tangible effect, since the first thing anyone does when a bright light is shined in their face is to either squint, shy away, or throw their hands in front of their face, usually a combination of all of the above. "They" also say that a bouncing dot on a bad guy's chest works for that purpose too (we can probably thank Hollywood for that, something good for a change) but it is also a possibility that the attempt to intimidate may fail and the trigger may have to be pulled. Crimson Trace has a great series of advertisements that you have probably seen. It shows a dude sitting in a mostly empty parking lot with his gun sitting next to him on the floor. He looks exhausted and over-

It's a good thing to have both iron sights and a laser supplement, particularly if you are in a rush. Adding a light is also a big bonus. Having both the light and laser in the same assembly is a super good thing. The final lighting device is a 37mm flare launcher.

whelmed, arms on his knees staring at the floor. The caption reads, "The guy with the laser won."

Whether or not the laser works as an intimidation tool, it can certainly work to enhance sighting of the gun. The reason it works for that purpose so well is that when the stress and adrenaline start messing up your finely tuned body chemistry, you get tunnel vision and the ability to focus on anything but the threat diminishes. Well the dot is on the threat and can be recognized and utilized easier than if you try to focus on the sights of your rifle like you would have to do without the laser. So you will find that this particular author is in the bag when it comes to lasers on defensive firearms. If deploying the laser or light somehow makes a bad situation worse, then I suspect that nothing would have defused the bad situation in the first place, since you've already passed the point where you presented your gun (this is assuming a weapon mounted light and laser).

Ultimately, lights and lasers are non-lethal defensive tools and should be part of any gun owner's arsenal. Get the lights first, then the lasers. The lights are cheaper and are useful for identification, and you can upgrade to the more expensive combos or laser units as you can afford to do so.

A final product to mention is the type of laser product used for training rather than as a shooting accessory. Brownells sent me a SIRT AR bolt from Next Level Training. This thing is really neat. One of the things that instructors always tell you to do is dry fire practice. This is when you take your UNLOADED UNLOADED UNLOADED gun and get used to the trigger pull, just as an experience in muscle memory, and trigger pull when aiming, to see how much your trigger pull instills movement in the firearm. If you can pull the trigger without the sights moving, you are golden. You can really measure this by having a laser, and this is the third excellent reason to have a laser: for training purposes.

The SIRT AR bolt replaces your bolt carrier and charging handle assemblies and uses a connector piece to mate with your trigger. This piece, when the trigger is pulled, activates a laser, which projects through the bore and out the barrel. Pull the trigger, release, do it again. Every time you pull the trigger, the laser illuminates and shows you on the wall or whatever. It's "semi-auto" in a way, too, since it automatically resets. Pull the trigger like you are doing a mag dump and you will see rapid dots on the target, hopefully all in the same place. This item incorporates the laser and trigger-pull practice into one unit. For the price of an extra bolt carrier assembly, it is also a pretty good deal.

(right) The SIRT laser training tool looks like this. Sort of reminds me of a cleaning rod guide. The round linear nature of the AR upper receiver bore makes it easy to fabricate all sorts of tools.

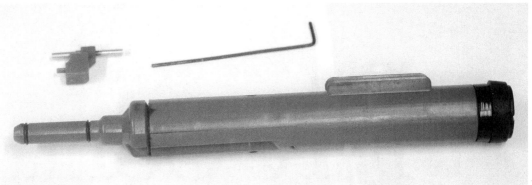

(left) The SIRT uses a connector to bridge the trigger SIRT gap. It is adjustable and sits right on the safety tab's front end. Care must be taken that the finger at the top actually goes into the hole in the bottom of the laser assembly.

(below) The SIRT laser is fully installed and ready to be practiced with. Installation requires removal of the bolt carrier assembly and the charging handle. Adjustments to the beam can be made through the ejection port or up through the magazine well where there are adjustment set screws. Magazine changes can be practiced at the same time.

Fire Control:
Triggers and Such

I f the barrel is the heart of a rifle then the fire control unit is the brain. Or at least the transmitter from the real brain, anyway – the brain in your head. That brain can be faulty, or have a bad interface with the transmitter. This is why we sometimes have gun safety issues like accidental or careless discharges, and thus why we can't have nice things. While it's possible to have accidental discharges that don't involve the fire control group (been there, done that), the vast majority of discharges, whether intentional or not, are the result of manipulating the fire controls. So what exactly do I mean by "fire control"?

I'm glad you asked. The term "fire control" encompasses all the parts necessary to initiate firing of the gun, and the parts necessary to keep it from firing. In a nutshell, on the AR series of rifles, it is the trigger, hammer, disconnector, safety/selector, trigger/hammer pins, and the associated springs or other miscellaneous hardware you might find. I have not mentioned the most important part of the FC unit, your own brain, because that should be a given, since you know the three NRA rules of gun handling by heart now, don't you?

It is these parts that cause the gun to fire. You pull the trigger, which releases the hammer, and the hammer then rotates forward to strike the firing pin. When the gun fires and cycles, the bolt

carrier then pushes the hammer back so that it is caught by the disconnector. The disconnector is attached to the trigger and, when the trigger is released, the disconnector then releases its hold on the hammer. The hammer then rotates forward slightly and the notch on its bottom then "resets" on the sear (the sear is the forward edge of the trigger; unlike on most guns, the AR has the sear and trigger combined into one piece) and the gun is ready to fire again. The selector can then be rotated to "SAFE" which restricts the movement of the trigger to prevent the sear from losing its grip on the hammer. Rotating the selector to "FIRE" will then allow the whole gosh-darned process to start over.

Wrong fire control. Author's note: You should have this kind of fire control too.

This is the fire control department. It has its own compartment.

SAFETY AND DISCONNECTOR

It should be said right now that anything mechanical will eventually break. For example, the disconnector does wear and might begin working poorly, allowing the hammer to skip past the sear on the trigger reset. This will eventually happen and requires the replacement of the disconnector, a not expensive part. I highly recommend purchasing a spare disconnector and keeping it as a spare part. Also, do not attempt to alter the disconnector. It is made the way it is for a reason. Don't screw with it. If the disconnector does not work correctly, and you are the one that intentionally made it work incorrectly and it winds up firing more than one shot at a time, then you are asking for not more than 20 years in the slam and/or a not more than $250,000 fine. If it's not working right, replace it. Match trigger units always have their own disconnectors and often times those disconnectors are of a much refined design.

The safety/selector rarely breaks. If it does, you will likely wind up somehow snapping the handle off. Replace it. I wouldn't keep a spare, since this is unlikely as heck to happen. Still, if it does, just

Several different disconnectors are shown here, with the standard on the top. These should not be altered, and when they stop working they should be replaced.

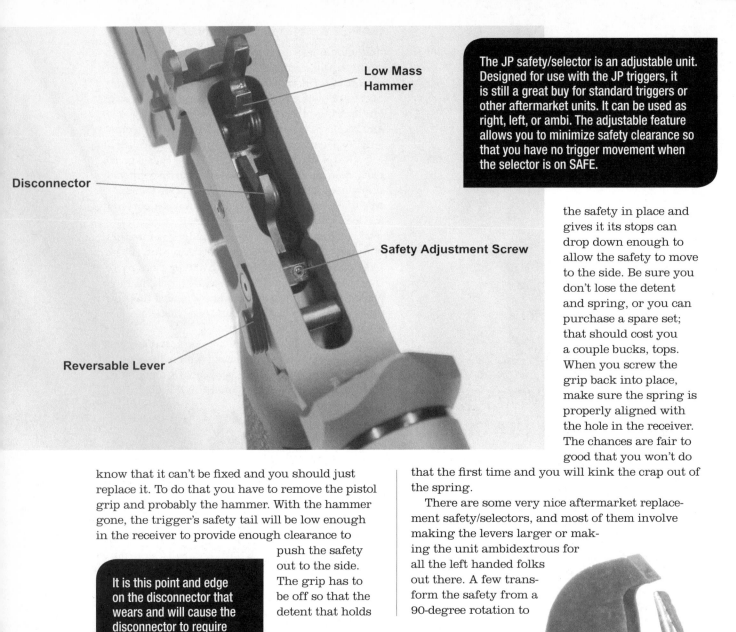

Low Mass Hammer

Disconnector

Safety Adjustment Screw

Reversable Lever

The JP safety/selector is an adjustable unit. Designed for use with the JP triggers, it is still a great buy for standard triggers or other aftermarket units. It can be used as right, left, or ambi. The adjustable feature allows you to minimize safety clearance so that you have no trigger movement when the selector is on SAFE.

know that it can't be fixed and you should just replace it. To do that you have to remove the pistol grip and probably the hammer. With the hammer gone, the trigger's safety tail will be low enough in the receiver to provide enough clearance to push the safety out to the side. The grip has to be off so that the detent that holds

It is this point and edge on the disconnector that wears and will cause the disconnector to require replacement. This is also something that should not be modified in any way or the rifle will become unsafe to fire.

the safety in place and gives it its stops can drop down enough to allow the safety to move to the side. Be sure you don't lose the detent and spring, or you can purchase a spare set; that should cost you a couple bucks, tops. When you screw the grip back into place, make sure the spring is properly aligned with the hole in the receiver. The chances are fair to good that you won't do that the first time and you will kink the crap out of the spring.

There are some very nice aftermarket replacement safety/selectors, and most of them involve making the levers larger or making the unit ambidextrous for all the left handed folks out there. A few transform the safety from a 90-degree rotation to a 60-degree rotation. Some folks like that, some don't care, but an ambi safety is much more comfortable to use when it only has a 60-degree throw. Regardless of the style, the safety is designed to prevent the movement of the trigger, or in actuality, to restrict the movement. Since factory triggers have gargantuan levels of sear engagement, the trigger will move a good amount when the selector is on "SAFE." The match trigger upgrades almost always, when installed, result in much less safety clearance, and some will remove it altogether, because the sear engagement on match triggers is so much smaller.

TRIGGER AND HAMMER

So now we look at the parts that we manipulate to make the rifle go !!!BANG!!!. The trigger and hammer interaction is very important and it is this interface that gives the rifle a trigger pull's feel. If the interaction is gritty because of less than ideal surface finishes, then the trigger pull will be gritty and jumpy and likely will be somewhat inconsistent. If the surfaces are polished like glass then the release will be very smooth. Do not mess with the sear/hammer engagement surfaces. This is a gunsmith job and he, if he's smart, won't do it either because the results will be temporary. Factory triggers and hammers tend to be only case hardened and playing around will often break through the hard skin to the (relatively) soft core of the trigger/sear. When this happens the sear will take a beating every time the hammer resets on the trigger, since on factory sets there is a big jump from when the disconnector releases the hammer and when the hammer resets on the sear. This can in short order require replacement. Your gunsmith will (should) suggest just buying a purpose-built, better trigger. You are better off doing this, even if the new fire control unit is four times what he would charge for smoothing out the factory trigger. No matter what he does, the trigger pull will not be as quality as a purpose-built match unit, and the match units

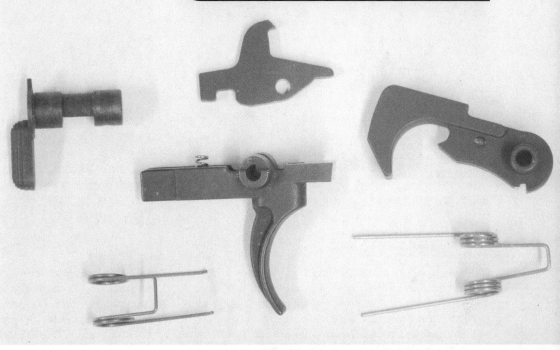

(below) The standard hammer and trigger come on the vast majority of factory rifles. They work well and can be horrible to halfway decent in pull quality.

(bottom) This is a prototype of yet another trigger from JP. This trigger has a round shoe that freely rotates. The idea is that the slight rolling motion compensates for the trigger finger's constantly changing orientation on the trigger during the pull. This trigger has a very different (but not in a negative way) feel to it. It also is a direct, non-adjustable replacement for factory triggers, with better sear geometry and way better surface finishing on the engagement surfaces.

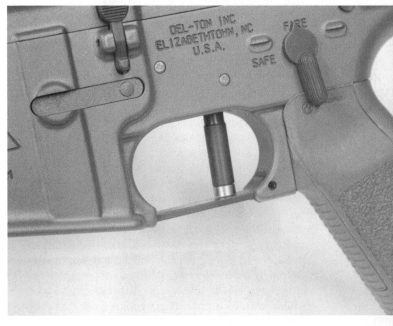

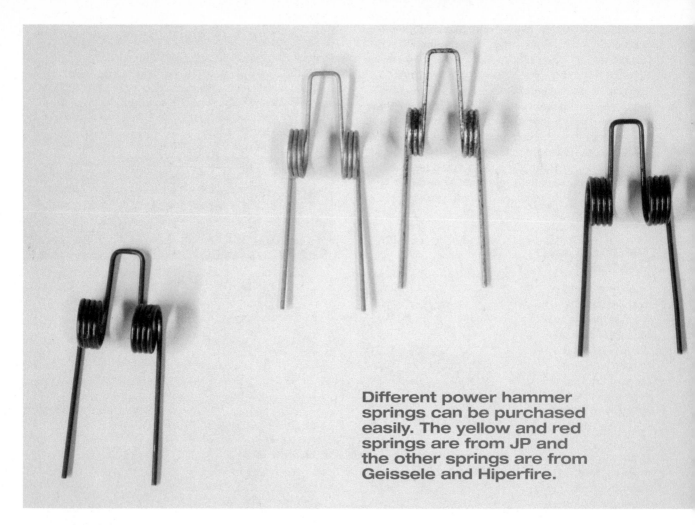

Different power hammer springs can be purchased easily. The yellow and red springs are from JP and the other springs are from Geissele and Hiperfire.

are generally made to a much more refined metallurgical and mechanical standard than the factory units. Better polished engagement surfaces, better interface geometry, better hardening, better machining and reduced sear engagement, not to mention perhaps reduced overtravel and pull weight, all combine to form a much better package than a factory FC unit.

So let's look at two of the drop in FC units that I always mention to people. Please understand that these are not the only quality units on the market, by far, but simply the two that I have had the most success and experience with, and for good reason: they are both really good. One is a single stage and the other is a two stage trigger. What's the difference you ask? Single stage triggers have short travel and break (release the hammer) with the full trigger pull weight at one time. Two stage triggers have a long travel, divided into two parts, the take up (or pre-travel) and the break. It is typical for most of the weight in two stage triggers to be felt in the pre-travel first stage, with the rest felt in the break itself. This gives the impression of a much lighter trigger. Where a quality four-pound single stage trigger will break with little movement when pulled with four pounds of pressure, the two stage

unit might exhibit a pre-travel pull weight of three pounds, and then break with the extra one pound of pressure exerted on the second stage. This gives the impression of a one-pound trigger pull, when it's still really a four-pound trigger pull.

There are adherents to both ideas and they rarely cross over. Some guys think the longer pull and second stage of a two stage trigger is safer. The single stage guys will say the pull weight is deceptive and to give it to them all at once. Decide for yourself which you like. Most guys who have transitioned from older military rifles like the M-14 or M1 prefer the two stage, as will most Service rifle competitors. Younger guys that went straight to the AR from the average traditional hunting rifle and the tactical competition crowd almost always prefer the single stage trigger. It just seems to work out that way.

On most single stage triggers, the biggest determinant of trigger pull weight is the hammer spring, followed by the trigger return spring, and then the quality of the sear engagement. Indeed there are several examples of different strength hammer springs, notably by JP Enterprises and Wolff Gunsprings, to allow adjustment of this trait. Furthermore, the tweaking of the hammer

spring legs will allow a small amount of adjustment of the hammer spring as well. On two stage triggers, this has less effect because of the completely different design of the parts and how they interact. The pull weight is much more a function of the trigger return spring and the disconnector spring. The second stage is formed by the disconnector contacting the hammer during the trigger pull, and so the disconnector spring is the determinant of the second stage pull weight.

Anyway, the two stage trigger that seems to be top dog right now is the Geissele series. There are a number of variants of the Geissele trigger unit but all are based on the old Browning double-hook design that you might see in other guns like M-14s, M1s, AKs, and Benelli shotguns. Some of them are adjustable for sear engagement and overtravel. These triggers have very smooth pulls and resets and, if they are adjustable, you can vary how much of the pull is felt on the second stage. They come as a full set with all the springs and their own oversized pins.

Probably the most popular single stage trigger is the JP Enterprises match trigger set. It incorporates a trigger that has an adjustment screw for minimizing overtravel, with very refined sear engagement fixed by the design of the hammer. The disconnector is easily adjusted by means of a set screw to perfect its timing, and the package also comes complete with oversized anti-walk pins and a replacement safety/selector that is set screw adjustable so that you can set the trigger and then set the safety to prevent any trigger movement when on "SAFE." The JP kit also comes with two hammer springs of different strengths.

On both of these triggers, the set screws are not "adjustable" as you might normally understand the term. They are intended to act as initial set up adjustments and then they are to be left alone. The set screws are to be thread locked in place once set and left that way, in a semi-permanent fashion. Indeed, the JP unit is shipped with high strength Loc-Tite to be used in installation to immobilize the screws fully, but allow for removal with the

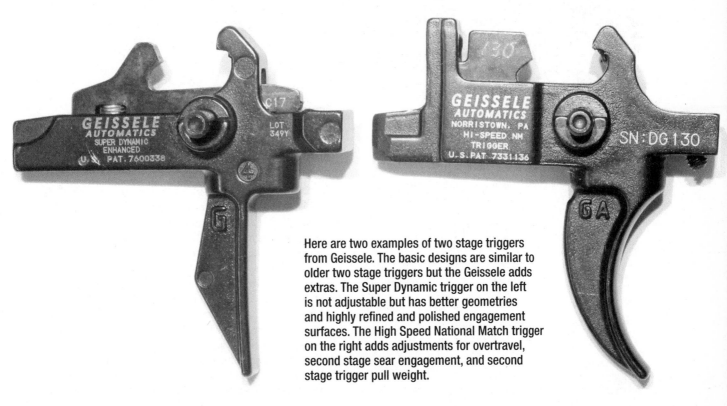

Here are two examples of two stage triggers from Geissele. The basic designs are similar to older two stage triggers but the Geissele adds extras. The Super Dynamic trigger on the left is not adjustable but has better geometries and highly refined and polished engagement surfaces. The High Speed National Match trigger on the right adds adjustments for overtravel, second stage sear engagement, and second stage trigger pull weight.

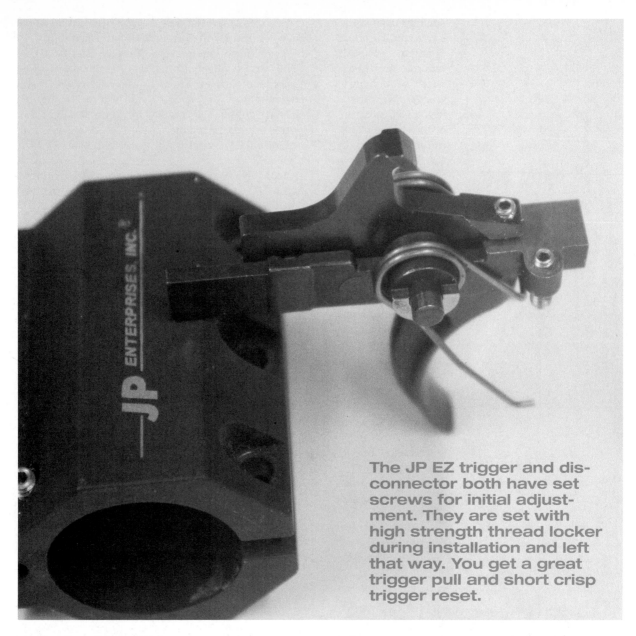

The JP EZ trigger and disconnector both have set screws for initial adjustment. They are set with high strength thread locker during installation and left that way. You get a great trigger pull and short crisp trigger reset.

application of heat. Set it and leave it. If this is done correctly (and it's not difficult to do) you will have a fire control set up that is so well refined and fine-tuned that there really is no comparison even to the best factory trigger set up. Furthermore, they are completely reliable and will have a longer service life than the standard factory FC assembly.

The point of the oversized pins is to more precisely fit the hammer and trigger, which generally have holes that are significantly bigger in diameter than the standard factory pins. The normal sizes are the results of tolerance run-out based on the mil-spec. The better the fit the more consistent the trigger pull will be, as long as the parts are still free moving with no binding, of course. Many aftermarket triggers will come with their own pins and they should be used in place of the original trigger pins.

MODULAR TRIGGER UNITS

Probably the easiest means of bettering your trigger pull is to install a modular trigger assembly. These have become all the rage. There are a number of examples available and every one of them is a genuine improvement on the factory FC. They will either be single or two stage, though mostly single stage. They install pretty much the same all over. The point is pretty much a function of your own ease. Emplacing a modular unit is child's play compared to installing one of the non-modular units and is quick and simple, if somewhat more expensive at times. You pull the existing safety to the side in the same procedure you followed earlier for the non-modular units. While in some cases in the non-modular units you can get by without doing this, you will pretty much always have to do so with the modular units.

Once you have the safety and pistol grip rein-stalled you simply go and shoot the gun. You don't have to set up any adjustments (while some, nota-bly the Timney unit, have adjustments, they are treated just like on the JP trigger, as set ups only; you don't mess with them). One of the original ideas was that if you had only one lower and you used it for two very different things, such as self-defense and varmint hunting, you could have two modular trigger units, one with a low pull weight for vaporizing rodents, and one with a pull weight more suitable for shooting Commies. Full brutal honesty took over and you don't see that market-ing much anymore, if only because the average AR owner typically winds up buying a second rifle for the second task. There's not much validity in that marketing point anymore, as a result of this.

There are only two minor drawbacks to the modular trigger, since the cost in my opinion greatly offsets the installation time and hassle. The first is that only some of them have some means of immobilizing them in the lower receiver. The ones

The new Hipertouch trigger is very unique. It uses two bal-ancing springs to lighten the trigger pull, essentially push-ing in opposition to the hammer spring when the hammer is cocked. When the trigger is pulled the hammer spring rotates the hammer forward and the springs that opposed before now enhance the hammer's fall. By adding heavier springs (the trigger pack has several sets) the hammer fall is faster and heavier, and the trigger pull is lighter. This trig-ger can be a good solution to the guns firing old Combloc cartridges with hard-hard primers such as 5.45x39 and 7.62x39. And it fills up all that extra space in the FC pocket of the receiver.

This is a small selection of modular triggers avail-able for ARs. The gold one is from Timney, the squarish one is from CMC Triggers, the gray one on the left is from Wilson Combat, and the black one is an AR Gold from American Trigger Corp. These range in price from around $150 to over $300. But they are easy peasy to install.

that don't place some sort of tension from the hous-ing to the receiver, and will exhibit play that takes away from the quality of the trigger pull feel. The other is that no modular trigger currently made can get to be quite as nice as the single install non-modular units, because each module is designed as a one-size-fits-all assembly. From a gunsmith perspective this is a big deal, but from a consumer perspective it really isn't all that bad. The modular trigger pulls, like the non-modular units, are so far above the standard factory models in perfor-mance and feel that there's no point in even com-paring them to those antiquated, inferior things.

So after free floating your barrel and hand-guards, the next thing I'd recommend greatly is installing a match grade trigger. Just make sure you take the time to get used to the vastly im-proved trigger pull. It's not unusual for someone who is used to the factory stuff to finger bounce a match trigger, just because it is so much more refined. This is a good time to remember to keep your finger off the trigger until you are ready to fire, and then be in for a world of goodness when you have a crisp, light, quality trigger release.

CHAPTER 13

Miscellaneous Accessories: Everything Else

I felt like I had to make a short miscellaneous chapter since there are several things that really don't fit to well into the previous sections of this book, and some of those are quite popular. These things tend to be various sorts of add-ons that often are also hang-ons, and are attached to the handguards or other part of the gun.

FORWARD VERTICAL GRIPS

This is probably the second most popular, and it derives greatly from the U.S. military, like many other aspects of the AR accessories market. The M-16A4 and the M4 are often seen with vertical foregrips under the handguard. To be fair, lots of people hold their rifles as if there were a vertical foregrip on their guns by placing their support hand around the magazine well. With the forward grip the hand can still be used vertically (many owners believe this give better leverage than if the hand was flat and wrapped around the handguard) just further down the barrel, where you will have arguably better recoil impulse control and dexterity. Vertical grips are seldom used in competition, but on tactical and defensive guns they are very common.

Filling the same role but in a slightly different manner are the angled foregrips. While the majority of forward grips are perfectly vertical, essentially a hollow aluminum or plastic tube attached to the bottom Picatinny rail of the handguard, the angled foregrip, as typified by the MagPul AFG models, attaches in a similar pattern, with a much larger footprint. The grip itself is literally angled, around 30 degrees

from horizontal, which is a much more (in this author's opinion) ergonomic and comfortable means of approaching the issue. It does take up a much larger section of rail than a vertical grip, which isn't necessarily a bad thing.

A rather important note is warranted here. Generally, if you have a pistol, you may not attach a separate, second, protrusive pistol grip to it or it becomes subject to the National Firearms Act. So then, if you have an AR pistol and you attach one of these VFGs to it you are committing a felony. There is an exception based on barrel length but I'm not going to go into it here.

The MagPul AFG does not in ATF's opinion constitute a protrusive pistol

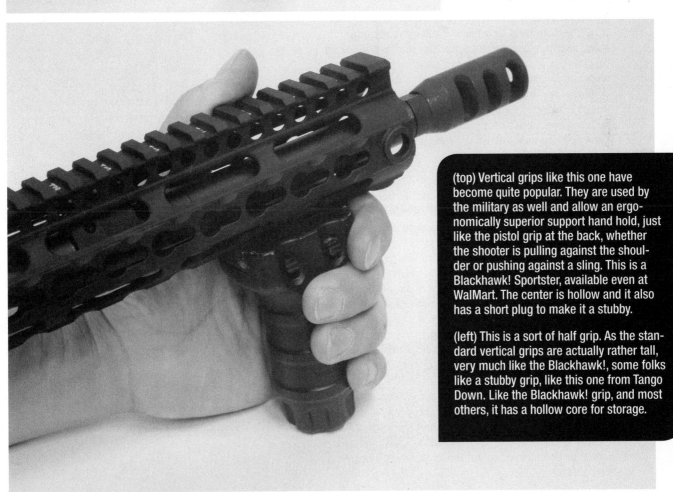

(top) Vertical grips like this one have become quite popular. They are used by the military as well and allow an ergonomically superior support hand hold, just like the pistol grip at the back, whether the shooter is pulling against the shoulder or pushing against a sling. This is a Blackhawk! Sportster, available even at WalMart. The center is hollow and it also has a short plug to make it a stubby.

(left) This is a sort of half grip. As the standard vertical grips are actually rather tall, very much like the Blackhawk!, some folks like a stubby grip, like this one from Tango Down. Like the Blackhawk! grip, and most others, it has a hollow core for storage.

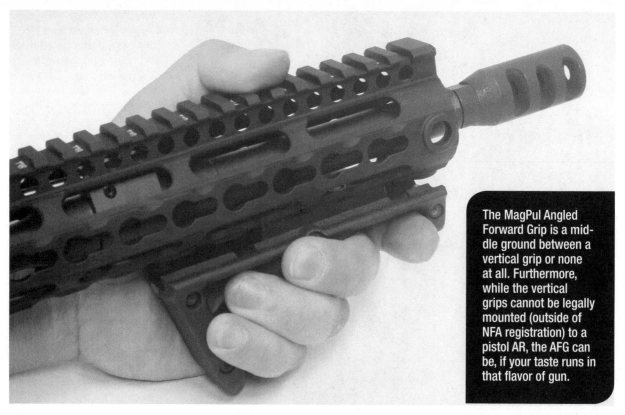

The MagPul Angled Forward Grip is a middle ground between a vertical grip or none at all. Furthermore, while the vertical grips cannot be legally mounted (outside of NFA registration) to a pistol AR, the AFG can be, if your taste runs in that flavor of gun.

grip and so may be used in this instance. Let's face it. AR pistols tend to be pretty heavy and using some sort of supportive apparatus under the barrel just makes sense, and the AFG fits that bill pretty well.

There are dozens of types of forward grips produced by almost as many companies. You shouldn't have any trouble finding one you like. You can even get one at Walmart nowadays.

SLINGS

If you have a rifle you will probably want a sling. It's just convenient to carry a rifle over your shoulder over distance rather than in your hand. Slings can also offer additional stability when firing. There are three main types of slings available: single point, two point, and three point slings. Traditional slings that attach at the front and back of the rifle are considered to be two point slings. Single point slings are generally a loop that wraps over one's torso with an extension that clips to the rifle, generally on the buttstock or on the receiver where the stock attaches. Three point slings are a hybrid of the single and two point styles, where a loop goes around the body with an extension to the gun. However, this extension then splits to attach to the rifle front and back like the two point sling. Unless you are a real fighting man, then you will likely be best served by a standard, traditional, two point sling.

A good sling will usually run over thirty bucks and can hit over a Franklin if you get really picky. Still nothing can replace freeing up your hands by hanging the gun on your body. So let's look at a few specific slings that you might want to buy.

Traditional slings

There are so many types of this sling that it would be literally impossible to cover all of them. They run from a piece of string tied around the front sight tower and stock to a multi-component, heavily padded, fully one hand adjustable quick release super sling. Slings will take up at least a quarter aisle in a sporting goods store like Gander Mountain or Cabelas and as a result choosing can sometimes be intimidating. So how about we look at it by application. Let's take it as a default for now that every long gun should have a sling, because at some point you are going to want to not carry it in your hand.

(opposite bottom) The Viking Tactics slings (the VT1 is unpadded, the VT2 is thickly padded), can be adjusted very quickly for tightness. In this pic your friendly author is cinching up to hold the carbine close to the chest for security and general carry.

(above) Your friendly author is about to get decidedly unfriendly with the local commies outside the back door (your friendly author has an enhanced fantasy life). In preparation, he loosens the sling so the gun can be maneuvered with greater dexterity by pulling the paracord tab on the cinch to expand the sling.

(below) Viking Tactics also makes a sling adaptor for Picatinny rails. Attach it to a rail and it offers you a QD sling swivel stud receptacle.

This more traditional style leather loop sling is designed for National Match use, but serves as a great traditional style sling for standard over-the-shoulder carry.

Single point slings

These are well represented in the tactical/self-defense world. Most, if not all, incorporate some sort of rapid release mechanism on the gun/sling interface, such as a hook or QD swivel, or on the loop in the form of a quick release buckle. They have one attachment point on the gun, and this usually is placed on the buttstock, either at the upper rear corner at the heel, or at the intersection of the stock and the receiver, sort of in the middle of the gun.

There are a number of aftermarket carbine stock plates that incorporate some sort of sling attachment point on them. Because of this placement, the long gun in question can be raised from the carry position quickly and can even be transitioned to either shoulder with little effort. When the shooter is finished, he can lower the gun so that it literally dangles in front of his chest. Traditionally, the rather short sling goes from the gun to a loop that the shooter places so that the loop crosses diagonally over one shoulder and under the other. Here is where there is a rather notable downside. The rifle tends to want to hang in such a manner as to make a male shooter appreciate the benefits of the internal placement of the reproductive organs of the female shooter. Single point-slung guns are often slung with one hand on the gun to control the

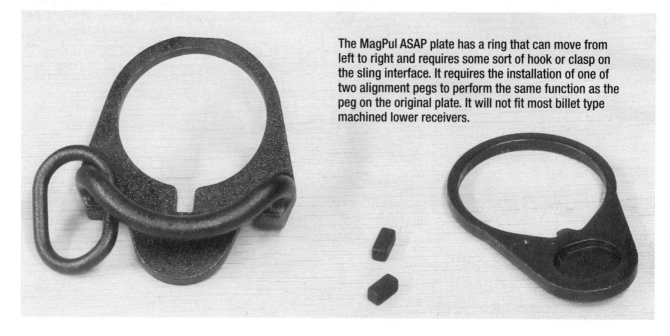

The MagPul ASAP plate has a ring that can move from left to right and requires some sort of hook or clasp on the sling interface. It requires the installation of one of two alignment pegs to perform the same function as the peg on the original plate. It will not fit most billet type machined lower receivers.

(top) Most single point sling attachments for ARs are incorporated into aftermarket carbine receiver plates. This unit from Midwest Industries uses a QR-type of interface but it slips over the carbine stock nut and clamps in place. It is installed on an AR pistol. An AR pistol can benefit (so can a rifle) from a single point sling. It can hang across the body or along the side if you like.

(bottom left) This is a Blackhawk! Sportster single point sling. It is inexpensive but still quite rugged and uses a snap clip to hook onto a sling loop, in this case a MagPul ASAP.

(bottom right) The firearm with a single point sling is quick to deploy. It does tend to flop around when hanging, so the wise male will spare a hand to steady it at times. No more children for the author.

bounce and sway to avoid some singularly male discomfort. This sort of mitigates the advantages of having a sling, since the point is to keep your hands free to protect your face when you trip and fall, and it tends to make the gun feel a little heavier because you are often resting one hand on it to keep the whole set up from sterilizing you. The extra hand weight can be felt, particularly if you are just looping the sling about your neck.

Three point sling

The three point sling started out with tactical applications but has proven to be useful in other areas as well. It's really just a refinement of the normal two point sling. People used to, and still do, carry their rifles equipped with a traditional two point sling by looping the sling over their neck and hanging the rifle across their chests, or alternatively, by making the sling really long and carrying it cross shouldered but with the gun in front of them, rather than behind them. The point is to be able to make use of the load bearing nature of the sling yet be able to quickly aim and fire the rifle without having to unsling first. The three point sling makes this possible, but in a more comfortable fashion.

These slings are usually set up in a way that there is a sling attachment point up toward the muzzle and an attachment point back toward or on the stock. These points are almost always at the heel of the stock and the forward end of the handguard or forend, not on the bottom but rather on the support hand side of the forend. This placement keeps the gun relatively upright when slung preventing discomfort that might be caused by magazines extended below the gun that would be caused if the sling attachment points were in the traditional bottom arrangement.

The nice thing about the three point set up is that it is almost as versatile as the single point sling as far as shoulder transitions and quick sighting from rest. Also, it's not as uncomfort-

able to the masculine mentality, since it tends to cause the rifle to hang slightly to the weak side, or is cinched up so tightly to the chest that it does not hang below the waist. Most three point slings have quick using adjustments to them so that shoulder transitions are easier or so that the sling can be converted to be used as a two point sling. The thing that typifies three point slings is the habit of connecting the front and rear attachment points on the gun and then both points to the loop or whatever is retaining the whole assembly to the shooter's body. This forms a triangle, and hence the "three point" moniker.

The means of attaching a sling to an AR have been heavily refined from the old stud system seen on traditional hunting rifles. Most sling systems on ARs recently are incorporating the quick release or detach pushbutton system. The loop is attached to a swivel mechanism that locks into matching holes in the rifle. These holes are commonly formed into the handguard and stock units. Some of the replacement carbine stock plates have these too. A large button is in the center of the swivel and depressing it unlocks four ball bearings in the shank of the swivel and the assembly can be easily pulled from the socket. It can be done with gross movements, such as when the hands are gloved, and can be reinserted just as easily. While not pretty and somewhat bulky, this is the only good way to be able to attach and detach your sling to your rifle with any speed. Plus the traditional sling placement points on a traditional rifle, the bottom, are not suited to a rifle with a projecting magazine and pistol grip.

(above) The Specter CQB sling is meant to be attached to an M4 or CAR buttstock. It has a completely secure front attachment utilizing the existing bottom sling loop as well as a wrap-around nylon strap.

(below) The front sling interface is paired with a simple loop strap at the rear. The sling can be worn with both straps together for a two point function, or encircling the torso for a three point function.

(opposite left) This is a 3 point sling from the makers of DuraCoat, Lauer Custom Weaponry. It's a nice pretty green and has a quick release buckle to get it off your torso in a hurry if need be.

(opposite right) The Spec Ops Mamba is a very versatile sling that can be arranged as a single point, two point, or even three point sling. Very helpful instructions are included for the AR and other firearms. Here it is set up as a two point sling, but with both points attached to the buttstock using two Quick Detach push button loops. Brownells sells QD swivel loops by the pair, made by Uncle Mike's. Not shown is the additional length of webbing that is used to turn the sling into a three point model, which also includes a large stirrup end for wrapping around an A2 stock.

There are a number of ways to use the sling to "sling up" or support the rifle, though the know-it-alls will likely say there are only a couple "proper" ways. Just do it somehow so that the sling partially supports and steadies the rifle when firing offhand. Here is one way.

(below) Here's another way.

SLINGING UP FOR STABILITY

Whatever your preference for sling type or attachment type, it should be stressed that almost any rifle is going to benefit from the attachment of a sling, purely for the ease and utility of carrying it around. Home defense guns would be the exception where I would expect a sling to get in the way. This kind of rifle should be short and handy and you aren't going to be toting it about much. Furthermore, the sling could snag on something just when you don't need that kind of headache, so if you have an AR for home defense, I'd recommend leaving the sling off. This is where the QD attachments come in really handy.

Aside from carrying your rifle, the sling has another use. Slings have long been used to add stability to a standing or sitting/kneeling shooting position. By wrapping the sling around the support arm, tension can be placed into the shooter/rifle combination that helps to settle the hold down a bit. There are several ways to do this, but what you are ultimately doing is attaching your elbow to your body via the sling, giving the support arm more support of its own.

Understand however, that you can easily flex the barrel or the entire gun doing this. There is a very good reason for free-floating the barrel with a large gap between the barrel and handguard or forend. When some guys sling up, they pull the forend or handguard, or tragically the barrel, an appreciable fraction of an inch out of line, through the sheer flexing of the part. This is why, on a gun from which you desire repeatable consistent accuracy, that you DO NOT attach the sling to the barrel, and why you MUST free-float the barrel and see that the sling attachment point is on the handguard or forend. There are a number of sling attachment points that affix to the barrel or the front sight tower of an AR, many of which use a Picatinny rail, and the sling loop is attached to that Pic rail. It's quite practical as long as you are okay with not hitting your target when you are slung up. If you must use one of these, be sure you shoot enough to get a good idea what the point of impact shift will be between the slung up shots and the non-slung up shots.

In competitions that allow sling usage when shooting, the most obvious being the Service Rifle match, the handguards are free floated with the sling swivel attached to the lower front end of the handguard tube, moved from the rear sight tower/gas block. The reason this is done is that service rifle guys sling up so tightly that it would very definitely change their points of impact. The downside is that the human body is not a CNC machine and cannot reliably exert the same amount of tension every time. Even if you could, your point of impact would change significantly when you

The AR is a decidedly non-ambidextrous rifle and there have been many attempts to make it more so. Some have taken the approach of modifying the receiver, which tends to require machined billet models, making them rather expensive. Much cheaper angles have been followed in regards to the most frustratingly monodextrous piece, the bolt catch. While there are several on the market, the cheapest and easiest to install is the B.A.D. Lever made by MagPul. It consists of a backer that affixes a long slender bent arm to the lever of the bolt catch. The arm extends down and through the front of the trigger guard to protrude slightly through to the right side of the receiver, just far enough for the trigger finger to manipulate it. This allows a much more normal application of the bolt catch to manually lock the bolt back. Extend finger, lift lever, and the left arm retracts the bolt to lock. This sequence, without such a lever, normally requires dismounting the rifle.

shot the same gun without slinging up. So as you see, the free-floating handguard or forend has a real purpose, to improve accuracy by removing stress from the barrel, particularly from the forces exerted upon the gun by the use of a sling. I have had customers call in asking why their gun shoots dead nuts on the bags at the range, but when they shoot from the shoulder the shots are grouping much less well and are six inches to the right. It's because they were slinging up on the rifle tightly enough to shift the group over and were doing it inconsistently enough that he groups were opening up like a shotgun pattern.

So the moral of the story is this: adding a sling to your rifle is a great idea in most situations and the best way to mount it is to do so in a way that minimizes interaction with the barrel in order to maintain precision in shooting. And, using a quick detach method is really handy too.

CHARGING HANDLES

There are the standard charging handles that come with every gun and then there are the rest. A great deal of effort has gone into making ambidextrous charging handles, which has resulted in much larger charging handles. A couple companies have gone to making replacement latches that are larger and easier to operate. The Badger Ordnance Tac Latches are wonderful, and as long as you don't mind the latch poking you in the belly you should be okay and happy to use them. A Gen II latch that is a bit smaller but still much larger than the standard handle latch can help alleviate that issue. Another option is to replace the handle entirely, and this is the approach that the ambi samples follow. The BCM Gunfighter charging handle is one that I really like. It is more robustly built than the standard handle, allows for more leverage if you have a stuck case, and has three options for latch size, all of which are significantly easier to manipulate than the mil-spec.

There are increasing numbers of side charging guns out there. The earlier and

still common method is to modify the upper receiver by adding a slot extending out the rear of the ejection port. A hole is drilled into the bolt carrier and a handle added. The more recent method is to redesign the upper receiver to incorporate a charging handle on the left side of the upper. Several different approaches have been used, notably by JP Enterprises, American Spirit Arms, and LWRC. These models are more expensive because

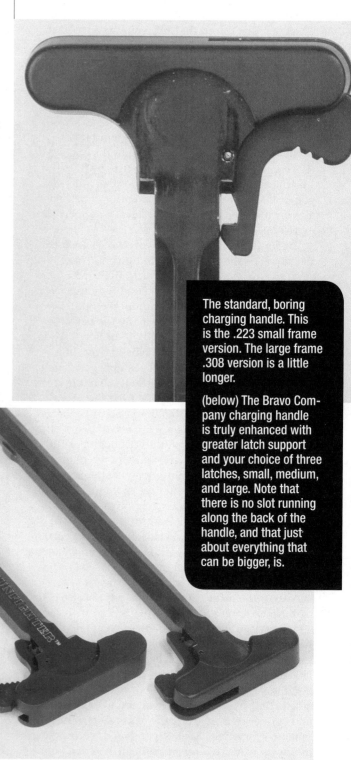

The standard, boring charging handle. This is the .223 small frame version. The large frame .308 version is a little longer.

(below) The Bravo Company charging handle is truly enhanced with greater latch support and your choice of three latches, small, medium, and large. Note that there is no slot running along the back of the handle, and that just about everything that can be bigger, is.

of the redesign, additional machining, and the relative complexity involved. They do have two very positive benefits. The side charging handle allows significantly greater leverage to be placed on a stuck operating system, and the rifle can be charged when mounted to the shoulder. A classic top-charge handle gun must be lowered (face removed) to be manually cycled. JP also makes a model with both top and side charge handles for the best of both worlds.

Here is one thing you should not do with any charging handle. You will eventually come to the point where you have a case head separation and wind up with a live round stuck inside the previ-

(below) Badger Ordnance has for years been making extended charging handle latches that have been the basis for many other companies' own designs. The Gen 1 tactical latch is large, square, and skeletonized. The Gen 2 tac latch is smaller, solid, and slightly more traditional looking. If you have a big gut these won't be the most comfortable, but they sure make the charging handle easier to find and grab without looking.

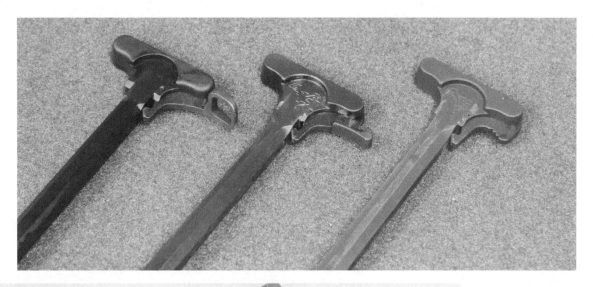

The PSC-11 upper receiver made by JP Enterprises is a high value upgrade that comes with top and side charging handles, as well as the jeweler's quality bolt carrier assembly. A rifle with a similar upper receiver minus the top charging handle can be purchased called the SCR-11. It is a good basis for a billet upper build and will match nicely with any forged lower, and especially nicely with most billet lower receiver assemblies manufactured by JP and other manufacturers, like this C3 Defense lower.

Samson Manufacturing makes a snazzy little tool that fits into several different pistol grip cores. The Survivor has several tools that you can find to be very handy. A small vial of oil is present as are scrapers, a brush, and most comfortingly, a broken case extractor.

(below) The broken case extractor is placed into the chamber where the hooks on the front grasp the case mouth, using the little prongs at the top. You then cycle the bolt to remove it (the extractor grasps the rim at bottom, just like with the case rim), which might require some force to do. When the broken case is extracted, the two halves of the tool are unscrewed and the case is removed from it. The broken case extractor usually, but not always, does the job, and if not, you should take the upper to a gunsmith.

ously fired case in the chamber. The only real way to fix this situation is to remove the magazine and use the "charging handle slam" to clear it. Do not hammer on the charging handle with a hammer. The handle will break or bend and become useless and require replacement. The correct means to clear this malfunction is somewhat unsafe but manageable if you are careful. You use the inertia of the bolt carrier combined with the rapid deceleration of the rest of the rifle. There is little to no chance of igniting the live round that is partially chambered since the firing pin is nowhere near the primer until the bolt is entirely closed, and in this case the bolt and carrier are nowhere near that state. It is a simple process of holding the charging handle and slamming the gun onto the butt plate with force, to try to jar the bolt carrier back and extract and eject the partially chambered round. This must be done with care and the muzzle pointed away from your face or anyone else's. If you can take the upper off the lower, you might pry the bolt carrier back and out of the receiver from the bottom. If you are uncomfortable (and you really ought to be uncomfortable) dealing with this situation, take the upper to a gunsmith. There could be several things at work here causing the issue.

Either way, once you get the live round out, you may need a broken case extractor to get the broken case out. This is one of the most invaluable tools you can have for an AR and you would be well advised to purchase one.

BRASS CATCHER

Some guys like to reload. A brass catcher is a means of not having to pick up your spent cases from the floor, by way of collecting them in some sort of bin attached to the gun. They are not perfect, as there are usually a couple cases per magazine

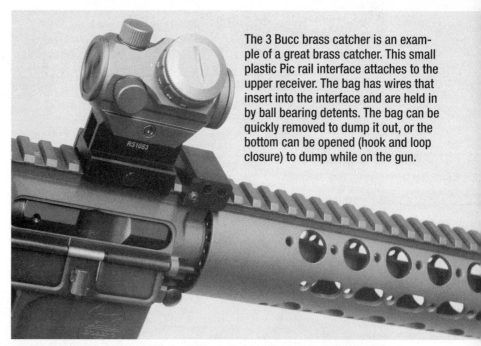

The 3 Bucc brass catcher is an example of a great brass catcher. This small plastic Pic rail interface attaches to the upper receiver. The bag has wires that insert into the interface and are held in by ball bearing detents. The bag can be quickly removed to dump it out, or the bottom can be opened (hook and loop closure) to dump while on the gun.

The 3 Bucc brass catcher mounted to a rifle. Like all brass catchers it is bulky, but the attachment interface is superior.

that get away, but the vast majority of cases are caught and can be dumped into a container of your choice for later reloading or recycling. The brass catchers tend to be bulky and may prevent the attachment of other accessories, but if you are one of those guys who wants to collect every case he fires, these are most definitely for you.

ASSORTED OTHERS

Everything except the kitchen sink is available for your guns and I won't be surprised when some wise ass decides to make a small kitchen sink miniature to actually attach to a Pic rail on the gun. You are spoiled for choices of stuff, so do some research and maybe test some stuff. Chances are you'll be able to find someone who likes it if you don't.

The SB-15 Pistol Stabilizing Brace made by SIGSAUER is an odd yet really cool AR pistol accessory. It does work as advertised.

(below) The Versapod bipods incorporate a quick release into the design, as well as a large hand stop interface.

Stabilizing braces

This is a pretty new concept and was initiated by SIGSAUER. The idea is that you make it easier to shoot an AR pistol by placing the brace over the pistol's buffer tube. The brace is a soft elastomer rubber that you insert your arm into. The brace wraps around your forearm and can be strapped down to rigidly hold the pistol to your arm. This brace has the general appearance of an M4 style buttstock and has become very popular in a very short amount of time. At first glance, a pistol with one of these braces might be confused for a short barreled rifle and this is why SIGSAUER made sure to have ATF approve it as a stabilizing accessory before they marketed it. It is quite effective at controlling muzzle flip in the pistols to which it is mounted, when strapped to the shooter's forearm.

Bipods and monopods

Okay, now we can get to the bipods, one of the most useful but least used accessories for an AR. A bipod is a device that you attach to the front of your rifle and has two legs by which you prop the rifle up above the surface of the bench or the ground.

The common style of bipod used with ARs is the small, lightweight, folding type that attaches via a Picatinny rail or sling attachment dome stud on the bottom of a handguard or rifle forend. I'd strongly encourage purchasing a bipod for use on a field rifle. The cheaper versions like the Rock Mount from Shooter's Ridge will do well for an amateur shooter. This model is closely modeled upon the Harris series of bipods but is made of thinner and lighter material. If you are not going to subject your gear to a beating, the Rock Mount is a good choice. If you want a much better resilience, go with the original Harris. These bipods typify this genre of accessory. The two legs use a spring to hold them in either the folded or extended positions. Folded, they point to the front, extended they point down. I should point out that folded forward is the correct position and this is addressed in the sidebar. Furthermore, all these folding bipods also have telescoping legs so you can adjust to some degree how far above the ground the rifle will be.

In the last couple years there have been a string of excellent folding bipod designs that have unfolded (ha) in the market. The Versapod is a cool

If the bipod legs fold, they should fold forward. The bipod in this picture is mounted backwards, though for an understandable reason. The legs are so long that they extend past the muzzle if they were to fold forward. However, the bipod is designed to dig into the ground. With the legs mounted to fold forward, the rifle can be pressed forward against recoil to lock the legs further and increase shooting stability and recoil control. If the legs are folded backwards (and if they cannot be locked open) you are not gaining as much stability as you could, and if you press forward, and you will, you may well collapse the legs entirely.

The Bobro is a newer design that is incredibly sturdy and versatile, and locks in place.

example that has a spud that inserts into a housing that attaches to the sling stud and serves as a handy hand stop. It has quick detach capability so you can pull it off quickly when you are bagging the gun back up for transport. It is quite heavy though and is best used on a bench gun or varmint rifle.

The Bobro bipod has an innovative locking mechanism that allows the shooter to open and close with little manipulation but will not do so without intent, by accident, and the legs lock open. Naturally, these more complex and featured units cost more, but the benefits are many to those who do a lot of outdoor shooting, whether it be hunting or competition.

It's hard to overstate the utility of a bipod. Even if you are not prone or bench-ridden a bipod can be used on a fence post or rock and since most of them pivot or have independently adjustable legs to some extent you can still obtain a level shooting position even if the ground is uneven in the extreme.

Cleaning and Maintenance

We're gonna assume that, since you've spent upwards of $500 on your first AR and upwards of $2000 on your second AR, you want to keep them spic and span so they keep operating at peak efficiency. Generally the principles of gun cleaning and maintenance that you follow (or not, depending on how particular you are about it) with your traditional rifle or pistol, if you own those, translate well to ARs. However, there are some differences and some additions that are typically not followed in the more traditional types of guns. Truthfully, the add-ons you will learn here should be just as scrupulously followed on your other guns too; it's just that AR owners tend to shoot their rifles much more than the old bolt action that Grandpa gave them, so they encounter all the likely problems that may not have been experienced by the older bolt actions or less-fired self-loaders.

It should be noted at this time that repeating firearms need more cleaning and mainte-nance than non-repeat-ing rifles. For example, a bolt action rifle with an internal magazine will have a higher incidence of malfunc-tions from any source than a breech loading single shot gun. (Gener-

ally, with all other things being "equal." I know, "apples and oranges," but work with me here.) For the same reason, self-loading firearms have more frequent incidences of malfunction than manually loading repeating guns. For example, the Rem-ington 7400 will malfunction faster than a 7600, even though the 7600 is merely a 7400 without a gas system. The more complex the mechanism, the higher the potential for breakdown; and the more required of the parts, the more frequent the breakdowns. ARs are not only self-loading (gas operated too) but they tend to get shot frequently (this is a good thing). This means that they will need, in general, more frequent cleaning, and thanks to the relatively dirty nature of the DI gas system, somewhat more specialized cleaning than most firearms.

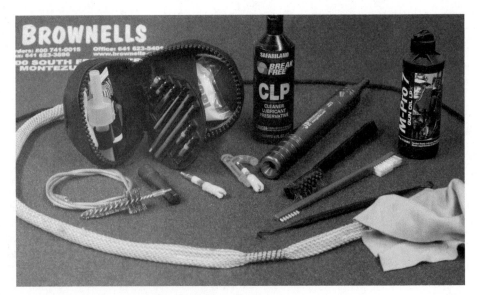

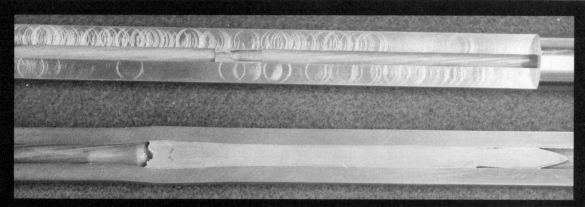

ARs tend to get shot lots more than other guns, and so barrel fouling can get pretty bad. It is believed that the upper barrel of these two cross sectioned samples failed because of extreme fouling. There are two bullet jackets but no bullet cores. The first jacket got stuck and the core continued on. The second bullet stuck into the first bullet's remaining jacket and its core also continued on out the barrel. Moral: If you shoot a lot, make sure you adopt a more frequent cleaning schedule. On the other hand, some calibers may be more prone to stuck bullets than others. The bottom barrel has six stacked up .300 Blackout bullets in it. The first five were subsonic that stuck. The very experienced shooter was unable to tell that these rounds did not exit, other than slightly increased recoil. He checked the fully ejected cases and found no indication of pressure problems. The final shot was a supersonic round and the difference in report was finally obvious, as was the blown out magazine. The receiver was undamaged. This was a 16" barrel with a pistol length gas port. This author highly recommends that owners of such characteristic barrels be aware of this. The subsonic .300 Blackout is a low pressure, short pressure curve round and the pistol length port barrel is the only one that will reliably fire and cycle both the subsonic and supersonic variations of the Blackout. If a shorter barrel length is available I'd recommend using it as a pistol build, rather than a rifle build, since some subsonic loads may not generate enough pressure to reliably function the gun. The problem with this example is not that a round stuck, but that the cartridge does not generate enough pressure to make such an event obvious to an experienced shooter, much less one who is less seasoned. Note that there is no bulging in the barrel until the supersonic round was fired.

BARREL MAINTENANCE

The barrel of your AR must of course be kept clean of obstructions. I still remember the famous words of wisdom from the movie "Surviving the Game", starring the marginally skilled actor, rapper, and pimp Ice-T, and the rather more capable Rutger Hauer. Ice-T finds a pistol and has a fellow homeless friend who exhorts Ice-T to always check the chamber for obstructions the first time you pick it up. Presumably, he meant "obstruction" to be synonymous with "live cartridge" as well as the cigarette that Ice-T used to blow up Rutger Hauer's Steyr AUG at the end of the movie. So what is the moral of the story? Obviously, it is that you shouldn't introduce a partially consumed cigarette into your rifle's chamber. This would be the same level of judgment required to put this steaming pile of horse crap movie in your DVD player.

Keep your barrel clean. Now, this doesn't mean you have to super scrub it every time you shoot five rounds. With an AR I'd recommend a barrel brushing and cleaning every 500 rounds, depending heavily on the ammo used. If you are shooting domestically manufactured, brass cased, pretty clean stuff, then go with this number. If you are shooting Com-bloc (past and future) steel cased ammo (and some other foreign brass cased ammo), then you will need to thoroughly clean your barrel far more frequently as these ammo types tend to leave large amounts of (usually non-corrosive) resi-due, which can harden in the barrel and chamber. If the steel cased ammo is lacquer coated (usually green, with the poly coated stuff being gray), then you will need to clean your chamber at least that often. The lacquer can burn off and stick to the chamber, and yes to the trolls this comment is sure to have uncovered, I have seen it with my own eyes.

The chamber is something that must be kept clean. Any stuff stuck to chamber walls can cause failures to extract of all sorts, and this could be from gunk, from poor machining in the chamber reaming process, or just random debris introduced to the

Cigarettes and guns don't mix. Cigarettes were also the subject that "Runaway Jury" was supposed to be about. No offense to Marlboro here, I hear some people like to smoke them. I just open the packages and throw them one by one at little children. It's particularly fun to put them in with the candy on Halloween.

Yuck!

chamber (think sand, grease, brass flakes, cigarettes, etc.). By far, the best way to keep your chamber clean is to use the appropriate AR chamber cleaning brush, available just about anywhere, including Brownells. Shoot, half the AR manufactures ship them with the guns. It is consumable and will wear out, particularly if you use it like I'm about to tell you to use it, but it's also only a couple bucks, so get a bunch of them and never run out. Put the brush on one segment of cleaning rod, put the rod in the chuck of your hand drill, slowly spin the brush as you insert it into the receiver (thereby partially cleaning the bolt way) and push it all the way into the chamber. Then spin it real good for a five count, with minor oscillation in and out. If you spin it fast when

This is a view into a chamber with a bunch of lacquer stuck in it. The lacquer is indicated by the extensive splotching in this image. This rifle came in for service because the case had jammed in the chamber, with the rim being ripped off by the extractor. The case had to be pounded out with force from the muzzle with a steel rod. Further examination of the chamber also revealed a very rough surface finish that required polishing.

(below) Domestic cases are all brass. Combloc cases are all steel. Go ahead and shoot either one, but the steel stuff generally leaves more residue and give you cause to follow a more frequent cleaning schedule. Also, if the case is gray, use it. If the case is green, save it for the AKs.

inserting it into the receiver, you run the risk of damaging the brush, the rod, and your face. But if you do this right, 99 times out of 100 the chamber and locking lug area will now be clean. If not, add a little solvent to the brush, but don't spin it at all until the brush is fully in the chamber. You can certainly spin it by hand, and this is what you will have to do if you are in the field, but employ the wonders of modern technology to help you in the shop or at home and use a hand drill.

If you are a neat freak, you might want to clean the outside of the barrel with some precision. The holes into the gas block and receiver through which the gas tube passes tend to get pretty gunky, and toothbrushing with basic solvent will clean these spots, since they can look kind of gnarly when the build-up becomes obvious. Piston-equipped uppers tend to vent under the handguard and will dirty that area. If you care about the surface of the barrel under the handguard then you can clean it up. Generally use the standard

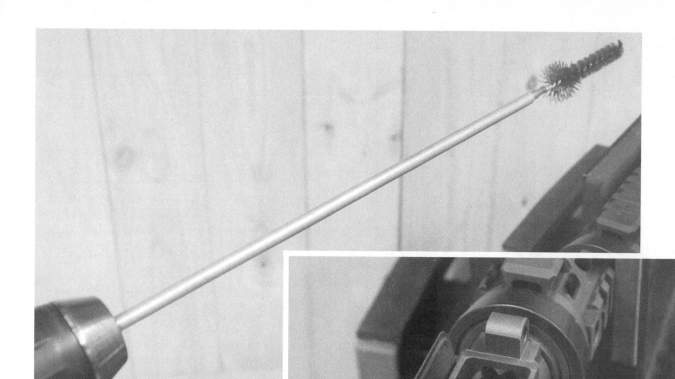

(above) This is a purpose-designed AR chamber brush attached to a single segment of cleaning rod (large frame might require two segments, depending on how long your segment is).

(right) Insert the brush from the rear of the upper receiver.

(below) Insert the brush into the chamber so that the largest diameter is inside the barrel extension and spin away for a few seconds with some minor push-pull action. The extension part of the brush is often made of steel bristles so don't push that largest diameter into the chamber. Trust me when I say that you can do it but don't want to.

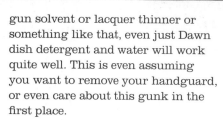

gun solvent or lacquer thinner or something like that, even just Dawn dish detergent and water will work quite well. This is even assuming you want to remove your handguard, or even care about this gunk in the first place.

A moment to examine the crown of the barrel should be taken on a semi-regular basis. This should only be necessary should you find your accuracy suddenly decreasing with no apparent reason, or if you drop the gun on the muzzle. It is vitally important that the transition edge between the bore and the muzzle face be kept undamaged. Any nicks or gouges to this interface will cause the bullets to exit the bore inconsistently. Or if you want to think about it this way,

Here is a false crown beginning to build up on the muzzle. A false crown is generally not something to concern yourself about if you have a nekkid barrel or one that has a flash hider attached to it. This one still has some time to go to build up to the point where it will start chipping.

the damage causes the bullet to upset slightly on departure, changing the point of impact, often significantly. Also, on guns that have muzzle brakes rather than nekkid barrels or flash hiders, after hundreds to several thousand rounds fired, a "false crown" can develop on the front face of the barrel. Powder residue builds up there because the muzzle brake sort of contains it more than a bare barrel or flash hider would. It can get quite thick. In fact, I've seen a couple ARs that had .020" - .030" thick false crowns on them. When the false crown chips (and they always will) the effect will be as if there was actual damage to the crown. Then the brake must be removed and the crown cleaned. You can carefully scrape it off with a brass tool, or even a dental scaler, and this is the quicker way, but you must be careful to scrape at the outer edge of the barrel and go nowhere near the bore. The stuff will chip off all the way to the bore if you scrape at the edges. The chips will fly with warp speed so this is one of those things that must be done with safety glasses. Honestly, everything gun related should be done with glasses, but this is one of those times when you really, really want to be wearing glasses.

The better way to clean the crown is to use cotton swabs and solvent to slowly dissolve away the false crown. It will take a while but will avoid the risk of damaging the crown or yourself. In either case, you can then use an extra-fine Scotch-Brite pad to polish the crown afterward. Take a small square about the size of the tip of your thumb, press it against the muzzle with your thumb and then rotate the barrel under your thumb. If done in this fashion, it will not damage the crown, but will scratch off any remaining stubborn stuff and put a nice finish back on the crown. Don't press real hard, just enough to put a slight amount of pressure on the pad.

If you are going to store the gun now, then run a lightly oiled patch through the bore and wipe the exposed outside of the barrel with a lightly-oiled rag. Even if the barrel is coated or stainless steel (which will rust in your safe, just you watch), a light coat of gun oil on the outside will look good for nobody to see it when it's in your safe, or when you take it out to impress your father-in-law when he visits.

Cleaning the actual bore should be done with the usual solvents available on the market. Ideally, the use of a standard one piece cleaning rod, or multi piece cleaning rod is perfectly sufficient, as is the use of the OTIS kit covered later in this chapter. Every cleaning kit will have instructions on how to do this so I won't cover it in detail here, save to say that clean means clean, no residue or odd colors coming out on the cleaning patches, and if it is done on a regular schedule (assuming you shoot a lot) you should not need to use any abrasives or super caustic chemicals.

MAGAZINES

Magazines are all disassembled by removing the bottom floorplate and pulling out the spring and follower. This process varies slightly with magazine design but is, in my experience, not difficult. You can buy an AR magazine brush to clean brush out the tube very quickly. You should do this if you drop the magazine in sand or mud or some other particulate. The springs should be kept dry of anything, unless perhaps, a very light coat of gun oil. Do not grease the magazine springs. You can clean the follower with a toothbrush.

Keep an eye on the feed lips. If the lips are damaged, discard the magazine. Mags are cheap, and damage to the feed lips, even apparently minor

Shooting Birchwood Casey's Gunscrubber or other aerosol cleaner into the upper receiver (do it in this fashion, since you don't really need it in the barrel) and scrubbing with a toothbrush works to clean your upper mighty fine.

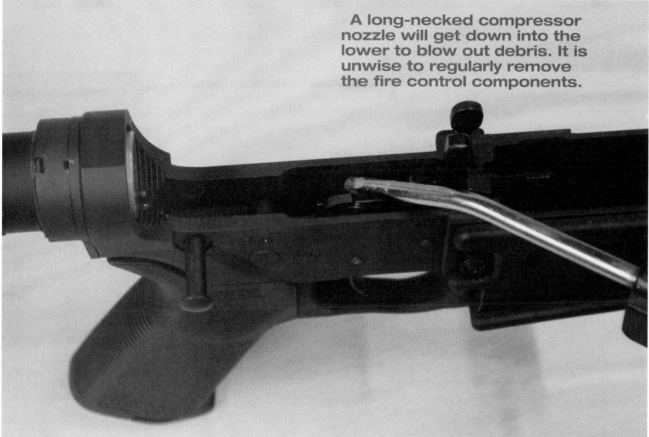

A long-necked compressor nozzle will get down into the lower to blow out debris. It is unwise to regularly remove the fire control components.

damage, can cause malfunctions. Some plastic mags are shipped with feed lip covers that incorporate lip gauges in them, GO and NOGO for the width between them. Some aftermarket cleaning tools like the Samson Field Survivor also incorporate feed lip gauges in the design of the tool.

RECEIVER MAINTENANCE – UPPER

The upper receiver receives much more wear and dirt and gunk than does the lower receiver. After you have cleaned your barrel bore and chamber you can use a toothbrush to clean the upper, using cotton swabs to get the little spots, like the area above the gas tube. The charging handle channel can be cleaned with an appropriately sized bore mop if your brush can't quite get into the channel. If you are using something like Gunscrubber, then hose it out by holding the upper over the trash can with the receiver in the can. Shoot the aerosol into the upper, pushing the spray to the rear of the receiver, and let it drain out the back. Scrub with the brush and residual solvent. It's easier to lubricate the bolt carrier and charging handle when you replace them rather than to lubricate the upper receiver directly.

RECEIVER MAINTENANCE – LOWER

A lot of owners make the mistake of removing their fire control components on a regular basis to clean the lower receiver. To be honest and as fair as possible, this is not a nonsensical thing to do. It can be difficult to get out the dust, dirt, seeds, and residue that eventually collect in the trigger pocket. However, frequent removal of the fire control pins can cause enough wear to the holes in the receiver that the holes will widen. You don't want this to happen, as it can cause some problems with the fire control, silly things like hammer follow-throughs, slam fires, release triggers, things like that. If this happens, and you can see the pins literally wobbling in the receiver, then you have one option to salvage the receiver. Go to using the large sized pins and Colt large pin fire control groups after reaming the holes from the original

.151" - 152" to the large pin Colt sized .169" – 170".

To clean the lower receiver, even if it looks ultra-crummy, use compressed air. Or an aerosol solvent like Gunscrubber in combination with compressed air. If you can do this outside, it is best, but otherwise shooting it into a trash can will contain it pretty well. When the stuff in the lower receiver looks clean, you can add a couple drops of oil to the trigger and hammer pins by introducing the oil with a needle tipped bottle. Add the oil to the side of the disconnector and it will find its way to the trigger pin. Adding oil to either side of the hammer pin bushing will find the oil getting down to the pin with simplicity. Add a drop of oil to the body of the safety/selector, and the takedown and pivot pins' bodies. Like with the barrel, wiping a thin coat of oil to the outside of the receivers will make the look a bit nicer.

BOLT CARRIER ASSEMBLY

This assembly may well be the dirtiest bit in the entire gun, even when the upper has a piston conversion, but particularly with the standard set-up. Since the gas that is tapped to operate the system is directed into the carrier's interior, this is where most of the residue winds up. The cylinder area of

The Real Avid AR-15 scraper is a multifunction cleaning tool. It has something to clean everything on the bolt and carrier and it is a very thin, easily-packed tool.

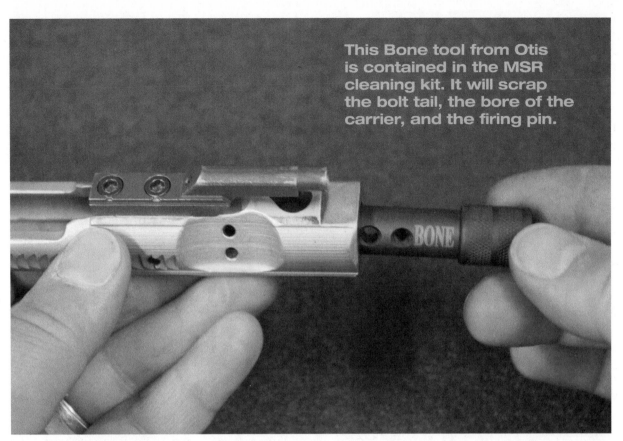

This Bone tool from Otis is contained in the MSR cleaning kit. It will scrap the bolt tail, the bore of the carrier, and the firing pin.

This line will develop on the cam pin. When it becomes an easily tangible shelf it would behoove you to consider replacing it.

the carrier, into which the bolt is inserted, should be cleaned regularly. There are tools designed to scrape this cylinder area, but for normal maintenance a .50 caliber bore mop is a great tool for cleaning. You will likely need solvent at some point sooner rather than later and the mop will carry it in quite efficiently. You can even use a .50 caliber bronze or brass brush if you so desire and use a hand drill in much the same way as when you cleaned the chamber. These tools may not effectively clean the rear wall of the cylinder and this is where the scrapers work well. There is some debate

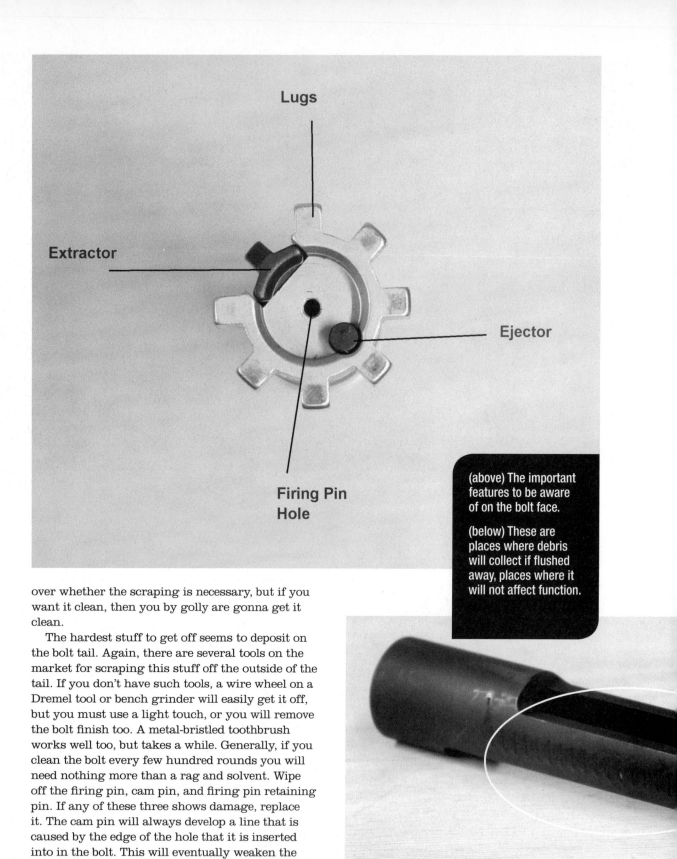

Lugs

Extractor

Ejector

Firing Pin
Hole

(above) The important
features to be aware
of on the bolt face.

(below) These are
places where debris
will collect if flushed
away, places where it
will not affect function.

over whether the scraping is necessary, but if you want it clean, then you by golly are gonna get it clean.

The hardest stuff to get off seems to deposit on the bolt tail. Again, there are several tools on the market for scraping this stuff off the outside of the tail. If you don't have such tools, a wire wheel on a Dremel tool or bench grinder will easily get it off, but you must use a light touch, or you will remove the bolt finish too. A metal-bristled toothbrush works well too, but takes a while. Generally, if you clean the bolt every few hundred rounds you will need nothing more than a rag and solvent. Wipe off the firing pin, cam pin, and firing pin retaining pin. If any of these three shows damage, replace it. The cam pin will always develop a line that is caused by the edge of the hole that it is inserted into in the bolt. This will eventually weaken the cam pin. Replace the cam pin anytime you replace the bolt, and if it develops a significant shelf, you should probably change it then too. The retaining pin should be replaced if it breaks, if it looks chewed up like your dog's plaything, or when you replace the bolt.

A properly lubricated carrier.

The firing pin is generally the most durable, in my opinion, of the internal bolt parts. However, if you have any primer punctures, you should replace the firing pin. The hot gases flowing past the tip when the primer is punctured will burn and corrode the tip off the pin, which will in short order incur enough damage that primer ignition may become questionable. Worse, since the tip becomes undersized as a result, further primer punctures allow more hot gas to be let into the bolt body itself to worsen the internal conditions there as well. The piece of primer that was punched out will be deposited inside the bolt and can affect extractor function. I've seen bolts that had twenty to thirty little punched out pieces that actually helped to gum up under the extractor and raise it enough to prevent proper functioning. When enough punctured primers occur, the round shape of the firing pin hole in the bolt will become not round and then the bolt should be replaced. Brushing

You can make a handy tool for installing your fire control group, or for disassembly should you be required to remove or upgrade these parts. Take a standard AR firing pin and cut off the front end, leaving only the main, large diameter of the pin. This is a perfect tool for pushing out FC pins and for guiding them back in again. For example, insert the trigger and disconnector, and run the firing pin all the way through to the other side of the receiver, touch the trigger pin to the tip of the firing pin, and then push the trigger pin all the way through while withdrawing the firing pin tool. Works just as well for the hammer. This tool is also good for tapping out tight takedown and pivot pins. Also, if you purchase any Geissele triggers, they come with a similar, but intentionally designed, installation tool.

(above) On the left is a hard chrome plated carrier. The middle is a Nickel-Boron plated carrier from WMD Guns, and on the right is a QPQ finished carrier from JP Enterprises. The QPQ isn't a plating really, more of a hardened case or skin, but the results are similar: high lubricity with enhanced cosmetics, better performance, and ease of cleaning.

(below) A variety of good lubes is available for your AR, some formulated intentionally for them.

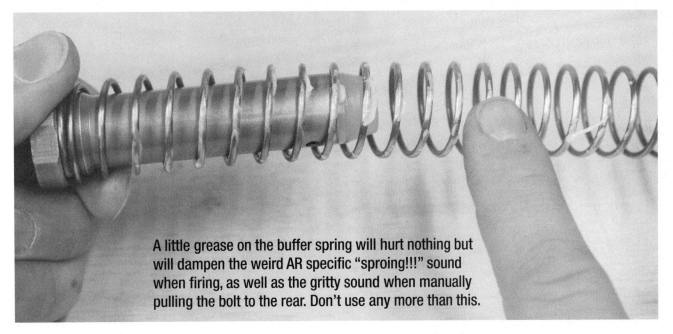

A little grease on the buffer spring will hurt nothing but will dampen the weird AR specific "sproing!!!" sound when firing, as well as the gritty sound when manually pulling the bolt to the rear. Don't use any more than this.

around the lugs will clean them up.

Examine the bolt lugs, particularly at the roots, for cracks or chips. If any are found, discard the bolt and use a new one. If the extractor and ejector are undamaged, remove them first and use them as spare parts.

The extractor often requires replacement before the entire bolt does, so keep one or two and the associated spring and pin on hand as spares. The ejector will usually last no problem, but a spare

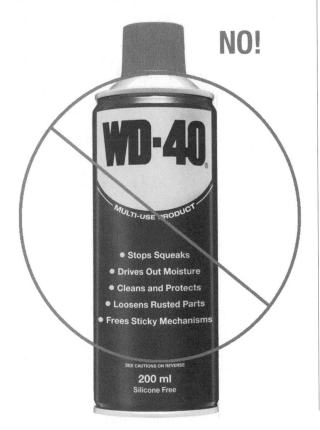

NO!

one of those and its spring and pin are good to have. Honestly, the ejector and spring are more likely to be lost than damaged, and the pin is often damaged during installation or removal. However, with cartridges that have been overloaded, a fun little symptom often occurs involving the ejector. You will notice this on the case headstamps first. The ejector will smear the letters right off the case head because the bolt is rotating when the pressure is quite high in the chamber. This chamber pressure is pushing the case tightly against the bolt face and, when the bolt rotates, the ejector scrapes across the case head, smearing the lettering. This is an indication that your loads are too hot, and a clear indication that you need to have your wife junk-punch you and then go about fixing your reloading practices. The worst part of this is that the ejector will smear some brass right off the case and it will collect in the ejector hole and jam the ejector. If the ejector is stuck in the hole, something is sticking it there and it is often brass flakes.

I know I'm going to draw some trolls from under the bridge with the following recommendation but here it goes, and this information is supported by multiple studies conducted by major manufacturers and the U.S. Army. The proper way to lubricate the bolt carrier assembly when you put it back in is to make it really wet. Use generous lube. Here's why. Lubrication serves another purpose in the AR (and all guns really) than just to make the parts slip past each other smoothly. Like in your car's engine it is also used to flush away debris that could affect the function of the mechanism. A light film of oil on the part will lubricate but not flush. This is why, and I would even challenge you to do this if you feel so inclined, you can just keep adding lubrication to the upper receiver

The JP Cleaning Rod Guide is one of several on the market and is a handy accessory if you need to clean a heavily-dirtied barrel.

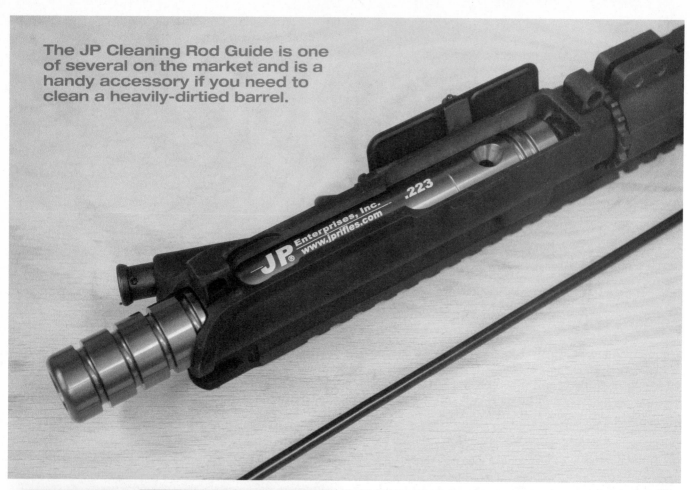

The JP Bore Compound is applied to a patch on a brass cleaning jag and inserted into the rear the emplaced bore guide. This should be done with the upper secured in a vise block for stability. Scrub the bore several times and then remove the compound with bore solvent. I recommend that the owner not use this product, as it is a mild, though non-embedding abrasive, until other bore cleaning methods and solvents have failed to fully remove the copper fouling from the barrel. It works very well and universally as a final option.

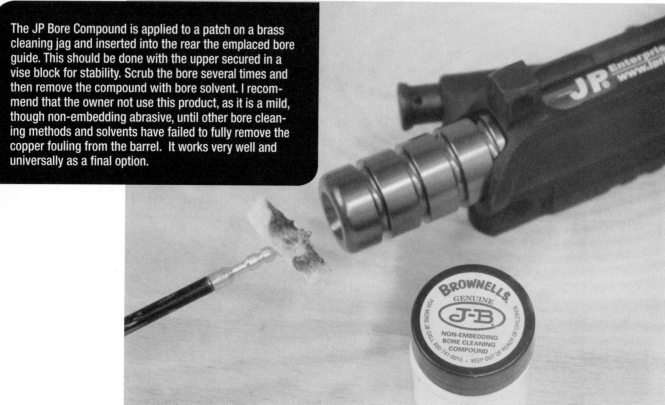

This little 4" black bag has everything you need to keep your AR clean and well maintained when you are out and about. You may run out of lube in short order, though, if you lube like you should.

and bolt carrier over and over again, keeping the system wet, not cleaning it, the gun will work for a surprisingly long time without failing. Like several thousands of rounds long time. It will get really dirty depending on the ammo, but because of the liquid lube still in place and being regularly replenished, the gunk doesn't get very hard and can be wiped off rather easily. Plus, the gunk collects in places where it does no harm because the movement of the bolt in combination with the fluid oil, flushes the gunk to those places.

Those who advocate a lubrication-free gun (particularly the AR) are mistaken in their desire. You should not want a lubrication-free gun, because you are then only addressing one half of the function of the lubrication. However, the new generations of platings that these companies are promoting are still very useful. Of course the point of the platings is to imbue the surface of the parts with a high lubricity. High lubricity contributes to lower amounts of friction between parts and therefore longer useful service lives. But frankly, it's my belief that the greatest benefit to the high lubricity coatings like hard chrome, Nickel-Teflon, Nickel-Boron, and others is that they make the gun so much easier to clean. In most

cases, particularly if they go to the trouble of polishing the plating as well, like the guys at WMD Guns do with their Nickel-Boron plated parts, you can simply wipe the gunk off with a dry rag. There is simply no comparison between polished plated and unplated parts when you want to clean them. These wonder-platings tend to increase the cost of the parts by 30-50%, but the convenience alone is worth the expense.

The findings have shown consistently that generous fluid lubrication is the best means of lubing up an AR, regardless of the environment. You may have to change up the lube selection in temperature extremes, and indeed, in the coldest of climes the use of a dry lube like fine powdered graphite may be necessary because all the fluid stuff will freeze. Hotter temps usually require a lighter, thinner-viscosity fluid. There are lubes that run the gamut, but there are several wide range synthetics that seem to be ideal for most guns in our country, in our temperate environment. The CLP and similar types that the military uses, such as Breakfree, MPro-7, and FP-10 are great general all-around choices that will clean as well as lubricate. There are others, of course, but my experience has been mostly limited to these and has been quite positive.

Don't use grease. There are two exceptions, but you will not be well served by using grease or anti-seize in the action of the gun. I've seen bolt carriers covered in grease and this can actually inhibit the movement of the carrier. Grease can be used, and is encouraged by the manufacturers in the engagement surfaces of the match grade fire control units, making mega smooth engagement

It's difficult to explain how to properly put the patch on the loop, so I won't. The kit has instructions on how to do it. Just realize that it gives full bore coverage and that is a very good thing, a very efficient thing.

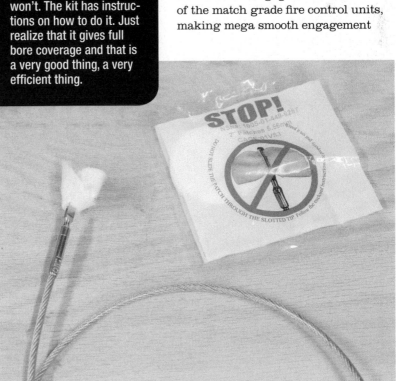

The patch is then pulled from breach to muzzle backwards. You may have to do this a few times, but the nature of the patch arrangement allows for multiple uses on each patch.

(below) This what the patch will look like pulled through once on a barely dirty barrel. Pretty good.

surfaces into Hyper-mega smooth engagement surfaces. This is a good application of grease. You might also apply a thin smear of grease to the buffer spring. A thin smear. This has the effect of lessening the raspy "sproing-ng-ng-ng" that you hear when you shoot your gun. Polishing a small flat onto the outer edge of the spring like the springs that JP Enterprises sells makes it even quieter. But do not use grease on the bolt carrier. Yes, it greatly (usually) increases the lubricity, but rather than flush debris it does the opposite – it keeps it right where it landed, and that is often the worst place for it to be. Grease is widely known to be a dirt magnet for good reasons. This is not a universal thing, as there are many guns that function better with grease in certain locations, but ARs are not them. The only real advantage to grease is that you don't have to replace it as often, but it does not outweigh the loss in fluid debris removal provided by generous lubrication with oil.

So my preferred means of lubricating a bolt carrier assembly is to hold it over the trash can and, using a squeeze bottle, squirt a stream on the right side, followed by a stream on the left side of the carrier. I then push and pull out the bolt a few times to make sure the lube is distributed inside the carrier, and I might drop a couple of oil drops into the vent ports on the right side of the bolt carrier as well. It will look wet and runny and I then reinsert it into the upper receiver and proceed to shoot it.

Use a commercially-manufactured gun oil. It's actually ridiculously inexpensive and every sporting goods department carries multiple formulations. Do not use WD-40. I know, I know, it says you can use it on guns right on the can, but it doesn't say you should use it on guns. It will gum up into a yucky solid and become very difficult to get off, and will jam the gun up if you use it generously. Old timers have been using it to their detriment for generations and just haven't learned their lessons in this regard, so break the cycle and don't let Dad or Grampa talk you into using it.

OTIS KIT

I've pretty much consumed the Kool-Aid when it comes to cleaning ARs. I do one of two things. I hose it out and brush scrub with Birchwood Casey's Gun Scrubber. I shoot Gun Scrubber on patches or use CLP to clean the bore. With ARs, I do not concern myself with copper fouling in

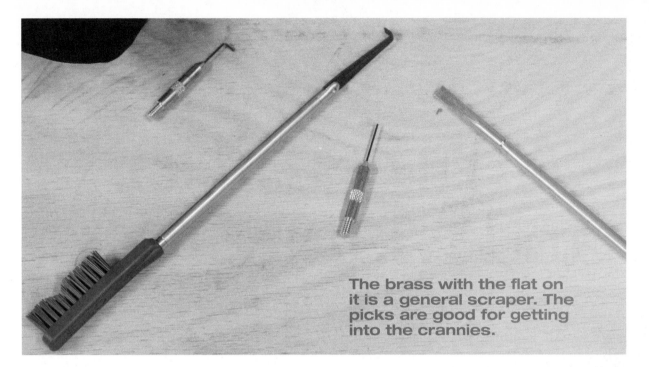

The brass with the flat on it is a general scraper. The picks are good for getting into the crannies.

the barrel. I will only do so if the accuracy has degraded significantly and every other potential cause has been eliminated, such as crummy ammo, crown damage, and caffeine let-downs. If I determine that copper fouling is the culprit (and you can see it in the barrel; it will have a yellowish green hue in white light [color blind; I think it's yellowish green]). I clean this out in a matter of five minutes with JB Bore Compound. It is a very mild abrasive that does not embed in the barrel. A few patches scrubbed in the bore with JB applied, and then rinsed with solvent has done an excellent job, in my own gunsmithing experience, of quickly and cheaply removing copper fouling, with no detrimental effect on the bore. There are reactionaries that will go flipping nuts after reading what I just typed, but I have cleaned hundreds of AR barrels in this manner and it works.

This should be done from the breach using a bore guide and preferably a one-piece cleaning rod, but that is something that most people don't bother to get. A break-down rod is fine, but make sure to use the bore guide if that's the case. The bore guide prevents chamber and receiver damage from over-excited people doing the cleaning. You don't want to have to clean JB out of your chamber.

Barring the need to use JB or if I am "in the field" (AKA: sitting on my ass at the range), then an OTIS cleaning kit is the method of choice. This is the second of the two things. OTIS has helpfully put together a Modern Sporting Rifle (MSR) kit that is fit for the AR-15. This is a very complete and well thought out kit. I'm sure most of you readers are familiar with Bore Snakes and similar products. The OTIS kits work in a similar fashion

but use standard patches and coated steel cables. You patch up the loop and pull it through the barrel. It cleans fast and quick. The kit has a long and a short cable and a loop and two bore brushes. A steel scraper for cleaning the carrier assembly and a stiff nylon brush with brass rods for a handle is included as are picks and a brass flat scraper. Rounding it out are an indispensable chamber brush in a case, and a tube of lube, with patches on the side. See the pictures for a step-by-step demonstration of usage.

The OTIS kits are not cheap. This MSR kit cost me $55, which is a lot more than a department store aluminum and steel assemblage that costs 10 bucks. Everything in this kit is designed specifically to clean your AR without damaging anything and it all fits into a pouch four inches in diameter and two inches thick. You can wear it on your belt. The only thing that a traditional kit will do better is to pound out a bullet stuck in the bore, but you can do that with a lot of things. If you don't want to spend the money on an OTIS kit (and you'd be foolish not to) then you can still effectively clean your AR with the $10 kit until you can afford the OTIS kit. Just follow the instructions in the kit for general rifle cleaning. Then go get a chamber brush. And a .22 caliber brass cleaning jag, because even if you get a jag in the 10 buck kit it will be soft plastic and a useless joke. Then get some lube. Then get a screwdriver and dental pick to scrape with. Then wrap it all up in your plastic bag and throw it in your range bag. By this time, with all the running around, you could have spent the $55 on the OTIS kit, saved some time, and gotten a far superior product for maintaining your AR.

Ammunition and Magazines

I f your AR doesn't feed properly, it will not shoot reliably. The most malfunctioning component of any repeating firearm is the magazine or the attendant feed system. On the AR, it's generally the magazine only, as there is no carrier or lifter or feed latch that you might find on a tube-fed firearm like most semi-auto or pump action shotguns or rifles.

Historically, the GI aluminum magazines have worked well as long as the springs haven't worn out. There have been some fixes for that, notably using a spring material that doesn't take a set and therefore a memory, like many springs are prone to do. Also, using more powerful springs has been an attempt to increase feeding reliability. If the gun is cycling at a very high rate, the bolt carrier may move to the rear and back forward into battery again before the magazine has time to lift another round into place under the feed lips. This will result in one of two malfunctions.

The first is that the bolt will simply close and lock without having picked up a new round. You

simply manually cycle the action again to load the chamber, but this will likely happen again unless you slow down the cyclic rate of the gun. With a standard rifle or carbine this can be done by using a more powerful buffer spring, or by increasing the reciprocating mass by using a heavier carrier or buffer. The latter solution is the more effective means of correcting this type of malfunction. If the gun has an adjustable gas block, then the gas port should be made more restricted by closing it off somewhat until the cartridges feed reliably and the bolt still locks back after the last shot.

The second malfunction is that the bottom of

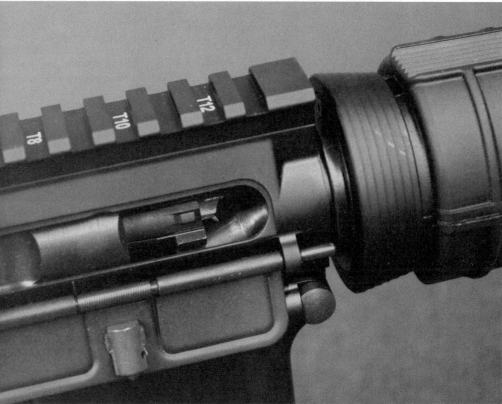

(above) Having a supply of extra magazine springs and followers can be a good idea. I don't shoot enough to have to worry about it but maybe someday I will...

(right) The bolt has dragged on the top of the cartridge with enough force push it forward to begin feeding. But since the bolt was not behind the rim, but rather over the cartridge, the bolt will jam the cartridge against the feed ramps and can impress a deep dent in the case wall (simulated here).

(below) This 6.5 Grendel magazine on the left next to a standard 30-round .223 magazine. Note the two rear stiffening grooves in the Grendel magazine. They are shallower to accommodate the fatter cartridge case body. The obvious groove at the front is also slightly shallower but is less easily seen. This magazine is stainless steel, made by C-Products.

the bolt will actually drag the top round forward rather than pushing it forward. The round will partially feed and the nose of the bullet will lodge under the bolt and against the feed ramp. The bolt will typically come to rest against the cartridge case body and make a large dent just behind the shoulder of the case.

Worn out magazine springs can also cause either of these two malfunctions.

Several manufacturers continue to fabricate aluminum magazines to the mil-spec, Brownells being one of the major ones. These magazines function quite reliably, are inexpensive ($10-$12 or so), and pretty much duplicate the function and performance of the GI magazines, both in 30- and 20-round capacities. Most factory rifles are shipped with this type of mag and you will not go

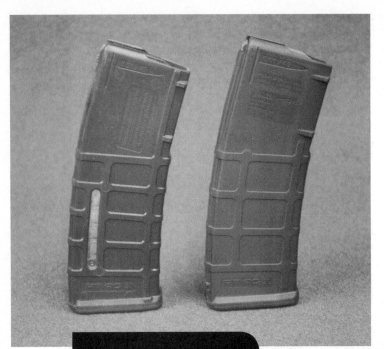

wrong sticking with the brands that you get with these guns.

There have been several examples of steel magazines over the years, but many of them are not of high quality, being poorly stamped, welded, and heat treated. There are several of high quality, specifically the mags made in Singapore. You can still find these magazines regularly and they are a good buy if you do. They are somewhat heavier than the aluminum standard. The generally well-made magazines made for one of the alternate calibers that have shown up lately are almost always made from stainless steel, as the walls can be thinner yet just as strong.

It seems that magazine technology has in recent years migrated over to the plastic and polymer end of things rather than steel and aluminum. The plastic molding technology industry has exploded in the last ten years and more gun parts are being molded in plastic than ever before. The biggest entry in the polymer molding bunch has been

(top) Two generations of MagPul PMags are shown here. The reinforcement waffle pattern has thinned out somewhat and the unshown Gen3 mag has some minor changes so it'll fit into a bunch of silly European rifles, but looks pretty much indistinguishable from the Gen2. The Gen3 also includes a dust cover. They are available with or without windows.

(middle) This MagPul enhanced self-leveling follower is designed to not tilt in any fashion. When in a standard magazine, you can push down at any point on the top of the follower and the entire follower will push down in a level fashion. This is sold as an upgrade to standard magazines with the mil-spec followers. The PMags have a similar feature.

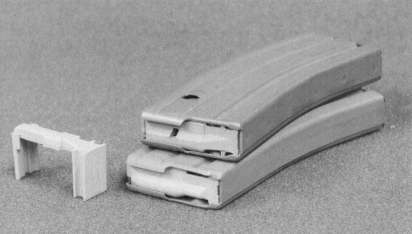

(bottom) There are a number of good polymer magazines on the market. The Lancer magazine is transparent, and has steel reinforcement on the feed lips. The Troy magazine has a slimmer than most profile and has the option of a grippy thingy on the base plate. There are others.

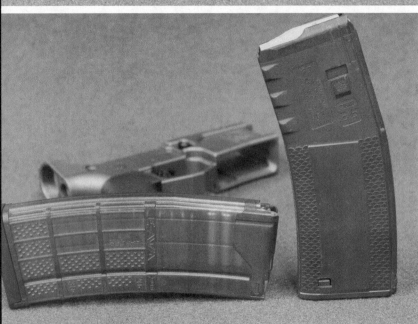

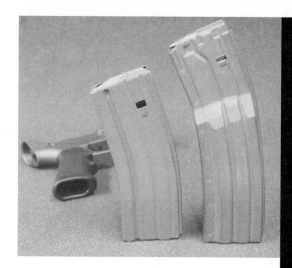

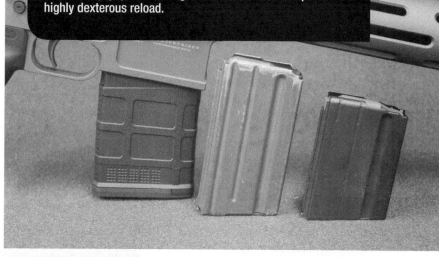

(left) A Surefire 60-round magazine is only a couple inches longer and twice as wide as a standard magazine. Below the magazine well, where the magazine well swells, it goes from a two wide stack to a four cartridge wide stack. Don't let this perspective fool you. This mag will hold twice the cartridges of the standard mag on the left. Surefire also makes a 100-round magazine that looks like a mastodon tusk sticking out of a caveman.

(below) This is a MagPul 20-round .308 PMag in a JP LRP-07. This magazine will also fit all the DPMS and Knight's pattern rifles, and honestly is the most common pattern of .308 magazines. The standard 20-round .223 magazine that saw use in Vietnam, and 10-round Grendel magazine lie next to it. ARs have also used FAL magazines, AK magazines, and others that are too scary to contemplate. The Armalite AR-10 magazine is also proprietary to Armalite and still in use by that company. This is only a sampling.

(bottom) This is the original MagPul product, the MagPul. Obviously it wraps around the base of the magazine leaving an easily grasped loop. The point is so you have a quick, secure, and no drop grip on the magazine in order to accomplish a highly dexterous reload.

MagPul and their magazines have been a big hit. The PMag can be purchased in multiple colors, for .223 or .308, and also can be had with windows so you can have some idea of how many rounds you have. The design incorporates a non-tilting follower (the GI mag followers went through several changes to address this, but not as successfully as the PMag follower) and a constant curve to the internal wall of the magazine. The standard metal mags have what are essentially two bends and the old followers that could easily tilt, so rumor says, could jam up at those locations. The constant curve and non-tilt followers supposedly cures this ill. MagPul also makes anti-tilt follower upgrades for standard GI magazines that seem to be a worthy upgrade as well.

Other companies, notably CAA,

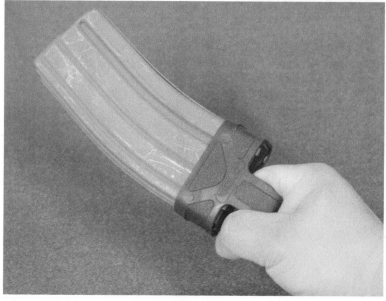

Tapco, and Lancer Systems, have pursued the plastic magazine as well. Each has their own strengths as each company followed their own priorities on the upgrade. For example the Lancer magazines are transparent. The Tapco and CAA magazines are heavily reinforced. There are simply a bunch of magazine manufacturers now and most of them are pretty reliable. I would state that there is a minimum price that the good magazines seem to cost (plus most cost under $25). If it regularly costs less than $10 at retail, I would not buy it. There are a couple brands (which will remain unnamed) that MSRP between 5 and 10 bucks and I wouldn't touch them with a sledgehammer. Okay, maybe I'd touch them with a sledgehammer, but I would not touch them with my rifle. Come to think of it, I actually have touched such magazines with a sledgehammer. That was great fun. These poor quality mags might be aluminum, steel, or plastic, but the $10 maximum price point seems to work well as an indicator.

The standard capacities of the AR magazines are either 20 or 30 rounds. Five- and 10-round magazines are common as well for use in rifles that will be in the hunting fields as several states limit capacities in that capacity. On the other hand, larger magazines have become common as well. The 100-round Beta C-Mag and the MWG 90-rounder are commonplace and functional drum magazines and the Surefire 60- and 100-round box magazines have become popular as well. These above standard capacity mags are, however, quite a bit more expensive. The dollar to capacity ratio is much higher with these magazines than the standard 30-rounders, so your money is more efficiently spent on normal mags, but the larger cap mags can be lots of fun. Get a stockpile of standard magazines first, and then buy one of the big boys for the fun times at the range or on the range.

The magazines made for use with the alternate cartridges (other than .223 or .308) will have capacities of whatever the heck fits in the box. Sometimes they are longer, shorter, or fatter. Just note that standard .223 magazines will not properly function with most of the alternate calibers, as the feed lips are optimized for the .223/5.56 or the .308/7.62 cases. .204 Ruger and .300 Blackout, two common alternates will work in .223 magazines. .260 Rem., .243 Win., and 6.5 Creedmoor will work in the .308 mags. Just about everything else will require a cartridge specific magazine and they may be difficult to track down at times. The company that seems to make the largest selection of magazine by cartridge is ASC. Their mags are sold by a number of dealers and distributors and are affordable

AMMO BASICS

Let's go over some ammunition basics and definitions.

A cartridge is composed of four components: the case, the primer, the powder, and the bullet. The primer is used to ignite the powder. The powder burns rapidly, producing a tremendous amount of expanding gas. The gas pushes the bullet down the bore and out the muzzle towards the target. The case is what holds it all together into one whole, the cartridge. Some of these terms are used interchangeably, such as bullet referring to the cartridge as a whole, but this is incorrect and just adds confusion.

The bullet is generally composed of a lead core surrounded by a thin copper jacket. The jacket serves two purposes: to prevent fouling in the bore (unjacketed lead bullets leave lots of lead in the barrel when going at high velocities); and to hold the core together. (Lead bullets traveling faster than 2000 fps tend to spin apart and disintegrate.

A cartridge is made up of a projectile (bullet), a primer, propellant (powder), and a case (in this instance I shot it off first; it's like when you really feel the need to crush an empty can against your forehead, so you slam a beer to get the empty can).

Modern bullets do not expand into the rifling, a common misconception. The rifling digs into the bullet. Shot cups, or wads, that hold shotgun shells are made of plastic and they often are designed to expand, as do the sabots holding sub-caliber bullets. But the bullets do not. This was not always true. The Minie style bullets used for a short time, notably in the U.S. Civil War, were designed to expand into the rifling. They were loose-fitting in the barrel, to allow easy repeated loading in heavily fouled barrels, and had a hollow base. The expanding gas behind the bullet pushed the walls of the cup into the rifling to form a seal and force the bullet base into the rifling to instill spin.

(top) Just to confuse you further, the case on the left is made of steel, and the one on the right has a black nickel plating on it. Even better, they have the exact same bullet, a 75 gr. Hornady match.

(above) Two kinds of primer, both can be volatile if used inappropriately. The primer in a can is for MyDipKit do it at home hydrographic kits. Pretty cool stuff, but it's stinky.

(right} This is the front side of a primer. The tri-lobed thingy is the anvil, which sits on top of the highly energetic priming compound sitting in the primer cup.

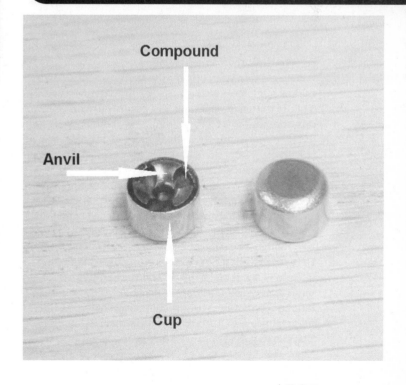

Compound

Anvil

Cup

You can see an example of this event by shooting a 40 grain bullet out of a 1:7 twist barrel. You pull the trigger and a gray cloud appears just past the muzzle. The bullet's jacket was too thin to hold the thing together.)

There are some bullets that are completely copper or brass. For example, the X bullets made by Barnes Bullets are usually solid copper with some sort of expanding mechanism in the nose, either a polymer tip, or a hollow skived tip. Other bullets may have more components. The service rifle cartridges of NATO and the former ComBloc nations use bullets that incorporate a steel insert on top of the lead core to contribute to armor penetration. Modern hunting bullets are often topped with plastic tips that serve to prevent point deformation and to initiate expansion of the lead core. The jackets may be mechanically or chemically bonded to the core in order to maximize penetration by preventing jacket separation when traveling through flesh. Partition bullets have two cores separated by jacket material. Remington Accelerator rounds were .30 caliber cartridges that used a .22 caliber bullet that was held by a .30 caliber sabot. The typical AR bullet is a solid lead core with a surrounding copper or bi-metal jacket (steel with copper plating).

The case is made of one of two metals. The most common, and pretty much universal domestically, is brass. Brass is ideal for case making, as it can be formed with just the right combination of harness, strength, and capacity. Steel is also used, but almost exclusively by foreign manufacturers, mostly in the former ComBloc nations. The steel ammo is cheaper but can cause potential extraction problems (we'll get to that in a minute). There have been attempts to make plastic cased ammo, but they have not borne much fruit as of yet. Aluminum is often used for pistol cartridges, but it is rare to unknown to see in rifles.

The primer is struck by the firing pin and makes a small explosion that ignites the powder. This is the most sensitive and potentially dangerous component of a cartridge, and the means of manufacturing them has changed little over the years. They are essentially all hand made by people with either no fear of death (who usually go missing when the primers they are assembling detonate in a chain reaction) or by people with an incredible fear of death who possess the skills and mental discipline to prevent it. Primers come in two forms. The American-designed Berdan and the British-designed Boxer. And go figure, the Boxer system is what we use, and the Berdan system is what everybody else uses. The Boxer priming system squeezes the priming compound between the primer face and an "anvil" that is inserted above it. The Berdan system incorporates the anvil into the case. The Berdan system is cheaper, but he Boxer system is much more readily reloadable, hence its use domestically. There are some cartridges made overseas that are reloadable, but most are Berdan-primed. No one else in the world shoots or reloads near the extent that we do.

The powder is called smokeless, as compared to the old black powder, which was decidedly not smokeless. Smokeless powder is derived from nitrocellulose and/or nitroglycerin and only "explodes" when tightly contained in a cartridge case; actually, the powder burns and is rapidly converted to gas, which then pushes the bullet. Outside the case, it burns brightly and with lots of smoke. It is not an explosive. Black powder is an explosive. If you light black powder outside of a case, it still blows up.

Some powders are "cleaner" than others. Early primers and powders were still rather corrosive and could quickly rust the bore of a gun if it wasn't cleaned. Much of the surplus ComBloc ammo that can be found, usually the stuff in the steel spam cans, has corrosive primers but non-corrosive powder. Modern manufactured stuff is non-corrosive, pretty much whatever you get. However, the powder on a lot of the foreign made stuff leaves all kinds of fuzzy, linty residue that, while not necessarily corrosive, is still dirty. If you

.223 Remington and 5.56mm look the same. You have to check the headstamp. If it doesn't say ".223 Rem." then it's 5.56 mm. It probably won't say "5.56mm".

are shooting ammo that leaves lots of residue, you should clean more frequently.

AMMUNITION CHOICES

We are going to spend some time on the ammo since ammo selection is a pretty important aspect of shooting any gun, including the AR. The first rule of ammunition selection is that you actually choose the correct ammunition for your gun. You'd be surprised how often this first rule is broken in the gun and hunting world. It's generally figured out the first time one tries to chamber the wrong cartridge, but it often is not. On that note we should first explore the differences between the .223 Remington and the 5.56 NATO.

We (or rather, you, since I already know) are going to find that there are many ARs chambered for .223 and others for 5.56, and frankly there is a difference that you should be aware of. .223 Rem-

ington is the original cartridge developed from the now uncommon .222 Remington cartridge. It is loaded with a bullet that measures .224" in diameter and is loaded to SAAMI specifications. When the rifle and ammo were adopted by NATO it was done so with a metric designation, 5.56mm NATO. Not only was the name altered, but the cartridge is loaded to a higher pressure.

Also important are the specifics of the chamber. The .223 Remington ammunition is meant to be fired in a .223 chamber. Ditto for the 5.56. The chambers are different. The largest differences, and the important ones, are that the freebore, or the distance from the beginning of the bore (corresponding to the location of the case mouth) to the beginning of the rifling is longer in the 5.56. The angle is also different. This allows for more generous acceptance of a wider variety of cartridges. Remember, at the time NATO was composed of over a dozen nations (now even more) and all of them

Look for the barrel stamp, like these. If it says 5.56 then you can shoot anything. If it says .223 Rem., then it probably is. If it says .223 [something] then it's likely a hybrid chamber and can shoot anything as well.

(below) The most popular cartridges for the various AR platforms look like these. .223/5.56, .204 Ruger, .300 AAC Blackout, 6.5 Grendel, 6.8 Rem. SPC, .308/7.62, 6.5 Creedmoor, .260 Remington, 9mm Luger, .22 Long Rifle.

would be producing ammunition to the specs, theoretically allowing any member nation to use the ammunition of any other member nation. Didn't really work out for real but it came close.

Because of the more generous nature of the 5.56 chamber and its higher pressure spec, .223 Rem. ammo can be fired from a 5.56 chamber with no concern, except for possibly having to deal with longer or excessive headspace on occasion. However, ammunition manufactured to 5.56 spec should not be fired through a .223 chamber. If the chamber is cut to minimum specs, and the 5.56 ammo is made to the grosser end of its specs, combined with the higher pressure of the 5.56 load, a negative result may occur. Broken and cracked cases, jammed cases, and head separations preventing extraction are the norm here, but in the extremes it can result in a functionally destroyed gun or damage to the shooter. Now, there are gonna be more trolls that say that it is no big deal to cross over this way and I say to them go ahead. The Darwin awards need some more gun-related entries. There is simply no reason to do so, since both types of ammo are readily available and there are other options to pursue to solve the issue.

The .308 Win. and 7.62 NATO have a similar

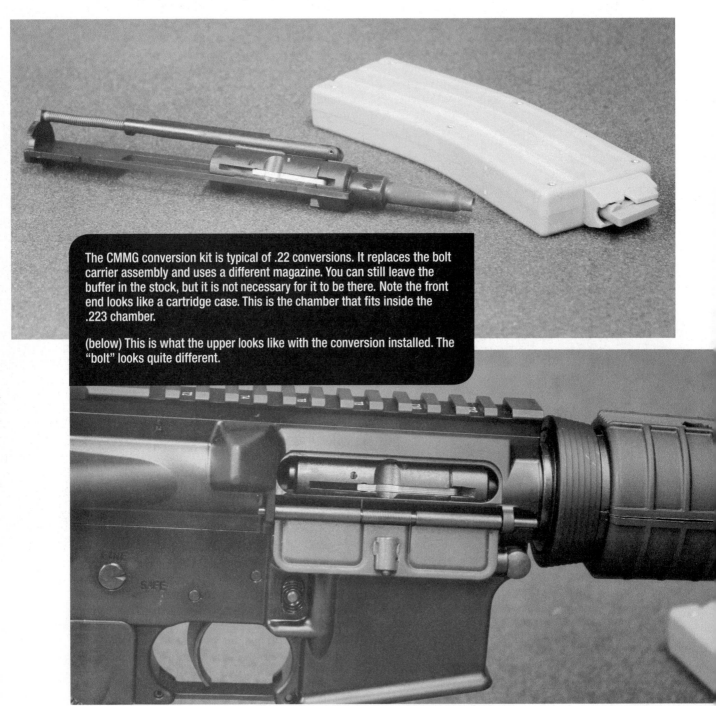

The CMMG conversion kit is typical of .22 conversions. It replaces the bolt carrier assembly and uses a different magazine. You can still leave the buffer in the stock, but it is not necessary for it to be there. Note the front end looks like a cartridge case. This is the chamber that fits inside the .223 chamber.

(below) This is what the upper looks like with the conversion installed. The "bolt" looks quite different.

story but somewhat in reverse. The .308 Win. cartridge is made to SAAMI spec as well, but unlike with the .223/5.56 the SAAMI pressure spec is higher than the NATO spec. The NATO chamber spec is still looser than the .308. And generally you should not mix the two as, technically, neither ammo is interchangeable for the other. Fortunately, in the AR world, pretty much every chamber is cut to 7.62 specs and is rated for .308 pressures. This cannot be said for the traditional rifle makes, which are all cut to .308 specs.

Some manufacturers have gone to using hybrid chambers to resolve this conundrum. The most common is the .223 Wylde chamber, which essentially splits the differences in half and allows both SAAMI and NATO ammo to be used with impunity. Furthermore, it preserves the accuracy potential of the .223 chamber. You may still find some guns chambered in the actual .223 chamber in the longer barreled varmint rifles, in order to gain the maximum accuracy, and many owners of these guns reload the ammo for them anyway. However the vast majority of barrels, even those that are stamped or listed as .223, are chambered in 5.56 NATO. If you are in the position of not knowing for sure, and you care, you can take the gun to a local gunsmith and he can figure it out for you. Another easier means might be to simply call the manufacturer and ask.

Why do they mark it .223 and chamber in something else? Often it's for some mundane exporting regulations that have no effect on the American consumer other than to confuse them. It's also cheaper to mark all your barrels in the same way even when some are exported and some aren't. Just call the manufacturer if you have reason to doubt what the marking indicates.

Furthermore, and a rant begins, is the habit of people referring to 7.62x39mm as .308 Short, .30 Russian Short or some other idiotic thing that isn't 7.62x39mm. Renaming a .31 caliber cartridge as .308 Stubbie or .30 Short does not make you sound trendy or smart. It just adds more confusion to already somewhat confusing cartridge naming conventions. I have experienced this conundrum first hand trying to find the correct ammo for a customer who insisted his brother sent him to find him some .308 Short for his SKS. I literally almost just about strangled the guy because he wasted ten minutes of my time arguing that there was such a thing as .308 Short. Rant over. The frigging box says what the ammo is. If you can't remember what it is, then save the damn ammo box.

Obviously, the vast majority of ARs built will shoot the 5.56 NATO and .223 Rem. The alternate chamberings make up only a fraction of the total but they seem to be gaining popularity. The military has looked at larger bullets for the service rifles and carbines. Two examples are the 6.8 Rem.

SPC and the 6.5 Grendel. The 6.8 is the more popular and common of the two. The 6.5 is the more flexible and better performing of the two at range. Despite their lack of adoption by the U.S. military, both of them make superb deer cartridges and are effective against many other forms of game. Magazines can be hard to find for the 6.5, with the only ones made coming from ASC, as my last internet search indicated. 6.8 magazines are manufactured by several companies and can be more easily purchased.

The flavor of the month is the .300 AAC Blackout, a further-refined version of the older .300 Whisper. The point of this cartridge is to neck out a .223 case to hold a .30 caliber bullet. Both supersonic and subsonic versions of this cartridge are available. Subsonic guns are suppressed effectively and easily with any number of sound suppressors and make really good deer guns (many are used for this purpose) in the states that allow suppressor use when hunting. The .204 Ruger is a superb varminting round and has vaporized many a prairie dog. When used in a rifle with a good muzzle brake, the .204 is effectively recoilless and is crazy fun to shoot. Both of these cartridges, especially the .204 are readily available, though both will require reloading to meet maximum effectiveness in any individual gun.

Of course, the most popular alternative caliber is .22 Long Rifle. Conversion kits have been around for decades to shoot the rimfire round through the

Steel cased ammo has to have a coating on the case to prevent rusting. All of the steel cases on the market originate overseas, and a thin hard lacquer coat is the usual means of protecting the cases. Hot chambers can melt this lacquer off, and since the steel cases contract faster than brass, hot propellant gases often get into the chamber between the chamber walls and the case wall, more so than with brass anyway. The result is that, in the rather straight-walled .223/5.56 cases and chambers, the stuff that is melted or burned off can build up on the chamber walls and inhibit extraction. It's best to use the polymer coated cases if you can find them, and most of the .223 and .308 with steel cases has this gray colored plastic coating that will behave much better in your chambers than the lacquer.

.223 barrel. The early kits were made by the Jonathan Arthur Ciener company, and others were soon on the market that copied or deviated somewhat from the original Ciener design. Ciener conversion kits are still popular, as are the CMMG units and Nordic Components types.

It has also become the in-thing to make fully dedicated rimfire versions of the AR-15. Several companies have done this to great success, Smith & Wesson being one of the first and best. The system is proprietary, with a proprietary magazine (most conversions are compatible with the Ciener style magazine) and bolt but it works well and is very lightweight. Colt, ATI, and others also produce rimfire only versions and these are almost always buyable for under $500.

Why rimfire you ask? Well, I'll tell you. It's cheaper. You can buy a brick of 500 rounds of .22 for the same cost as two boxes of 20 rounds of .223. That's a lot more shooting and a lot more practice with the .22 than with the .223. Sure it's not exactly the same thing, ballistics and felt recoil significantly differ, but it's better than nothing and rimfire is just plain funner to shoot than anything else. Yes. I. Mean. FUNNER!

If you are just on your first AR or are about to buy your first AR then stick to the 5.56 NATO uppers. This is what the huge majority of guns are chambered for and it will shoot 5.56 or .223 ammo with impunity. The ammo, at least of the time of this writing, is plentiful. I should digress for a moment here. It seems during every election, or after every stated intent by politicians to ban one thing or another, that there is a run on certain guns and accessories. 30-round magazines and the ammo that they hold, particularly 5.56, seem to disappear the fastest, even as fast as the guns. At the moment, the industry has caught up to the last run on stuff caused by legislative threats after the Newtown, CT, school shooting. But it's an industry that gets cleaned out every time something like that happens and the industry is still struggling

The Hahn Precision conversion is a great way to turn your .223 lower into a pistol caliber carbine. This kit from Brownells includes the 9mm Hahn conversion magazine block that inserts into the mag well and is tensioned in place, combined with a Brownells 32-round Uzi-style Colt magazine.

(below) The Brownells magazine will work with some bolts and conversions to hold the bolt back after the last round in the magazine is fired. Some 9mm magazines will not, and this Brownells mag has the little tab on the back of the follower that actuates the bolt catch (you can barely see it in this picture between the feed lips). The JP 9mm bolt and SCS assembly functioned perfectly with this upgrade kit, including locking the bolt back after the magazine emptied.

When you start reloading, don't listen to people who want to sell you something. Start with a simple single stage press like this RCBS Rockchucker. This model is as old as I am and still working strongly. You can get a Rock Chucker Supreme loading kit from Brownells for a little over $300. Just add a set of dies and components and you will have all you need to begin reloading. Do not start with a progressive press. Get your legs under you with a single stage like this one first. And don't reload rifle ammo with a progressive press either, stick to using it for high volume pistol reloading.

to resupply the .22 Long Rifle shortage, which by some irrational means, was caused by the same events. So there is some wisdom in having an alternate caliber upper as a backup. It used to be that the .22 upper was the ticket for that show, but perhaps a 6.5, 6.8, 7.62x39, or 5.45x39, or 9mm upper might be a good choice as a secondary upper as well, so that you can keep shooting.

A PRIMER ON RELAODING FOR ARs

So many treatises have been written on reloading ammunition that it seems foolhardy to get into it, since that would be replicating a number of works released by this publisher alone, as well as by much more experienced (read: crankier, wiser, wider, and more ancient) writers than I. However, since the AR owner tends to shoot frequently even if he or she is a new owner, we'll go over some important reloading information, should you want to pursue that hobby right away. Like many of the things I say and write, this will likely tork some people off and counteract a piece of propaganda or two, but that's okay. If they fire me I have more time to play with my kids.

I'm going to approach some of this stuff as do/do not. Reloading is not at all difficult, truthfully it's as much art as science. Just like when painting or drawing a picture, there are rules to be followed, and as you gain experience you will produce a more superior product. In the art world, you may start out with stick figures and later on be painting portraits of world leaders. In the cartridge reloading realm, you start with the low-ball recipes listed in the many reloading manuals (you must start with these manuals; get several for cross referencing), simply so you can make more ammo cheaper than you can buy it already assembled. Pretty soon you are loading with much detail to determine what particular recipe or recipe modification makes your gun shoot the tightest groups. So let's start.

Do purchase as many reloading manuals as you can. You can get old manuals that still have a great deal of valid info, and many manufacturers actually give out free sample reloading books to whet your appetite for destruction. You can't have too many reloading manuals.

Do not have distractions. If you can't do it without watching the TV, your kids, or listening to the

radio, then you need to come back and reload when you can. Or just don't. Again, reloading is not difficult, but you must pay absolute attention to details. Distractions cause you to skip powdering a case and then double charging the next one. When you then shoot them, the chargeless cartridge sends a bullet two inches down the barrel, followed by the double charge which then blows up your gun and sends pieces of barrel into your face. For better perspective, these pieces of barrel are steel shrapnel being propelled by an explosion.

Do not do what so many do and exceed the maximum listed loads. There are unfortunately a great many people who think published safety data somehow doesn't apply to reality in their little corner of the universe. See, in fantasyland, every attractive woman in the world sits on the couch with me to watch Firefly, and catches every joke and laughs their tweezed eyebrows off and the curls out of their purple hair every time Jane makes stupid wisecrack. I don't reload in fantasyland and neither should you. The published load data is not shadow-fudged to be lawyer proof, nor should it be treated as such because you just have to break 4500 fps with that .204 Ruger.

Do not use a progressive press for reloading rifle ammo. Progressive presses do multiple things at once to multiple cartridges. Single stage presses do one thing at a time. You are starting out, and you need to do one thing at a time, particularly seating primers. Progressive presses conceal the primer seating step; you don't feel the tension as the primer is being pushed into the primer pocket of the case. You need to be able to feel this so that you know there is tension and that the hole is tight around the primer. Insufficient primer seating tension leads to popped primers and damage to your gun and possibly you. If you use a single stage press or one of the several excellent hand priming tools you will be set. The hand primers use a lever slung beneath a shell holder. The shell holder is fed primers from a tray attached to the handle. You can feel primer seating tension with great sensitivity. Pistol cases may be reloaded with a progressive press, as he majority of pistol cartridges do not develop the intense internal pressure that rifles like .223 and .308 develop.

If you are reloading your own brass and not someone else's you can use standard reloading dies. If you got your brass from a source that even in the remotest possibility has been fired through a machinegun, you should use small base dies. These reloading dies like standard sizing dies reshape the case to a certain "factory" dimension (depends on how you set it up). Small base dies also slightly undersize the bases just in case. Machineguns tend to blow out the bases more than normal guns do.

Never, f%$&*#g, never shoot reloads reloaded by anyone else, especially by your best friend. Never! Only shoot your own reloads or those sold in a factory box that has the word "remanufactured" on it somewhere. When it comes to reloading, always remember this maxim: your bestest buddy wants your guns.

Do not mix powders together, and never have more than one powder canister open at one time.

Do understand that reloading requires a substantial initial investment. It may take several thousand rounds to break even. You need a press, a scale, manuals, components, reloading die sets, a bench, and other things at a minimum. There are kits that you can get from every press manufacturer, such as Hornady, RCBS, and Lee, that contain most of what you need for $300 or so.

Do understand that reloading isn't really cheaper than shooting factory ammo. 99% of the time, you just wind up spending the same amount of money shooting more often.

Do follow common sense gun handling safety considerations. Wear safety glasses, and some

Primers are sold in boxes of 100 or in bricks of 1000. Depending on your frequency of reloading, it may behoove thee to purchase by the brick. The CCI 41 primers are significantly harder than standard or match primers. Low mass hammers or reduced power hammer springs may not strike with sufficient force to ignite them.

(below) To reload, you need a set of dies. This .308 set from Lee belongs to the author and has seen moderate use. You will occasionally have to clean them. Treat them well and they will last longer than you will.

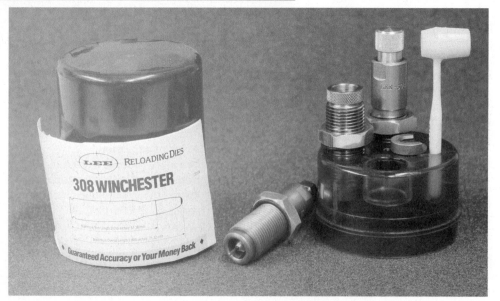

might want to wear latex or nitrile gloves. Don't mix things. Your reloading bench should be only your reloading bench and used for nothing else.

Do keep your guns well maintained. Well-made ammo is worthless if the firearm is not well-maintained as well.

Reloading equipment is available from many places. Sporting goods stores such as Cabelas carry a grand assortment, as do smaller department stores like Mills Fleet Farm. Brownells sells it. Some Gander Mountains still carry it, but mostly

they've flaked out of the reloading business. You can get anything online, but will wind up paying more when factoring in shipping. The best place to get reloading equipment and supplies is your local small gun shop, most of which will stock at least some bullets and reloading dies.

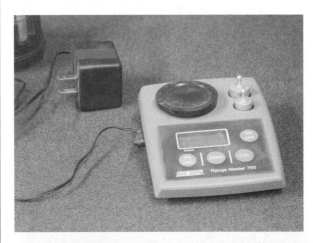

(below) Here is just a pair of the large variety of smokeless reloading powders on the market for your .223 or .308. Ramshot TAC is an especially versatile powder that can be used for almost any of the cartidges that are fired from the AR systems such as .223, .308, 6.5 Grendel, 6.8 SPC, 6.5 Creedmoor, and .260.

(bottom) There are even more selections of bullets than powders. .223 bullets that can be shot in an AR run from 45 grains up to 100, but 80 grains and over generally don't fit in the magazine. Match your bullets to your barrel. Faster twist barrels will stabilize heavier bullets. Slower twist barrels will better shoot lighter bullets and will not spin them apart, as can happen with light bullets in fast twist barrels.

(top) The reloading scale that comes with your kit is almost always a balance arm type of scale. Personally, I can't stand these, so I bought a $115 Rangemaster 750 scale. It's easy to use and calibrate, and it's small too. It will run on A/C or you can take it to the range and run it off a 9V battery.

(above) There are a number of small tools you will need to have. Many of them come in the kits, but you will definitely need case lube (dip or spray on), extra reloading trays, and any convenience tools like bigger handles or hand priming tools that you might like to have.

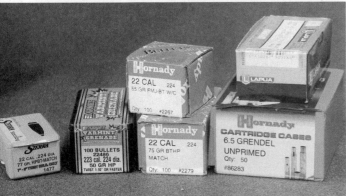

Receivers

The parts that hold everything together, or if you will, the box that contains all the parts of the gun to one degree or another, is called the receiver. On most firearms like the average traditional semi-auto hunting rifle, that box is composed of one piece and the bottom wall is missing, usually filled by the trigger housing. On the AR and a lot of modern sporting rifles, this box is split into two parts, the upper receiver and the lower receiver (on some rifles this is called the trigger housing, FAL, G3, etc.). Usually the upper receiver is the serial numbered part, but perversely for a rifle but rather normally for pistols, on the AR it's the lower half that has the all-important engraved number.

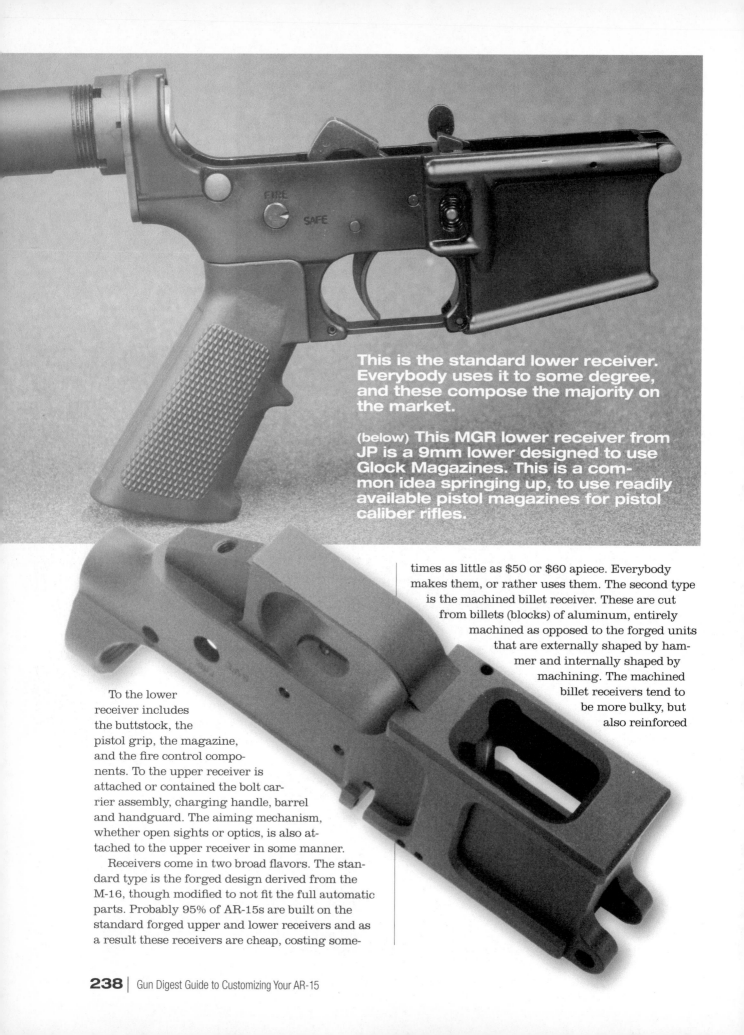

This is the standard lower receiver. Everybody uses it to some degree, and these compose the majority on the market.

(below) This MGR lower receiver from JP is a 9mm lower designed to use Glock Magazines. This is a common idea springing up, to use readily available pistol magazines for pistol caliber rifles.

To the lower receiver includes the buttstock, the pistol grip, the magazine, and the fire control components. To the upper receiver is attached or contained the bolt carrier assembly, charging handle, barrel and handguard. The aiming mechanism, whether open sights or optics, is also attached to the upper receiver in some manner.

Receivers come in two broad flavors. The standard type is the forged design derived from the M-16, though modified to not fit the full automatic parts. Probably 95% of AR-15s are built on the standard forged upper and lower receivers and as a result these receivers are cheap, costing some-

times as little as $50 or $60 apiece. Everybody makes them, or rather uses them. The second type is the machined billet receiver. These are cut from billets (blocks) of aluminum, entirely machined as opposed to the forged units that are externally shaped by hammer and internally shaped by machining. The machined billet receivers tend to be more bulky, but also reinforced

This is a typical machined-from-billet lower receiver.

(below) This is a typical billet lower receiver and upper receiver set. Note the heavy reinforcement around the stock interface at the rear of the receiver and around the magazine well, and the much thicker upper receiver, lacking forward assist and port cover. It is also typical for these receivers to have an integral trigger guard, and for the reinforcements to be cosmetic enhancers as well. If it looks angular with faceted features, it is a billet receiver.

in all the right places, making a structurally stronger receiver. The companies that make them also tend to incorporate enhanced cosmetics into the reinforcement making more visually appealing receivers in the process. They will come in sets of complementary upper and lower receivers, when available. However, the trade-off is a substantially higher price. While they have been as low as $150 per piece, this is uncommon and most will cost upwards of $250 per piece or $400 or more per set. This is significant, but for those who figure the looks as an important part of a personalized rifle, the billet receiver sets are a necessity.

Manufacturers all purchase the forgings from a very few forges that make the raw materials for the receivers. The forging is then internally machined and the holes are drilled. Occasionally the forges can't keep up with the demand and then you generally see another billet set introduced by somebody.

The billets tend to be easier to acquire since many other industries use big blocks of aluminum. Relatively few use forgings that already look like AR receivers.

LOWER RECEIVER

The AR-15 is quite possibly the most home-built firearm in existence. It is easy to assemble and there is, as we have touched upon in previous chapters, lots of stuff to stick onto the gun in the world of the aftermarket. While you can certainly update an existing rifle, to build one you need a lower receiver, and this is the part that most people start with. With few exceptions, the receiver choices are pretty universally of decent quality. On occasion you will find issues of fitting to the upper receivers being poor, but this is generally the result of run out between the parts from two different manufacturers, and this is really to be expected. The next most common issue might be a magazine well that is marginally too tight or slightly loose. This results from the fabricator using a certain type or brand of magazine as a model for the magazine well and, of course, everybody uses something different. Even so, if the mag well is too tight, some minor modification to the interior of the magazine well or to the magazine will fix the problem.

UPPER RECEIVER

The upper receiver tends to see as much variation as the lower. The standard forged receiver incorporates an ejection port cover and forward

The MGI Hydra lower receiver is modular and can accept a number of MGI's magazine wells. They are simply exchanged and range from .223 to 9mm to 7.62x39. The AK magazine wells allow the use of AK magazines, which helps to solve the problem inherent in 7.62x39 AR-15s, the lack of large amounts of reliable magazines. In that caliber, they are kind of hit and miss, because the straight  nature of the magazine well does not well comport to the rather steep taper of this cartridge. The Hydra mag wells gives new life to that caliber in the AR. Modular upper receivers are available from MGI as well. This rifle has not yet been built but the author is greatly anticipating the result.

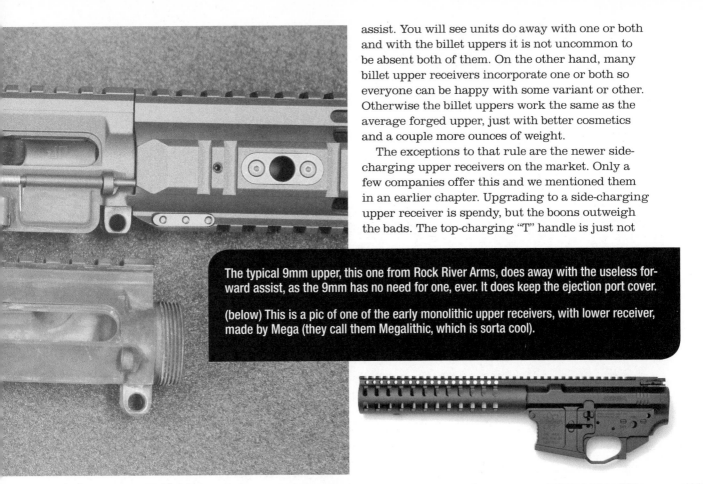

assist. You will see units do away with one or both and with the billet uppers it is not uncommon to be absent both of them. On the other hand, many billet upper receivers incorporate one or both so everyone can be happy with some variant or other. Otherwise the billet uppers work the same as the average forged upper, just with better cosmetics and a couple more ounces of weight.

The exceptions to that rule are the newer side-charging upper receivers on the market. Only a few companies offer this and we mentioned them in an earlier chapter. Upgrading to a side-charging upper receiver is spendy, but the boons outweigh the bads. The top-charging "T" handle is just not

The typical 9mm upper, this one from Rock River Arms, does away with the useless forward assist, as the 9mm has no need for one, ever. It does keep the ejection port cover.

(below) This is a pic of one of the early monolithic upper receivers, with lower receiver, made by Mega (they call them Megalithic, which is sorta cool).

In order from the left is a 9mm RRA upper, a standard AR upper from Del-Ton, and a PSC-11 from JP. Note the differences in design, and also the similarities. They will all work on a standard lower receiver.

With a side charge handle, you can keep your cheekweld and eyes on target even when pulling the handle fully to the rear, unless that is, you shoot with "nose to charging handle," choked up on the stock.

that user friendly, even though everybody is used to operating it. It's relatively fragile and you have to move your face off the gun to use it. The reason these side charge uppers are more expensive is that you generally have to get a matching side-charging bolt carrier (or modify your standard carrier) and that they are universally billet cut uppers. The proprietary side-charging uppers (not to be confused with the modified standard chargers with slot cut receivers and knobs drilled into the right side of the carrier) are all designed with the handle on the left side, to be operated with the support hand. As mentioned already several times, this keeps the face on the stock cheek weld, and the firing hand fully emplaced where it should be, on the pistol grip, ready to fire. Pew. Pew. Pew.

One interesting, fairly new invention is the monolithic upper receiver. This is nothing more than the upper receiver and handguard being machined from a single piece of aluminum. These uppers are the most rigid and theoretically will allow slightly greater accuracy, since the interface between the receiver and handguard is technically a minor weak point. Only a few companies make these and they are expensive, but really something to look at. The specialized tools needed for barrel installation are either included with the monolithic upper, or the upper utilizes some sort of quick-change capacity.

INGREDIENTS

AR receivers are almost always made of aluminum alloy. DPMS used to make a stainless steel lower receiver that was sort of attractive (though much heavier) and Turnbull has begun making rifles with steel upper and lower receivers that are color case hardened with wood furniture to go along with it. These rifles are absurdly attractive (and high sale price) and give a much appreciated traditional look to a thoroughly modern rifle.

For years Bushmaster, and previously Professional Ordnance, has been making carbon fiber receivers. These receivers worked well and produced guns that tipped less than four pounds on a scale. They are still available from Bushmaster and Windham Weaponry, but do have a few non-cross compatible parts in them. Plastic receivers are the new thing and a bunch of smaller manufacturers are trying them out. The plastic by nature is not as resilient as aluminum, but it can be much less expensive. The Omni Hybrid receivers that American Tactical Imports is making MSRP for $50 and that is a pretty, pretty price. They look good too, being very reminiscent of a billet lower receiver, for the same reasons regarding cosmetics and structural integrity.

Regardless of what type of receiver you choose to build into a rifle, make sure it makes use of standard components (as the vast, vast majority do).

80%ERS

As a final note, I want to address the 80% lower receivers available. An 80% lower is a forged or machined billet lower that is incomplete to the point that ATF does not consider it to be a firearm yet. Basically, the outside has been shaped, but the interior specifics like the trigger pocket and extension tube threads have not been machined, nor have any holes been drilled. No serial number is present as it is not yet a firearm. The magazine well is generally present, as you need an EDM machine or broach to properly form it and most people don't have those next to the drill press in the garage.

Since it is not yet considered legally to be a firearm, no federal background check is necessary to purchase one. You pay your $25 and take it home and finish the fabrication yourself, which is and always ought to be, perfectly legal. Here's where the problem lies. First, even though you can get fixtures to help you do it right, it's still not the same as a professionally made receiver and frankly, most people do not have the equipment or skills to adequately finish the receiver. This means you have to take it to someone else to do it for you, which possibly opens a can of worms, depending on how ATF is feeling that day.

Secondly, the powers-that-be really don't like these things. They can't control them. They have already gone after one company that makes a ver-

sion of this and confiscated their customer lists, I assume to ostensibly go confiscate from them since they decided that this particular model of unfinished receiver did not satisfy the 80% receiver rules. Honestly, you are better off not messing with these unfinished or 80% lowers. Because really, the big reason people are drawn to these things is that they are paper free. But the guys who pursue this option already are multiple gun owners anyway. This means that at some point they have undergone a NICS background check, which means that the .gov already knows you own some kind of gun. At this point, getting an 80% lower and finishing it yourself, and only you know you have it, no longer applies because if they decide to get around to confiscating guns, they will come after your other guns too. And let's be really straight here. It's only a secret if only you know about it, and none of you guys is going to be able to resist showing it to your current buddies. "Current" being the key term here.

I don't find the advantages of finishing an 80% lower to be worth the converse. In this I disagree with many other writers and consumers. Make your own decision, but if you are a new gun owner or a recent convert to the AR side of things, leave it be.

> This ATI Omni Hybrid lower receiver has the 9mm conversion installed in it. The Omni Hybrid is plastic and has been reinforced heavily in some areas, as well has having an aluminum insert to hold the receiver extension. This receiver has a $50 MSRP, an extremely good value.

AK Accessorization

he AR-15 is America's rifle, and for good reason. A significant percentage of Americans now owns at least one and it can be used for anything on the continent, provided it has the appropriate upper and cartridge for the task. It is certainly the most popular rifle for the consumer to build on their own, and probably the easiest, requiring only a couple of specialized tools.

Well, the AK and the FN-FAL are the world's rifles. When we used the M-14, everybody else that didn't openly hate us used the FAL. The rest of the world used the AK, and still does. Fortunately, we still have the opportunity to own these guns if we purchase them from a few sources that manufacture them here in the U.S. For the most part, they are purchased as parts from overseas sources and then built here with American receivers and other parts to comply with U.S. law. Like ARs, these guns are commonly built at home, and that's why I'm including them in this AR book. All three guns are quite popular; all three are fairly easily assembled with basic tooling and a very few specialized, affordable tools; and all three are very, very good rifles. When a guy has an AR and then he wants something different, he gets an AK. When he wants something else, he gets an FAL or HK. The order might change, but there's a good chance that if a gun owner has one of the above, he will soon get one or both of the others.

So in this chapter and the next we'll explore some of the options for accessorizing the AK and the FAL. The AK opportunities are numerous, though nowhere near as vast as the stuff that's available for the AR platforms. The FAL accessories are actually pretty limited, but it is still a very popular rifle, and the affordability of American parts and the value in imported parts kits ensure that it is often homebuilt as well. So we'll cover the limited selection of parts for that rifle as well in the next chapter. In either case, we'll briefly discuss the building of a rifle from a kit, though that will not be the focus here. We're concentrating on the parts that are easy to replace or upgrade, rather than building from scratch, since doing so is much more time- and tool-intensive than it is with ARs.

AK RIFLES ON THE MARKET

The typical AK is chambered in 7.62x39 Russian and is sold with the standard rifle barrel of a hair over 16" in length. A fixed wooden stock, pistol grip, and forend assembly is typical and will usually be shipped with a single 30-round magazine. This was the original configuration of the AK-47 when it showed up and the basic pattern remains true.

The early guns had a stamped receiver, but the Soviets weren't all that good at stampings yet so went to a machined receiver. Later they figured out how to do it and the AK-47 became the AKM,

This is the classic AK-47. This is what everyone envisions when they hear the word "AK-47." It's a classic, it's a reliable gun, and it's boring. iStock photo.

and this is the pattern that most of the AKs on the market seem to follow. There are several, notably from Arsenal, Inc., that can be purchased with the stronger yet heavier machined receiver. All the receivers that are sold on the market for private

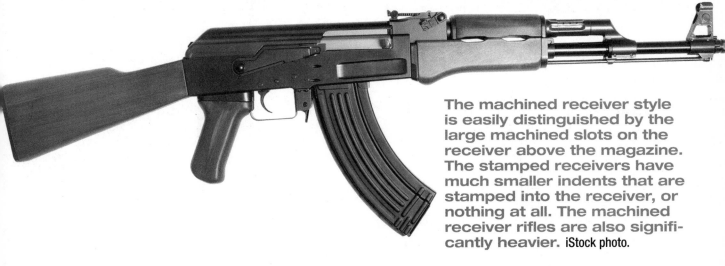

The machined receiver style is easily distinguished by the large machined slots on the receiver above the magazine. The stamped receivers have much smaller indents that are stamped into the receiver, or nothing at all. The machined receiver rifles are also significantly heavier. iStock photo.

gun assembly are stamped, though there are little idiosyncrasies in all the variants that must be taken into account. For example, there are side folding stocks, underfolding stocks, pistols with no stocks at all, wire frame stocks, etc. There are Polish, Russian, Romanian, Chinese, Bulgarian, Hungarian, Yugoslav, and a few East German types out there. The majority lately has been Bulgarian, Romanian, and Yugoslav and most of these different styles have slightly different articles in their designs that may not be compatible with the others. Most of the stuff does cross over though.

Since all these guns are subject to 922(r) regulations they have to be built with no more than 10 of the parts on the list. So as we go through the options, please remember that you must keep an accurate count and that there can be no more than 10 foreign-made parts from the list. While there are a few ARs that are imported, they are few in number and we don't at the moment need to consider that gun and its relationship to the 922(r) restrictions. However, the AKs and FALs are very much subject and attention must be paid. You don't want to be prosecuted for not having a U.S. made piston. While I don't know if anyone has been successfully nailed because of 922(r) violations, it doesn't pay to take the chance. Check Appendix A for a comprehensive breakdown of the 922(r) regulations and the listed parts. Each part is considered a major required part for the functioning of the firearm, so the list is not quite as random as an initial glance might suggest.

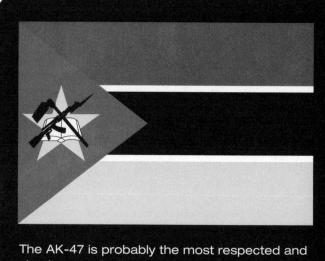

The AK-47 is probably the most respected and simultaneously the most hated gun in the world. The West cordially hates it because the West has had to fight against it for so many years. To Third World nations like Mozambique, on the other hand, it contains enough symbolism to appear on the national flag.

BARRELS

It's virtually unheard of to replace an AK barrel unless that barrel was horribly damaged. It cannot be changed as easily as an AR barrel. The AK barrel is press fit and pinned into its trunnion, which is riveted into the receiver. Indeed, you might

After you gain some familiarity with your AK you might consider building one, sort of like an AR, but not. There is a bit more labor involved, and a couple expensive tools. This is what you start with, in this case a Bulgarian AK-74 parts kit. Frankly, it's a big mess.

Unlike most kits, this Bulgarian AK-74 kit had the receiver scraps completely removed. This saves time and effort of removing them from the front and rear trunnions. The old rivets must still be removed and replaced.

(right) AK barrels are heavily pinned in place. The front sight and gas block both have cross pins. These stubs of barrel must be removed so the other parts can be used. These are the remnants from the original rifle, built, but never apparently fired. The rifle was disassembled, the receiver cut, and the parts put into a bag and shipped to the U.S.

While ARs' barrels are retained by a simple barrel retaining nut, the AK has a front trunnion that is riveted to the receiver, and a barrel that is held in the trunnion by a press fit and a large cross pin, here.

even be better off just buying a new gun than paying to have the barrel changed. As a result, the aftermarket support for barrels is pretty much restricted to replacements for the barrels that are cut in the parts kits.

The downside to building your own AK is that the barrel is probably the most difficult and gear-intensive part to install. Most folks who build their own AKs will do so with the basis of an imported parts kit. A U.S.-made barrel is almost always used. The original barrel trunnion, gas block, and front sight are still attached to the barrel, but the barrel sections that used to connect those parts has been cut off and thrown away. Since the barrel is pressed into the trunnion, you need to press it out and for that you need a hydraulic press. It also helps to have a fixture for this and an excellent example made by AK Builder is sold by Brownells. After

(above) This is a pistol version of an AK. The I.O. Hellpup is basically a short-barreled AK without a buttstock, which allows it to be classified as a handgun. Its weight makes it pleasant to shoot as well, if somewhat heavy for one handed firing. It is to this pistol that we will add stuff in the rest of this chapter.

This replacement barrel was made by High Standard and purchased from Brownells. Just like with AR parts, AK parts of all varieties (and tools too) can be obtained there. This 5.45x39 barrel was also finished with Graphite Black Cerakote.

(left) For many years, the AK rifles were manufactured with a muzzle device that had a simple "slant" in it. It worked by directing some of the propellant gas up and to the right, compensating for a right handed shooter. It actually worked pretty well, and many factory rifles still use it. The muzzle threads are protected by a simple nut if the slant brake or other device is not present.

(below) This Liberty Suppressors Phoenix flash hider is long enough to make a 14 ½" barrel legal if permanently attached. This is one of many options available from Brownells.

(bottom) The AK-74 brought to the AK family a large muzzle brake and compensator that actually attaches to the front sight housing rather than the barrel. It has a huge internal expansion chamber with exit ports to the top and right side, and a large baffle forward of the chamber which performs as a brake. It is quite loud but is also one of the most effective re-coil- and muzzle-flip-reducing muzzle devices ever made. The basic design has been robbed and modified for years.

you push the barrel out, you have to push the new barrel in, drill the gas port, and then install the gas tube and front sight, drill the holes for the cross pins for those, rivet the whole thing together, and then stamp and refinish the whole thing. It is enough trouble that most people find a gunsmith or AK armorer to assemble at least the barrel area of things onto their receiver. The result is good, but here is where the AK deviates greatly from the ARs and shows that changing the barrel is not done on a whim.

This is not to say that different length barrels are not available. There are pistol length barrels for the pistol builds based on the short barreled AKs. There are long heavyweight barrels for the RPK builds. There are 7.62x39 barrels for the AK-47 builds and there are 5.45 barrels for the AK-74 builds. You can even find .223 barrels and magazines, but those guns are usually only available from the factory.

As far as muzzle devices go, there is a pretty good selection. All kinds of stuff from the usual manufacturers like Yankee Hill Machine, Surefire, Primary Weapons Systems, Troy, and others can be screwed onto the muzzle of an AK-47. There is much less choice for the AK-74 since the muzzle device on that rifle is usually directly affixed to the standard front sight assembly. Furthermore, the basic AK-74 comp/brake is often kept since it is a very effective model. Muzzle attachments, be they comp or flash hider, and the barrel threads,

are regulated under 922(r) as well, so don't forget the count. Taking an American-made brake off and replacing it with an original Bulgarian may put you in violation.

STOCKS

The buttstocks are frequently replaced, mostly because the owner wants to use an American-made part. The parts kits come with original buttstocks (made overseas) and the stock is a cheap way to get a U.S. part on the gun. Straight up replacements (which are essentially identical) are the most common, but the AR-style collapsible stock is well-liked on the market, and several companies have made adaptors that allow the use of these stocks.

Most AKs came with a simple, fixed, plastic or wooden stock. It was rather short by American standards (because American stocks are way too long), though there are "NATO"-length stocks available to lengthen the pull to better accommodate taller shooters. Underfolding stocks were also very common. These required a pivot point on either side of the stock, and are not very comfortable. The stock was formed from stampings and can be folded when a magazine is seated in the receiver.

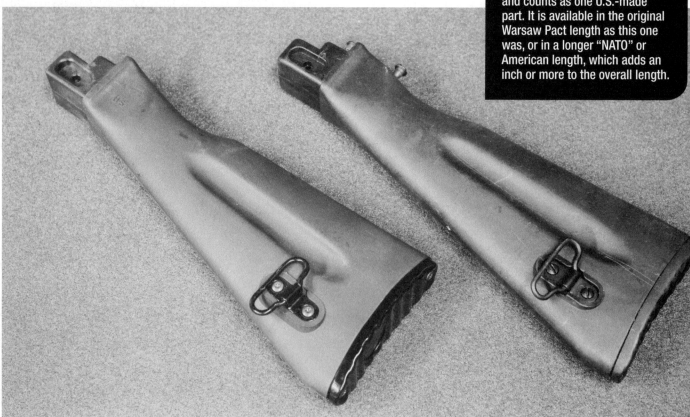

The stock on the left is a U.S.-made replacement for the Bulgarian stock on top. They are identical, though of course the U.S. stock is and looks newer even though it was a blem (the shininess of the metal should give that away). This cost $30 and counts as one U.S.-made part. It is available in the original Warsaw Pact length as this one was, or in a longer "NATO" or American length, which adds an inch or more to the overall length.

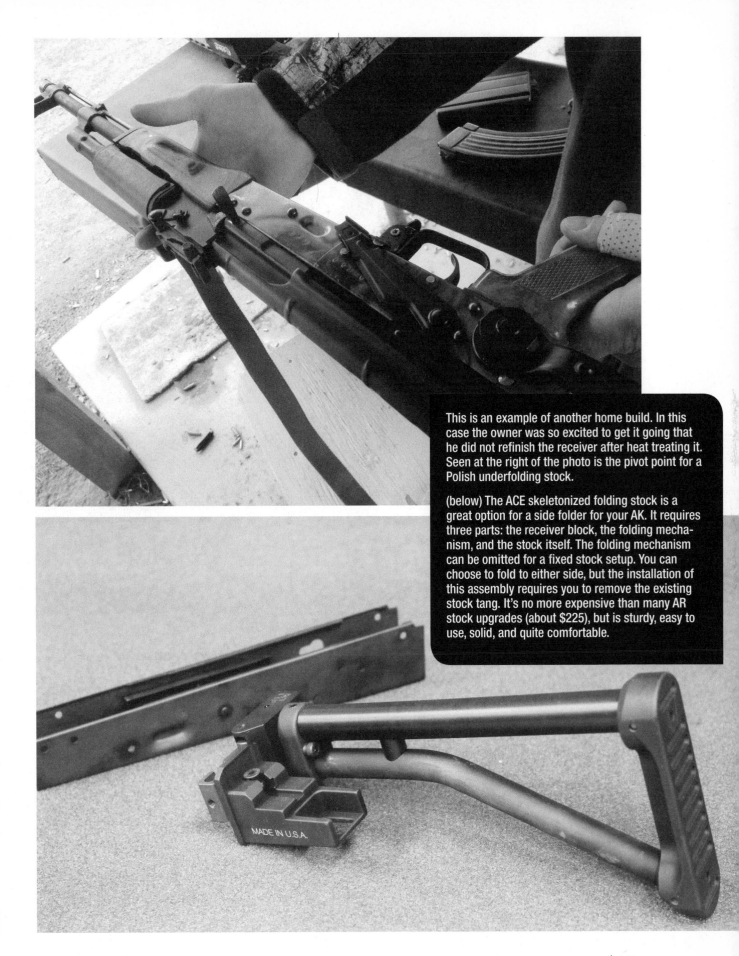

This is an example of another home build. In this case the owner was so excited to get it going that he did not refinish the receiver after heat treating it. Seen at the right of the photo is the pivot point for a Polish underfolding stock.

(below) The ACE skeletonized folding stock is a great option for a side folder for your AK. It requires three parts: the receiver block, the folding mechanism, and the stock itself. The folding mechanism can be omitted for a fixed stock setup. You can choose to fold to either side, but the installation of this assembly requires you to remove the existing stock tang. It's no more expensive than many AR stock upgrades (about $225), but is sturdy, easy to use, solid, and quite comfortable.

MADE IN U.S.A.

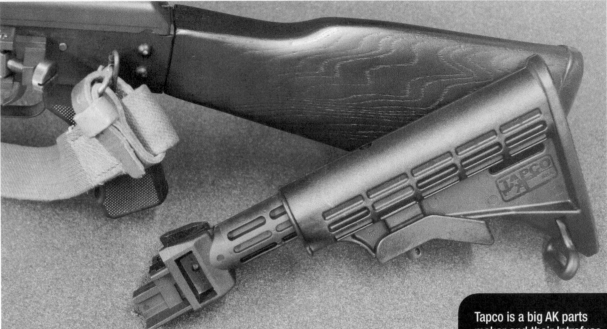

It is virtually identical to the underfolding stock that the Germans had on the MP-38/40 series of submachine guns in WWII. More recent versions, particularly in the Russian and Bulgarian designs, might display a folding stock that looks like a fixed standard stock. These are pretty neat because they are sturdy and much more comfortable than the underfolding style. The side folding wire frame stocks are very light but uncomfortable, and furthermore, they look like hell. It's like you have a full gun that someone decided to stick a clothes hanger into the back of. I'm sure someone will, but I can't imagine why anyone would want to install something like that on a gun if they have other choices. This stock is the kind you'll find on the Polish Tantal 5.45x39 and its clones.

Still, whatever you want, you can probably find. There are several options only available domestically, such as the ACE skeleton stock that can also be used in one of its versions in the AK series. Throw in the other folding and collapsible stocks, there should be something for everyone.

Be aware that you may have to do some fairly significant alteration to your rifle if you want to change the stock, say, from a standard fixed to something else. You may have to grind off the top tang from the rear trunnion. You may have to remove the rear trunnion (grind or cut off the rivets) and put a different one in. If you are home-building, then simply use the right parts to begin with. It's a lot easier to get the receiver designed for the underfolding stock than to modify a fixed stock receiver for the underfolder. In particular, the Russian style left side folding mechanism is a very good design, but the receiver must have

several holes and a machined slot, and it's much easier to get this in the receiver from the factory than to do it yourself.

HANDGUARDS

Most of the handguards that you will find for the AKs are like the buttstocks, simply American-made replacements for the original foreign-made pieces. Of course since this falls in the parts counts, it like, totally makes sense to upgrade since you have to replace it anyway. There are a few more options for AK handguards than just for the replacement. Like with the AR units, there are four-railed options for the AK, or one rail, or whatever. Samson, Troy Ind., Midwest Ind., CAA, The Mako Group all make railed forends for the AR platforms, and they also produce railed forends for the AK systems. These are just the big name guys; there are plenty of less well-known companies that make them as well. Again, just like with the AR. Let's look at just one of them, the Midwest Industries AK47/74 Universal Handguard.

This is a direct replacement unit and can be purchased with some options. The standard top half has a Picatinny rail. You can also get a top with a scope ring designed to mount an Aimpoint

Tapco is a big AK parts maker and their Intrafuse AK T6 stock is sold by the thousands to consumers and by the thousands to manufacturers as OEM equipment. It is essentially an M4 stock with an AK stock adaptor piece. Just remove your standard buttstock (two screws) and insert this unit in its place. It comes with screws and a drill pin to make the pilot holes in the stock adaptor. This allows it to be used with a number of AK variants.

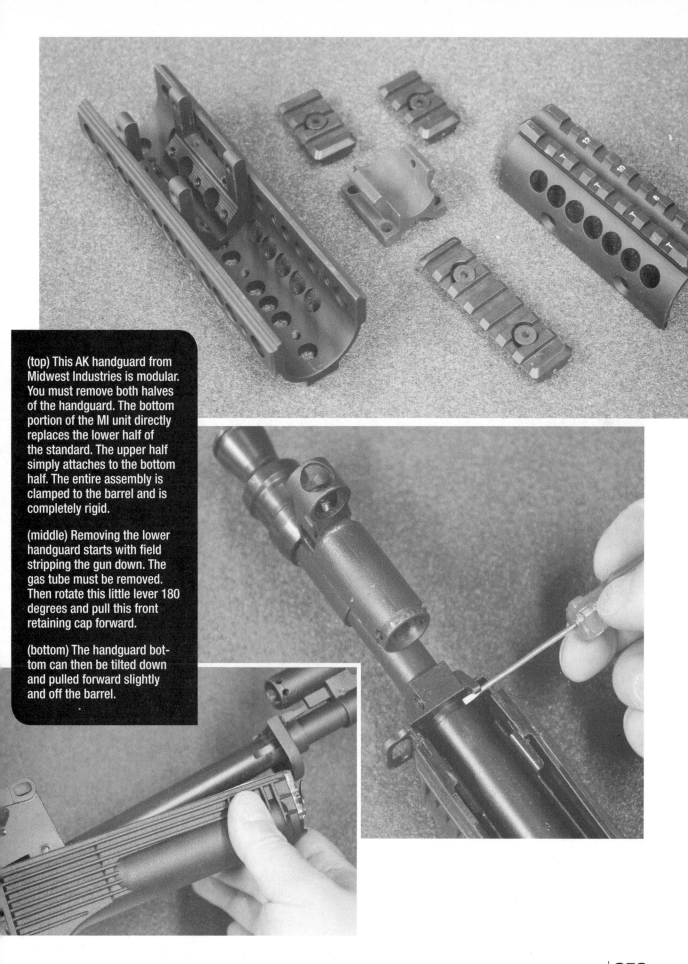

(top) This AK handguard from Midwest Industries is modular. You must remove both halves of the handguard. The bottom portion of the MI unit directly replaces the lower half of the standard. The upper half simply attaches to the bottom half. The entire assembly is clamped to the barrel and is completely rigid.

(middle) Removing the lower handguard starts with field stripping the gun down. The gas tube must be removed. Then rotate this little lever 180 degrees and pull this front retaining cap forward.

(bottom) The handguard bottom can then be tilted down and pulled forward slightly and off the barrel.

The MI lower half can then be attached to the barrel and clamped down tightly.

CompML2 red dot. Other options include a number of micro-red dot sights such as the Vortex SPARC, the Trijicon RMR, or the Burris Fastfire. This upper half is attached to the lower half which clamps solidly to the barrel.

They tend to take a bit more effort to install, but not horribly so. Of course, when you are building from the ground up, you can avoid some of the disassembly issues. For example, you will often have to replace the stock piece that is attached to the gas tube. For most users this means simply rotating the old one off and rotating a new one on, as the retaining cups holding this wood piece are crimped in place. Many of these handguards and rails also incorporate a top piece that covers the gas tube, so removal of the wood in this location is mandatory.

(opposite bottom) The upper half of the MI universal handguard installation requires the upper wood or plastic piece to be removed as well. It looks hard, but isn't. Place the back of the gas tube, where the flats are, into a crescent wrench and hold it. Take your other hand and rotate the handguard piece so that it is on the bottom of the gas tube and pull it off.

(top) Reinstall the gas tube and then the upper half of the universal handguard can be attached to the lower half via these screws.

(bottom) The Picatinny rail, while universal, will usually make the irons unusable. Still, this Bushnell TRS-25 makes a good match for this handguard.

Unfortunately, there does not appear to be any way to free float an AK, simply because the gas tube and piston are housed right above the barrel. It's doubtful that a huge increase in accuracy would be possible anyway, as so many other parts are made to such loose tolerances to accommodate dirt that the benefits of free floating would be nowhere near that which the AR receives.

PISTOL GRIPS

A lot of people find the standard AK pistol grip to be uncomfortable. I find that the taper of the grip is just the opposite of what I want. I like the grip to taper slightly at the top, with a slightly wider bottom, and on the AKs it is perfectly straight with a hump on the bottom. I find it more difficult to feel like I have good control and leverage with the shooting hand, so aftermarket grips are a good solution. In fact, the Tapco SAW style grip follows this concept, is much larger in circumference, and also changes the grip angle rather sharply. The U.S. Palm pistol grip changes the angle and keeps a somewhat thinner profile and is quite comfortable.

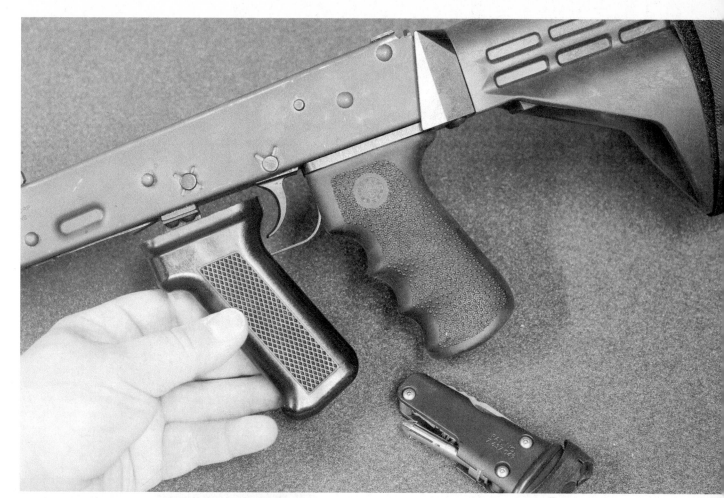

(opposite top) AKs use an angled square nut that protrudes down through the receiver to attach the pistol grip. The standard grip uses a very long screw to affix. Most aftermarket magazines are hollow and us a much shorter screw.

(left) The U.S. Palm AK Battle Grip next to the original. You can see that this is a completely different style and shape than the original "factory" Combloc grip.

(above) The AK grip by Hogue can be purchased in a package that includes an AK survivor tool set.

Like with the U.S. Palm grip, we here see a comparison between the standard grip and the MagPul MOE AK47 grip. Note that the MagPul grip much more closely duplicates the angle of the original, but adds a moderate palm swell to the back of it. Just that little palm swell makes the pistol handle and feel completely differently.

(below) The SB-47 brace is made by Century Arms. Similar to the SIG-SAUER stabilizing brace for AR-15s, this allows an AK pistol to be fired with great steadiness with one hand. It has an L-shaped steel cup/bracket at the front, whose bottom is sandwiched between the pistol grip and the receiver.

I have yet to see a replacement grip that doesn't do away with that "straight" taper.

Samson manufacturing makes a Field Survival Tool that fits inside the pistol grip of an AK Ergo grip. This has all the most useful tools for maintaining an AK in the field, including cleaning equipment and a broken case extractor, which is most handy. It simply slides up into the grip. There is a comparable model for ARs that fits up into the standard A2 pistol grip.

One interesting accessory that is grip related is the pistol brace made by Century Arms. Similar to the SB15 brace that SIGSAUER makes for the ARs, the SB47 brace is attached to an AK pistol and wraps around the shooter's forearm. It does a surprisingly good job of reducing muzzle flip when used as designed, though some older stiffer people may not be able to comfortably contort their shoulder, neck, and arm sufficiently to aim this pistol with an SB47 attached with only one hand. It's also a heavy combo and you had better have strong deltoids to hold the thing on target.

The shorter screw of the MagPul grip allows a much better clamping force on the brace's bracket than the much longer screw of the original grip. With the original grip, it is difficult to tighten the screw enough to prevent side to side rotational play with the brace bracket.

MAGAZINES AND AMMO

The majority of ammunition that you will find for an AK is foreign made, steel cased and relatively inexpensive. Unlike the choices available for domestic cartridges, you will be quite limited in selection of bullets. For example, there are reloading options with U.S. manufactured bullets but they are pretty limited to simple soft pointed or ballistic tipped hunting rounds, and you can't really use those in the steel cases anyway. While a lot of people use SKS rifles, very few use AKs when deer hunting for example. To reload, you would have to purchase domestically made ammo from say, Winchester, Federal, or Hornady to get the cases, though some unloaded virgin cases might be found at times. Mostly, it's just much more affordable to shoot the cheap stuff, and you will find a couple hunting cartridges out there too.

Fortunately, the AKs have always been designed to fire steel-cased ammo, and the cases have sufficient taper to make extraction a bit easier than the much more straight-walled cases used in most AR calibers. Plus, you don't need to worry so much about chamber and receiver fouling as you would with the American rifle.

This is a .223 round and a 7.62x39mm round. Note the vast difference in the case wall taper. This more acute taper in the 7.62x39 enhances its reliable extraction ability. The much more straight-walled .223 case works against it in the short carbine gas systems and is a factor in the extraction problems frequently encountered in those rifles.

This is a representative example of AK amoo. From the left is the basic full metal jacketed 69 grain 5.45x39mm bullet in a polymer coated steel case made in Ukraine. Next is a hollow pointed 7.62x39mm model made by Wolf in Russia (it does not expand). Then we have a remanufactured domestic hunting load using a soft nosed bullet loaded into used Israeli cases by Wisconsin Cartridge Corp. Finally is a Hornady brand cartridge using a 60 gr. V-Max 5.45x39 bullet loaded into an out-sourced lacquered steel case.

(right) This is one of the gajillions of Korean steel magazines imported recently. They are reliable and cheap. They are also made in the pattern of the millions upon millions of standard stamped steel magazines made in the last 65 years.

(bottom) This is one of the many brands of domestical-ly-made plastic magazines without steel reinforcement. They work pretty well but the feed lips can, on some rifles, deform without the steel inserts. The magazine on the right is a Bulgarian manufactured magazine which includes the steel reinforcement. It is priced more accordingly. The bright line on the feed lip of this magazine, barely visible in the lower right corner, is the exposed steel feed lip reinforcement.

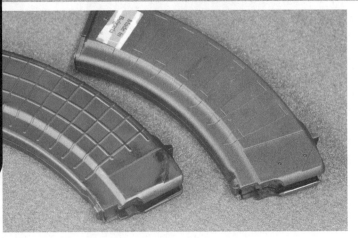

models, are quite long but otherwise identical to the standard 30-round steel mags. Some peoples' kids just have to buy the 75-round drum magazines, but be warned that some of these are a bit iffy in reliability. They aren't too expensive, actually, so if the one you bought doesn't work, sell it to your sucker of a buddy and buy one that does.

As magazines go, the surplus magazines from the old ComBloc are generally pretty good, regardless of the source. AK magazines, at least the steel ones, were made to take a beating, and even forty- or fifty-year-old examples are often found in excellent working condition. New steel magazines are still imported, oddly enough many from Korea, and work well, as do the majority of plastic magazines made by every Tom, Dick, and Harry. Rumor has it the best magazines are the Bulgarian "Circle 10" models made by Arsenal, Inc., and they are indeed well constructed, with rigid polymer bodies and steel reinforced feed lips and lugs. They are also the most expensive.

You may find the need to fully satisfy the capacitor level in your brain/magazine interface unit and purchase a larger than 30-round magazine. The 40-round mags, originally designed for the RPK

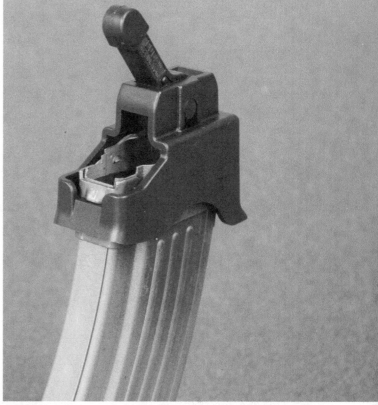

(top left) The steel reinforced polymer magazines made in Bulgaria are often considered the highest quality and most resilient on the market. This one on is a 5.45 AK-74 magazine with the valued "Circle-10" stamp on it.

(above) The Lula magazine loaders are really effective. You can get a sore thumb pretty quick when you are working 30 rounds against a stiff mag spring. The magazine fits into the Lula loader just as it would a receiver. The toggle on top is simply pushed forward and a round inserted, then pushed rearward and another round is inserted. This is repeated until the magazine is full. It can rapidly be unloaded in the same way, then adding in gravity to pull the rounds out from under the feed lips (hold mag top forward down so rounds slide out front). You are making use of a great deal of leverage with that toggle. These loaders are available for zillions of firearms and are only about $25 each.

(left) A standard 30-round magazine, next to a 40-round RPK magazine, next to a 75-round drum magazine.

FIRE CONTROL PARTS

You are going to want to get a U.S.-made set of fire control parts if you are building a gun on your own. The retail available guns will all have them already. Match triggers are mostly unheard of; Timney triggers was said to be working on one a couple years ago, but I haven't seen it yet. You will have a couple of choices for standard triggers. Tapco makes the most popular model and it is used as OEM equipment in a lot of the rifles on the shelf.

High Standard, makers of the famous .22 pistol, have entered the AK market in force and make trigger/sear/hammer combinations in addition to barrels and all kinds of other parts for the AKs. I should note that some of the more "sporting" style AK models, particularly the shotguns, the ones without pistol grips, have a separate connector piece between the trigger and sear, as the trigger is mounted several inches farther to the rear on these guns. Fortunately, they are already 922(r) compatible, so it shouldn't be much of a concern.

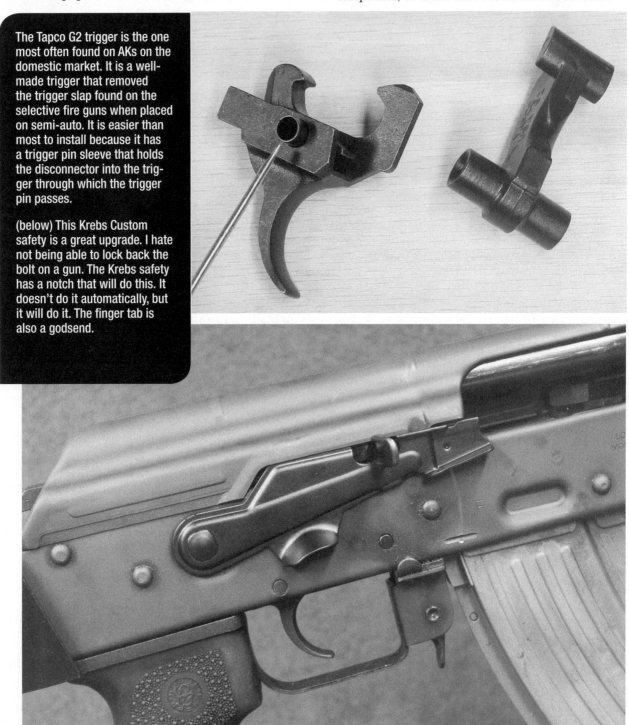

The Tapco G2 trigger is the one most often found on AKs on the domestic market. It is a well-made trigger that removed the trigger slap found on the selective fire guns when placed on semi-auto. It is easier than most to install because it has a trigger pin sleeve that holds the disconnector into the trigger through which the trigger pin passes.

(below) This Krebs Custom safety is a great upgrade. I hate not being able to lock back the bolt on a gun. The Krebs safety has a notch that will do this. It doesn't do it automatically, but it will do it. The finger tab is also a godsend.

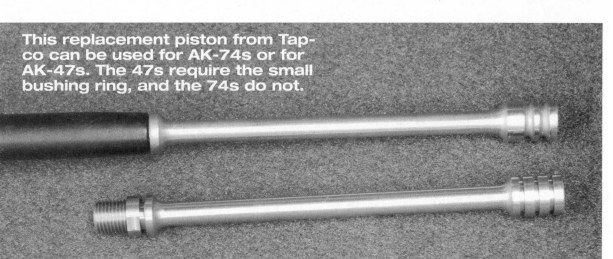

This replacement piston from Tapco can be used for AK-74s or for AK-47s. The 47s require the small bushing ring, and the 74s do not.

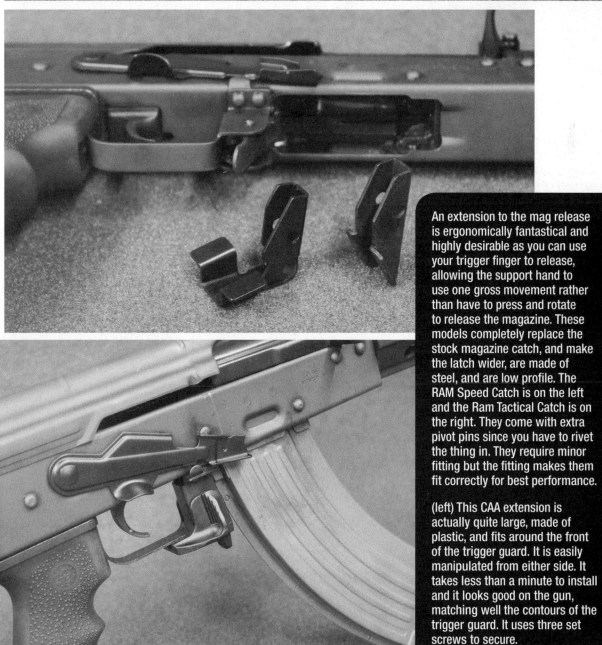

An extension to the mag release is ergonomically fantastical and highly desirable as you can use your trigger finger to release, allowing the support hand to use one gross movement rather than have to press and rotate to release the magazine. These models completely replace the stock magazine catch, and make the latch wider, are made of steel, and are low profile. The RAM Speed Catch is on the left and the Ram Tactical Catch is on the right. They come with extra pivot pins since you have to rivet the thing in. They require minor fitting but the fitting makes them fit correctly for best performance.

(left) This CAA extension is actually quite large, made of plastic, and fits around the front of the trigger guard. It is easily manipulated from either side. It takes less than a minute to install and it looks good on the gun, matching well the contours of the trigger guard. It uses three set screws to secure.

If you have an AK, you need a bayonet. Need it. Need it bad.

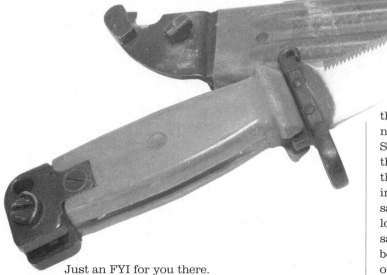

Just an FYI for you there.

There have been some alternate or enhanced safeties. The Galil, the Israeli version of the AK, had a thumb lever (on the left side) attached to what was essentially the standard right side safety lever. You might find this on the really expensive AKs, like those made by Krebs Custom. Krebs also makes a drop-in replacement for the safety lever that is normally standard on all AKs. This lever normally on the standard safeties only goes from SAFE to FIRE, or if the gun is a machinegun, there is an extra full auto step in there. When the lever is on SAFE, it also blocks the charging handle from being fully retracted. The Krebs safety lever also has a cutout that you can use to lock the charging handle to the rear, a handy user safety, as it makes good sense to be able to lock the bolt back. Furthermore, it has a shelf that sticks out halfway back the lever so that you can reach your trigger finger up to disengage or engage the safety. This is impossible to do on a standard safety lever without having to take your hand away from the grip. This is practically a must-have for AK owners and you wouldn't go back once you have it. Brownells sells these handy little things and I bet they are a great seller.

This is the usual means of attaching an optic to an AK. The receiver has a rail fastened to the left side to which clamps a mount that reaches up and over the top cover.

MISCELLANEOUS ACCESSORIES

There are a number of other replacement parts that might spark your interest. Of particular note, the presence of U.S. made pistons is a boon, since that is a relatively easy part to install for your parts count purposes.

Several manufacturers make magazine catch extensions. It's easier to use your trigger finger to release the magazine and your support hand to then remove the magazine than for your support hand to do both. All these extensions, either the clamp on ones or the longer latches themselves, allow this difference in manipulation to work.

All sorts of bayonets are on the market, should you want that accessory to complete the rifle. Many of the AK bayonets are neat in that they have a wire cutter incorporated in to the bayonet, to be used in conjunction with the sheath. Some of the older Chinese AKS rifles, should you run across them (you probably won't because the owners will be loath to sell them), will have folding

Installation of the TWS mount requires the replacement of the button of the recoil spring assembly. It comes with a modified version of the button that puts downward tension on the machined top cover, by means of an angle on the button's bottom.

(below) This Texas weapons systems mount replaces the usual top cover and fits on rigidly. The first thing you do is remove the rear sight. Set it to 1000 meters and then push down in the middle slot above the pivot point with a screwdriver. It may need a light tap on the handle. The sight when freed will travel at least seven feet so be careful. In this picture, the sight has been retrieved from the dog's shoulder and placed close to its original location for purposes of this illustration.

spike bayonets, much like some of the SKS rifles. There are some jurisdictions that require these to be removed. I hope you don't live there, and if you do I feel really sorry for you, that you live with such irrational municipal leaders.

Optics can be a bit complicated when it comes to AKs. Quite simply, they were not designed to accommodate them. You will often find AKs with a rail-like fixture on the left wall of the receiver. This is designed to accept a ComBloc style clamp on scope mount that hangs over the top of the receiver. The mount is necessarily high so that the receiver's top cover can be easily removed for cleaning, which means the optic is too high for an adequate cheek weld to be maintained on the stock. Several approaches have been attempted with success to address this boggle.

The first was probably by a company called Ultimak that makes gas piston tube replacements that incorporate a Pic rail on the top of them. You could then mount a forward red dot scope and this works really nicely, but since the tube has this unfortunate tendency to heat up, so does the optic that sits on top of it. So if you are doing mag dumps you might find your optic getting too hot, potentially ruining it. Similar methods of attaching an optic directly to a replacement handguard have become common too. If the rail does not touch the gas tube, then the heat problem is largely dissipated.

The rising method that several small companies

The front of the cover attaches and replaces the rear sight for rigidity at the front. A small spring tab, in conjunction with the angled button, tensions the rear.

have attempted is to run a rail over the top cover that attaches to the stock trunnion, or to place a rail on the cop cover itself. The best example of this is the AK rear sight rail system made by Krebs Custom. Normally, the top cover would be a horrible place to mount an optic, since it is not a secure surface. Both the top cover rail and the separate rail methods generally require removing the rear sight and using the rear sight housing on the barrel trunnion to secure the front of the cover or rail. The rear sight is then usually changed to an aperture sight and attached in some way to the rail at the back. Different approaches are used to make the cover or rail stiff so that a return to zero can be achieved after cleaning. Placing the scope low and over the receiver allows a proper cheek weld, the use of traditional or tactical magnifying scopes, and removes the heat problem of mounting over the gas tube.

With the optic mount on the top cover, the traditional style scope (with small objective) is much more usable. The average AK will shoot somewhere in the area of 3-4 MOA, though some shoot much better than that. So some surprising accuracy might be witnessed if you have a good rigid setup.

Slings and other articles are attached in the old familiar ways, or with the Quick Release types that have become popular with the ARs.

When you buy or build an AK you will want to get some form of front sight tool, even if only for the initial zeroing. Mikhail did not want his fellow illiterate conscripts taking the gun apart too much, so adjusting the front sight windage

requires the press that is built into all of these sights. They typically also include a wrench for adjusting the elevation. You can get these tools everywhere, online, in shops, at gunshows.

So it's pretty clear that the AK style of rifles is to a great extent upgradeable by the owner. It's certainly encouraged, as the upgrades will make the gun more ergonomic, more fun to shoot, and more your own, which means that you will get out and shoot it more.

Completed, the Texas Weapons Systems Dog Leg Scope Mount almost looks like it belongs on this AK pistol. This pistol is now completely optimized for fantasyland and Tannerite effects. With the sturdy scope mount and stable pistol forearm brace, hits at 800 yards are only a weekend away.

Many replacement handguards now have Quick Release swivel interfaces integral to the assembly.

This aftermarket QR socket and swivel from Uncle Mike's can be installed in just about any rifle. The socket can be glued into a hole drilled in a stock.

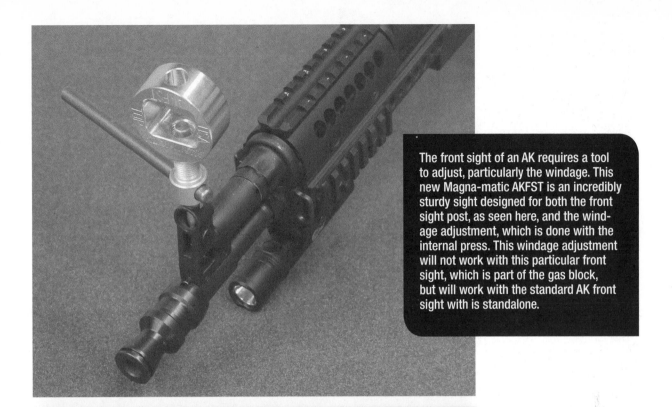

The front sight of an AK requires a tool to adjust, particularly the windage. This new Magna-matic AKFST is an incredibly sturdy sight designed for both the front sight post, as seen here, and the windage adjustment, which is done with the internal press. This windage adjustment will not work with this particular front sight, which is part of the gas block, but will work with the standard AK front sight with is standalone.

(below) Should you choose to build an AK from a kit, or for whatever reason, change out your barrel, you will need this selection of tools made by AK Builder and available from Brownells. The big tool and associated parts at the top is the riveting tool, the block at the lower left is for removing and reinstalling the rivets holding the trigger guard in place on the receiver, and the stuff on the right, including the long square bars are for removing and installing the barrel. One other big tool is needed and this is…

(right) …a 12 ton hydraulic press. The barrel press kit from AK builder fits right into this press. This thing cost close to $180 and works perfectly well for barrel installation. This is the only reason that I purchased this press and it was worth the money. It is not really a super high quality press, but it works for the job intended.

FAL
Customization:
The Free World's
Right Arm, Only Better

The FN-FAL was the 7.62mm competitor to the M-14 when the Army was looking to replace the old M1 Garand rifles in the fifties. It was designed by the firm Fabrique Nationale Herstal, located in Liege, Belgium. The firearms historians in the readership, amateur or professional, will realize the importance of Liege, Belgium and the FN firm, to world arms making history, and to American arms history as well. But the newcomer may not, so a very brief history lesson is in your immediate future.

FN has been making guns for centuries. They have been supplying firearms the world over for many of those years and still continue to be a major arms supplier to both government and private interests. Where the FN and American stories first conjoin is in the late nineteenth century when John Browning decided he didn't want to deal with the guys at Winchester anymore. See, the people running Winchester had been purchasing Browning's gun designs for years, manufacturing some, and sitting on the rest, to prevent other companies from building them. They paid for the designs outright. Browning desired to change the arrangement when he made his famous Auto-5 shotgun. Winchester did not share the desire. As a result of probably the poorest decision in firearms history, Winchester came out the big loser. Browning went to FN in Belgium and found a new partner much more interested in building his designs on a more equitable royalty basis. FN built and sold the shotgun outside the U.S. and Remington was contracted to manufacture and sell the Auto-5 as the Remington Model 11 inside the U.S. The Auto-5 was the first functional and mass produced semi-automatic shotgun and remains the most reliable auto-loader to this day. (I know, I know, argue, argue, but as long as the friction rings were set up correctly by the user it shot completely reliably and softly as well. A story for a different book.) Now, Browning has his revenge, since Winchester has long ceased to exist as a rifle maker, and the rights to the Winchester name now belong to FN, as do the rights to the Browning name.

So the engineers at FN designed a modern battle rifle to counter the AK-47. It was 7.62mm, had a 20-round magazine, was decently accurate, could be adjusted for various ammunition, and most models were select fire. Folding stock paratrooper

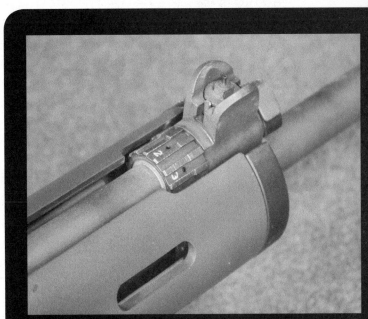

The FAL has an integral gas adjustment system to allow the shooter to adjust the gas system for different ammo. This was a necessity for this rifle since so many nations used it and may have had to borrow other nations' ammo. It works by regulating the amount of gas vented rather than the amount of gas allowed into the system.

It's this one.

Perhaps the most famous design made by FNH before the FAL was John Browning's Auto-5 shotgun. It is humbly sitting here among lesser creations by lesser men. (Actually, Browning designed the fifth from the left too, the Winchester 94.)

(below) Several types of FAL receivers are manufactured by several companies. Some will have lightening cuts, some will have provision for a carry handle and some won't, some might possess some other alteration. Regardless, they will be of steel and significantly heavier than an AR receiver. This model is made by Coonan, Inc.

models were also made. This rifle was adopted by everybody but us, it seems (the M-14 beat it out in the Army trials, but only because the M-14 cheated). The rifle was manufactured under license by India, the U.K., Austria, Germany, Brazil, Argentina, and more. Whoever didn't make it, bought it from those who did and so the FN-FAL in some form or other was used in every theater of war for over fifty years, up to this day.

FAL TYPES

There are two major derivations of FAL (stands for Fusil Automatique Leger, in case you were wondering), the Metric version, and the Inch version. The metric versions are the original and encompass the majority of the rifles built. The British Empire was at the time still stuck in the Imperial system of measurement and used such silly units of measurement as inches to build theirs, which means that many parts are not interchangeable between the two types. The inch pattern rifles and parts were used by the various nations that were or had been part of the Commonwealth, such as Canada, India, and Pakistan. Even among the different patterns, there were proprietary modifications on occasion and you will find parts incompatibility there as well. For example, the trigger housing for the Argentine version has a small difference from the standard Belgian type, so that the standard receiver will not fit without making a minor modification.

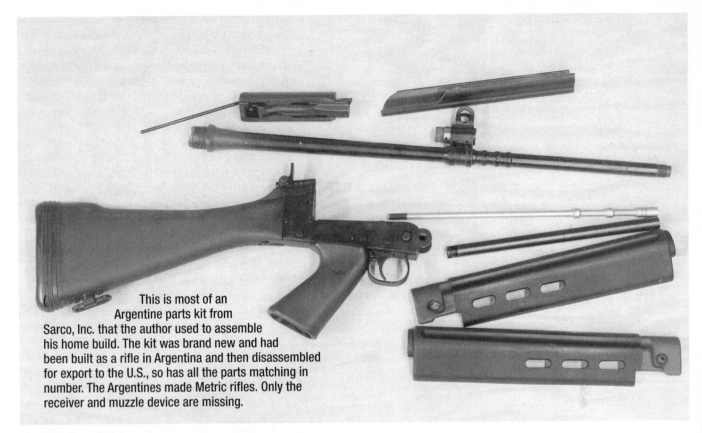

This is most of an Argentine parts kit from Sarco, Inc. that the author used to assemble his home build. The kit was brand new and had been built as a rifle in Argentina and then disassembled for export to the U.S., so has all the parts matching in number. The Argentines made Metric rifles. Only the receiver and muzzle device are missing.

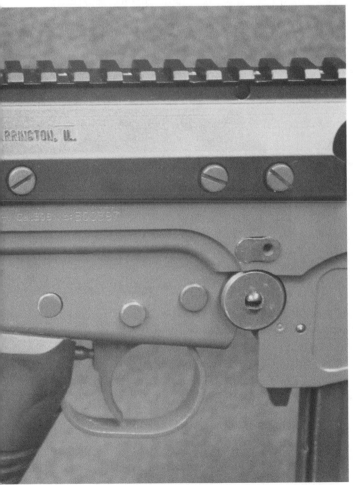

BUILDING YOUR FAL

Except for the full-out rifles made by DS Arms and Entreprise Arms, you are not likely to find a new FAL on the market. DSA manufactures all the parts in the U.S. and you will get a really good rifle for the money you spend on it. They build on the Austrian STG58 pattern, since they are using the tooling they purchased from Austria some years ago. Standard rifle, paratrooper, and even sniper versions are built by DS Arms, and you can get AR stuff from them too. Entreprise Arms builds their rifles mostly on imported parts kits and they make excellent rifles as well, though the selection is not quite as large as DS Arms. Several different variants of the FAL were imported by different companies in the U.S. back in the seventies and eighties, but not in large numbers. Most of these were of the metric pattern.

If you are building your own, you will have to start with some kind of surplus parts kit. They can still be found pretty easily online and will run around $350-$600. Of course, you will need to find a few U.S. made parts to ensure compliance to the same old 922(r) regulations that the AKs (and many other guns) are subject to. However, we will still concentrate on relatively easy upgrades here, rather than complete builds.

RECEIVERS

The best place to start is with a U.S.-made receiver, since the parts kit will not have a receiver in it anyway. You can get these from DS Arms, Entreprise Arms, and Coonan Arms. All three of them will work just fine for your build and are of high quality, with prices running in the $300 - $500 range.

STOCKS, HANDGUARDS, GRIPS

The next thing to do is to get a U.S.-made furniture set. The stock, pistol grip, and handguard will all count against the parts limit and direct replacements are cheaply available. More expensive alternatives are available, such as MagPul PRS stocks. If you want to accurize your FAL then the PRS stock is a great choice. Just like on the AR style, the PRS allows the length of pull and cheek height to be adjusted to suit the user – whether tall and skinny or short and fat. It also adds significant

weight to the gun, which will soak up some felt recoil. If you are building a paratrooper model, you can do so with a standard parts kit, but will have to purchase a number of extra parts. The bolt and recoil spring system are contained under the top cover to allow the stock to fold, so these parts will be necessary to purchase, as well as a paratrooper trigger housing. DSA manufactures U.S.-made paratrooper trigger housings and all the rest, so the parts are available to build the paratroopers if you like. The paratrooper stock folds to the side and looks very much like an ACE skeleton stock.

Handguards are not common. Sure you can get replacement standard types, but the availability of aftermarket handguards is sparse, nowhere near the AR or AK cornucopia. DS Arms has a neat free-float handguard that actually does free float. The effect is arguable since the FAL has a really big reciprocating piston that has an effect on the accuracy of the barrel, but it does help. The free-float tube is also rather heavy, despite being fabricated from aluminum. Again, this is a great choice if you want to tighten up the accuracy of your FAL and, together with the PRS stock, makes a heavy shooter that is comfortable to shoot all day long. You might find a few railed handguards, DS Arms makes a model for example, but they attach much the same way as the standard handguard and therefore do little for accuracy. They can, however, be used to attach any number of gun boogers to the rifle so you can act as tough as the AR couch commandos at the range when you walk up with your bedecked-out FAL.

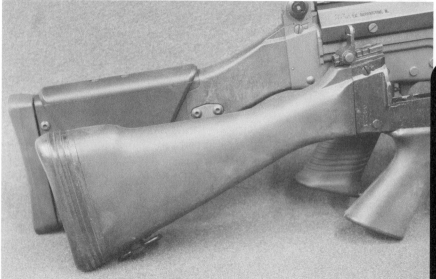
By now, everyone knows that MagPul makes stocks for ARs. They also make a PRS stock for the FAL (and the HK G3 too) that has all the adjustments that the AR stock has.

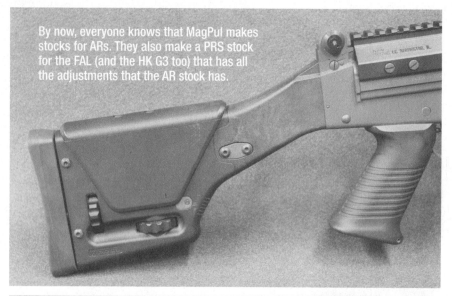

The standard FAL stock is comfortable, but unlike the AR and AK, is a little lower in relation to the barrel, making muzzle rise a bit more prevalent. The design was sort of a transition between the older wood stocked rifles and the newer high-plastic inline rifles. Starkly triangular, it attempted to lower the bore axis by dropping the cheek area below the heel of the stock.

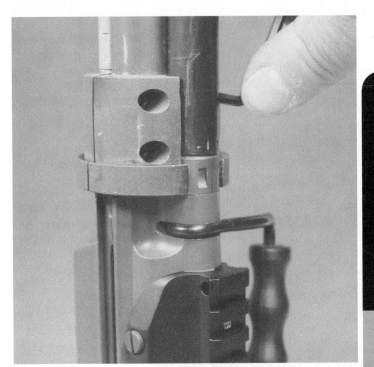

(left) The tube has a two piece clamping bracket at the rear that clamps around the chamber of the barrel. Four screws secure it tightly to the barrel. Make sure it is perfectly aligned with the piston hole in the receiver. The darker black tube is a specially made cover to conceal the back half of the piston, and is not standard.

(below) The tube is then passed over the barrel, carefully avoiding the gas block and is slid around the bracket at the rear. This rather large-diameter thick-walled tube is a true free-floating handguard tube. Long bolts run the length of the tube and fasten the endcaps together with the tube in between.

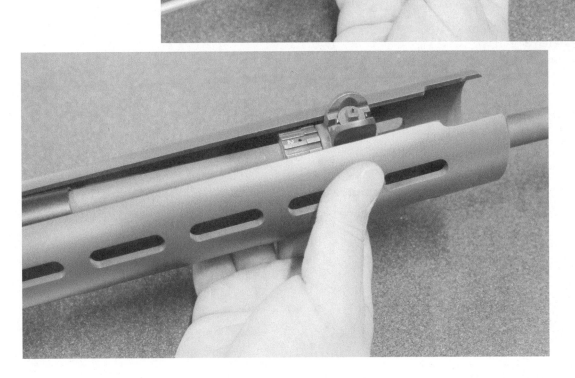

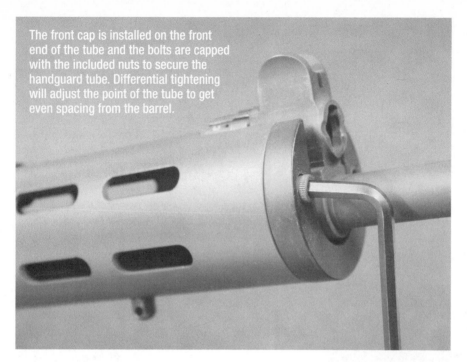

The front cap is installed on the front end of the tube and the bolts are capped with the included nuts to secure the handguard tube. Differential tightening will adjust the point of the tube to get even spacing from the barrel.

part, this is true. You might on occasion need to remove a thousandth or two from the rear of the barrel's receiver seat, or if the barrel will over-tighten, a steel shim will be required to be installed between the barrel and receiver. It is generally accepted that this shim, in order to be perfect, be surface ground to the correct thickness so that the barrel times on correctly.

Unlike the AR and AK that use rotating bolt heads, the FAL uses a dropping hinge-type bolt. The carrier carries the bolt itself through its movement, and then forces the

BARRELS AND BOLTS AND RELATED ITEMS

Barrels of various types are available, but most builders keep the original, since the parts count is usually obtained with other items. New U.S. barrels are available from DS Arms and surplus barrels from any number of surplus parts dealers like Sarco, Inc. in New York. The barrels and receivers should all be threaded by the manufacturer so that any barrel will fit any receiver, and for the most

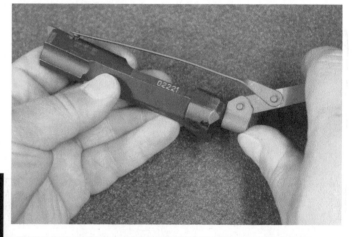

(above right) The FAL extractor is a bear to get out with your fingers or conventional tools. This removal tool is available from Brownells and makes the job a lot easier.

This rifle has a DS Arms medium weight barrel. It has a somewhat heavier contour under the handguard than the standard barrel. It has also been shortened by three inches. The DS Arms barrels come with the gas block pretty much permanently attached.

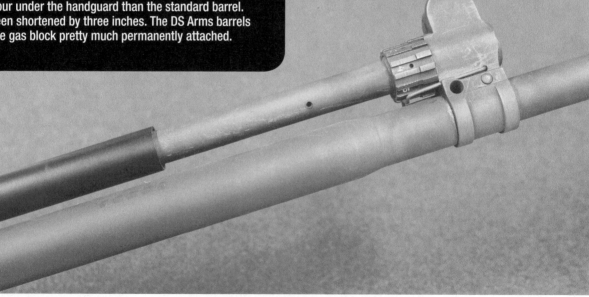

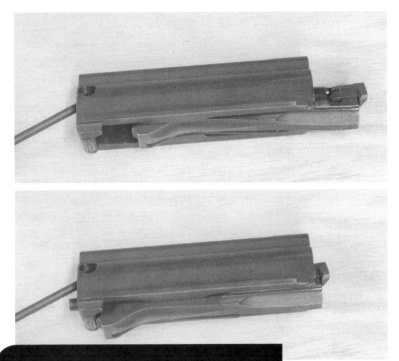

bolt tail to drop into a locked position. The bolt tail then bears on a hardened steel locking block that is pressed into the receiver. This locking block must be appropriately sized. When you torque on a new barrel, you must then headspace the new barrel and choose the correct locking block for the bolt that you have in your pocket. There are tapered rods that are designed to help you figure out the proper size. You insert it from the side with the bolt in the locked state, with a GO headspace gauge inserted in the chamber. Where the rod stops when inserted indicates the proper thickness of the locking block that needs to be popped in. You then buy that thickness locking block and then pound it into the receiver. The headspace should then be checked again with the locking block in place. The bolt

(top) The bolt tail has a flat that bears against the locking shoulder. Note in this picture where the bolt is in an unlocked state that the back of the bolt raises up into the bolt carrier. The muzzle would be to the right.

(above) The bolt tail is now dropped down from the carrier due to the face of the bolt making contact with the rear of the barrel. As the bolt is pushed to the rear, a camming surface inside the bolt carrier forces the tail of the bolt down to engage the locking shoulder.

(right) A locking shoulder looks like this. All you need to headspace an FAL is a set of gauge pins (any auto repair or machine shop will have them) and the chamber headspace gauges.

(below) A stainless steel gas piston can be purchased from Coonan Arms. Below it is an original Argentine piston that is hard chrome plated.

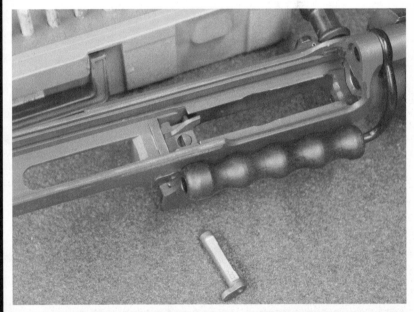

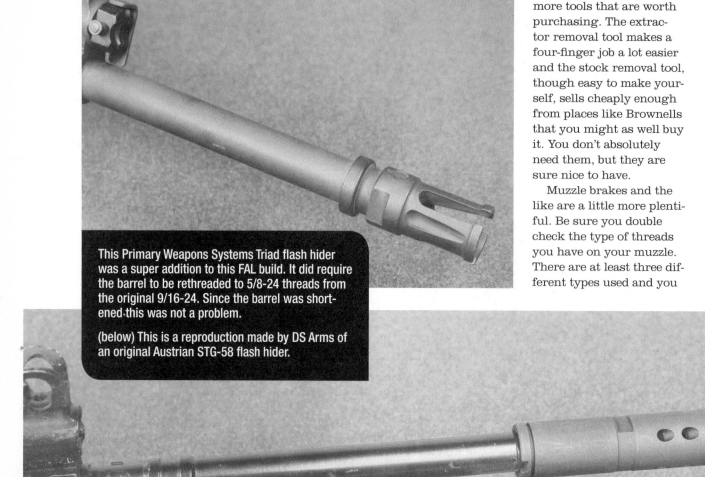

This Primary Weapons Systems Triad flash hider was a super addition to this FAL build. It did require the barrel to be rethreaded to 5/8-24 threads from the original 9/16-24. Since the barrel was shortened this was not a problem.

(below) This is a reproduction made by DS Arms of an original Austrian STG-58 flash hider.

There are a couple more tools that are worth purchasing. The extractor removal tool makes a four-finger job a lot easier and the stock removal tool, though easy to make yourself, sells cheaply enough from places like Brownells that you might as well buy it. You don't absolutely need them, but they are sure nice to have.

Muzzle brakes and the like are a little more plentiful. Be sure you double check the type of threads you have on your muzzle. There are at least three different types used and you

should then lock on the GO gauge, and not lock on the NOGO gauge.

Rather than buying one of the rods, I'd highly recommend getting a gauge pin set. For an imported gauge pin set in the range you need for an FAL you will spend around $100, about two to three times what you'd pay for the rod. However, the gauge pin set can be used for all kinds of other things, and if you have any machinist history, you'll know that pins can be really nice to have. From a home accessorizing standpoint, you can use the gauge pins to fixture parts for stoning or filing, or for gauging other items such as gas ports, carrier keys, and all sorts of things. Money far better spent than on a single-use tool.

I'd suggest getting a U.S.-made gas piston from Coonan as well. This is a part that requires no fitting and can be used to double check your barrel torque. If the piston binds in the receiver, then the barrel is not installed correctly.

wouldn't want to get the wrong one. If your muzzle is not yet threaded to accept a comp or whatever, then I'd recommend having it cut to 5/8-24. This is the standard on domestic barrels for .30 caliber bullets and you will find a lot more options for the muzzle device, including sound suppressors, suppressor adaptors, and just about anything made for the large frame AR series of rifles. Barrels can be recut to this thread if desired, but remember, the addition of threads or muzzle device will count against your parts total.

FIRE CONTROL

U.S.-made replacement parts for the trigger, sear, and disconnector can be obtained from Entreprise and DSA. These are direct replacements and will not disappoint. The only enhanced or match trigger that I know of for the FAL is made by Jard, Inc. This trigger, hammer, and sear set changes the standard trigger set up that is based on a Browning design, to the double hook trigger seen on many AR aftermarket models, also designed by Browning. You basically keep the pins and retainers and the safety lever, and replace the rest of the parts. This single stage trigger is a vast improvement over the original design and is well worth the $175 it costs. You can get it with different springs and the trigger is adjustable for overtravel and sear engagement.

The Jard, Inc. FAL trigger is significantly different from the original design, and is indeed identical in function and feature to their AR match triggers.

(below) The standard FAL fire control looks like this. You will see it again in modified form if you have an M1 carbine or Ruger 10/22.

OTHER STUFF

Optics rails directly replace the top cover of the receiver. Two models are largely available, one from A.R.M.S. and the other from DSA. The A.R.M.S. model slides in and is tight because of spring tension placed on the rails, is lightweight and will function with paratrooper rifles too. However this is not adequate for long range precision because, even though it is tight to the receiver, it is still not rigid enough for high precision riflescopes to maintain a zero. It is more than adequate for red dots or other close range optics and with the long Picatinny rail it can mount just about anything.

The DSA model is similar but uses clamps to hold it rigidly in place. It is a bit heavier and more spendy, but it allows the use of high power optics with maximum precision. Two versions are made, depending if you want a standard rifle or a paratrooper. If you want a sniper FAL, then go with the DSA cover. If you want a CQB gun then go with the

The rails that ride in the receiver also direct spring pressure to the side to tension the top cover.

(below) This A.R.M.S. top cover is lightweight and has a Pic rail on the top of it. It also closely follows the contour of the receiver.

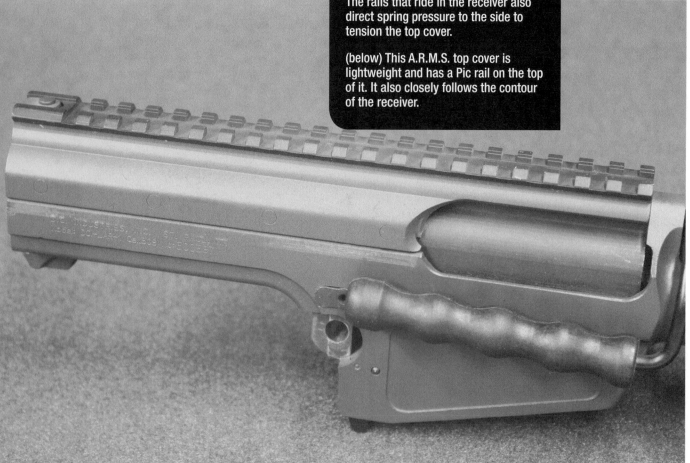

(below) **The DSA top cover also has an integral Picatinny rail and is machined from an aluminum block.**

(bottom) **These clamps rigidly affix the DSA rail/cover to the receiver. This mount is solid enough to mount long range optics and retain a zero for a sniper FAL.**

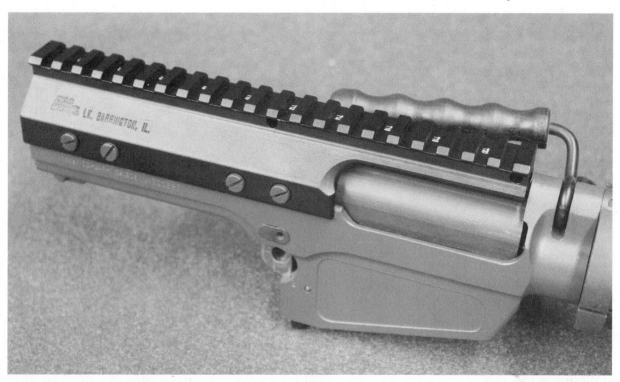

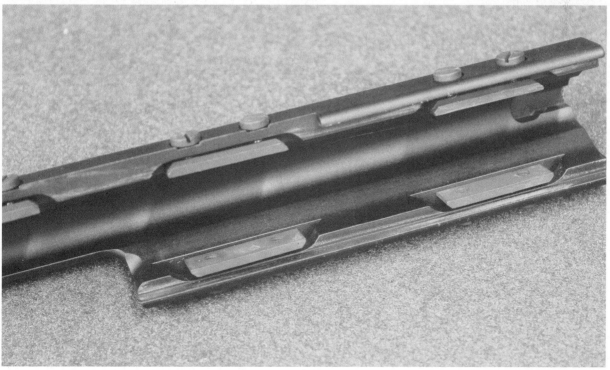

lighter A.R.M.S. model. Either way you have a vast improvement over the nekkid standard sheet steel top cover.

I'd also highly recommend replacing the standard rear sight with DS Arms' PARA rear sight assembly. The standard model works well but is unprotected. The PARA assembly is derived from the AR rear sight and has a flip dual-plane aperture that is protected by the sight body. It can also be installed with and adjustable side windage wheel so you don't have to adjust the sight with the two opposing retaining screws, but with the wheel. This is quicker and can be done without a screwdriver. This sight assembly is only sixty bucks and is practically a steal (actually, it is steel).

Magazines can be purchased surplus in good shape or purchased new from DS Arms. They are only $20-$30 depending on capacity and are well made. The surplus stuff can be had for $10 or less, but usually could use some refinishing. Twenty rounds is standard, but five and ten rounds for hunting is only a phone call away.

Buffer Technologies makes recoil reducing synthetic buffers for a heck of a lot of guns. This is FAL version placed right at the back of the receiver.

(below) The FAL gas adjustment can get fouled up and stuck so the FAL gas wrench is a handy tool. It will give you enough leverage to unstuck a stuck gas adjustment wheel. DSA makes this and sells it to Brownells who sells it to you.

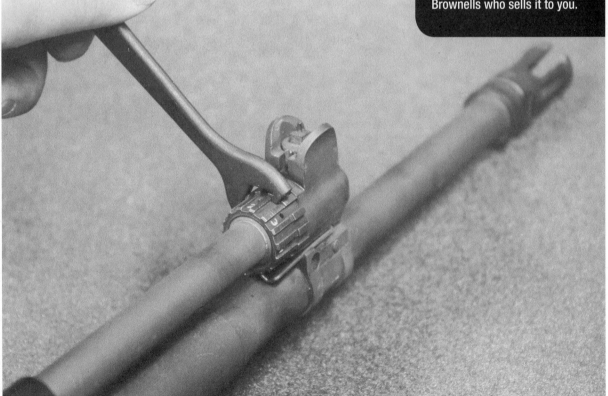

(top) This is the standard rear sight assembly for an FAL. The aperture will slide forward to elevate and slide rearward to lower. Windage can be adjusted by alternating the loosening and tightening of the two side screws.

(above) The PARA rear sight retains the two windage screws but uses them only for retention. The windage is adjustable via a large wheel on the right side of the housing, similar to the AR-15 A2 rear sight. The aperture is also an "L" style flip sight with two apertures. Best of all, the housing better protects the rear sight itself, a feature lacking in the standard sight.

(left) The DS Arms mags on the left are duplicates of the old original Austrian mags on the right. Both work just as well as the other. Both mags tend to run in 15-20 buck range now.

Appendix 1: Parts Subject to 922(r)

If you are building a rifle (or pistol) based on a foreign made firearm that may not be legally imported because it "does not have a sporting purpose" you will need to replace a certain amount of foreign made parts for parts manufactured in the U.S. These specific parts are listed here. If fewer than ten of these parts are present, then it is considered a U.S. made firearm and is legal to manufacture.

1. .... Frames, receiver, receiver castings, forgings or stampings.
2. .... Barrels
3. .... Barrel extensions
4. .... Mounting blocks or trunnions
5. .... Muzzle attachments
6. .... Bolts
7. .... Bolt carriers
8. .... Operating rods
9. .... Gas Pistons
10. .... Trigger housings
11. .... Triggers
12. .... Hammers
13. .... Sears
14. .... Disconnectors
15. .... Buttstocks
16. .... Pistol grips
17. .... Forearms, handguards
18. .... Magazine bodies
19. .... Magazine followers
20. .... Magazine floorplates

AK pattern rifles have fourteen of the above parts used (including front and rear trunnions and two piece handguard), seventeen if a foreign magazine is. The normal procedure is to replace the receiver, barrel, muzzle attachment (if one is present), gas piston, trigger, disconnector, hammer (sear is part of trigger), pistol grip, buttstock and handguard. This replaces ten foreign parts with U.S. made parts, leaving five remaining foreign parts, or eight if you are not using domestically manufactured magazines. This leaves a cushion of two parts, a wise option.

FN-FAL pattern rifles have thirteen of the above parts, sixteen if a foreign magazine is used. The normal procedure is to replace the receiver, muzzle attachment (if one is present), gas piston, trigger disconnector, hammer (disconnector is technically a function of the sear and trigger interaction), pistol grip, buttstock, and handguard. This replaces eight foreign parts with U.S. made parts, leaving nine if you are not using domestically manufactured magazines. This leaves a cushion of one part.

It should be noted that while the sear of the AK is an extension of the trigger, and a separate disconnector piece in the FAL is nonexistent, there may be those in positions of gun law enforcement that will still consider them to be two different pieces, so the extra one or two part inclusion cushion is recommended. If you are using only domestically manufactured magazines, then you can get away with more original foreign made parts than stated in the previous paragraph. Also, in the case of both the AK and FAL, the piston and operating rod are both the same piece. This cannot be said for the G36 or its imported "sporting" version the SL8. These rifles have both a gas piston and a separate operating rod piece. On the other hand, G3 rifles have no gas piston or operating rod.

For those who might care, the AR-15 or AR-10 have the following: receiver, barrel, barrel extension, muzzle attachment, bolt, bolt carrier, trigger, hammer, disconnector, pistol grip, stock, and handguard for a total of thirteen parts (including two receivers). This only applies to guns imported to the U.S. or to guns built from parts kits imported to the U.S. Imported kits are considered imported even if it started out life here in the U.S. There are a bunch of M-16 kits that have surfaced in the U.S. formerly from the butt crack of South East Asia or somewhere, wherever Uncle Sugar sent them to back in the sixties and seventies. These reimported parts kits, if assembled into rifles, will technically be subject to 922(r) under my understanding of the law. You will need to replace the barrel, lower receiver, and fire control parts, as most of them have the original full auto parts included in the kits. Then throw the old fire control parts in the lake or sell them to a dealer that has the legal ability to deal in machineguns. You will then have an eight parts count rifle with a two part cushion.

Appendix 2: Manufacturers

The following is a far from exhaustive list of manufacturers that produce quality rifles. It is by no means complete and for some part is based on my own experience and observations. It should be obvious that there will be others and to those folks, please understand, I only have so many opportunities or years in my life. Or room on the page. Virtually all of them make excellent retail parts as well.

Armalite	www.armalite.com
Alexander Arms	www.alexanderarms.com
Adams Arms	www.adamsarms.com
American Spirit Arms	www.americanspiritarms.com
Barrett	www.barrett.com
Bushmaster	www.bushmaster.com
CMMG	www.cmmginc.com
Colt	www.colt.com
Daniel Defense	www.danieldefense.com
Del-Ton	www.del-ton.com
DPMS	www.dpmsinc.com
DS Arms	www.dsarms.com
Double Star	www.star15.com
Fulton Armory	www.fulton-armory.com
JP Enterprises	www.jprifles.com
LaRue Tactical	www.laruetactical.com
Les Baer	www.lesbaer.com
Mega Arms	www.megaarms.com
Noveske Rifleworks	www.shopnoveske.com
Olympic Arms	www.olyarms.com
Primary Weapons Systems	www.primaryweapons.com
Remington	www.remington.com
Rock River Arms	www.rockriverarms.com
SIGSAUER	www.sigsauer.com
Smith & Wesson	www.smith-wesson.com
Spike's Tactical	www.spikestactical.com
Stag Arms	www.stagarms.com
Wilson Combat	www.wilsoncombat.com
Windham Weaponry	www.windhamweaponry.com
Yankee Hill Machine	www.yhm.net

Appendix 3: Aftermarket Support

All the manufacturers in Appendix 2 support the aftermarket of AR parts, many in great volume, and some also the AK and FAL parts too. The following list, again not complete, adds some of the massive volume of aftermarket support for these rifles. This list is limited in the same way for the same reasons as Appendix 2.

Advanced Armament Corp. .... www.advanced-armament.com
Badger Ordnance... www.badgerordnance.com
Bravo Company USA .... www.bravocompanyusa.com
Command Arms Accessories... www.commandarms.com
Falcon Industries... www.ergogrips.net
Geissele Automatics... www.geissele.com
Hahn Precision .... www.hahn-precision.com
Hera Arms .... www.hera-arms.com
High Standard .... www.highstandard.com
Hogue.. www.getgrip.com
Lancer Systems.. www.lancer-systems.com
Magpul .... www.magpul.com
The Mako Group .... www.themakogroup.com
Jard, Inc. .... www.jardinc.com
KNS Precision.. www.knsprecisioninc.com
Midwest Industries .... www.midwestindustriesinc.com
NexTorch.. www.nextorch.com
Smith Enterprises.. www.smithenterprise.com
Streamlight.. www.streamlight.com
Surefire .... www.surefire.com
Tapco Weapons Accessories... www.tapco.com
Troy Industries .... www.troyind.com
Timney Triggers .... www.timneytriggers.com
Vltor Weapons Systems .... www.vltor.com
WMD Guns... www.wmdguns.com
Wolff Gunsprings .... www.gunsprings.com

Distributors include but are not limited to:
Brownells .... www.brownells.com
Midway USA .... www.midwayusa.com
Optics Planet... www.opticplanet.com
And the list goes on and on and on.

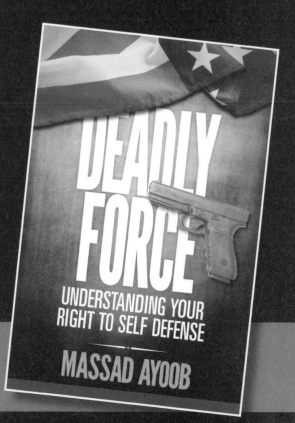

IT'S BACK!

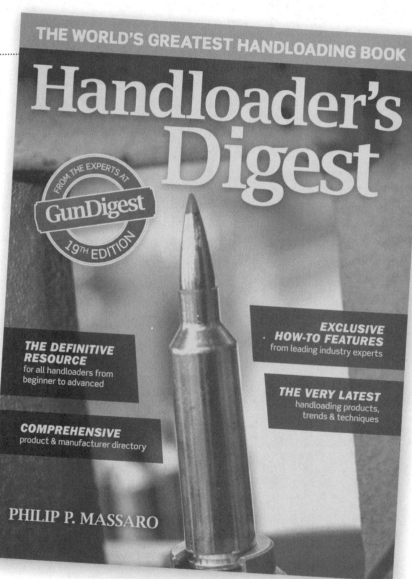